THE CAITHNESS INFLUENCE

THE
CAITHNESS
INFLUENCE

Diverse lives of distinction

VALERIE CAMPBELL

Whittles Publishing

Published by
Whittles Publishing Ltd.,
Dunbeath,
Caithness, KW6 6EG,
Scotland, UK

www.whittlespublishing.com

ISBN 978-184995-039-8

Printed and bound in Great Britain by Bell & Bain Ltd., Glasgow

For Doug

CONTENTS

ACKNOWLEDGEMENTS

I would like to express my deepest thanks to the following for their help: Cora Ovens at the Van Riebeeck Society in South Africa; Irene at the Boys Brigade in Scotland Headquarters; Paul Dew at the Metropolitan Police at New Scotland Yard; Gary Gleeson at Wanganui District Council; Denise Anderson at the University of Edinburgh; Derek Lamont, Minister at St Columba's Free Church; Susan Mills at Clackmannanshire Council; Graham Cormack, Coaching and Development Manager for the Camanachd Association; and Lisa Snider at AABC. I would especially like to thank David Graham Scott and Ian Charles Scott for their time and patience in answering my many questions.

I would also like to extend my deepest thanks to the following: Colette Robertson, Leanne Kempton, Lorna McPartlan, Morag McMillan Wilson, John Allan, Morag Anderson, Julia Lee-Taylor, Maria Gallagher Shankland, Pauline Hurst, and Amanda Dawson. Lastly I want to thank my husband, Doug, and my children Sam, Lauren and Kirsty for allowing me the space and time to write this.

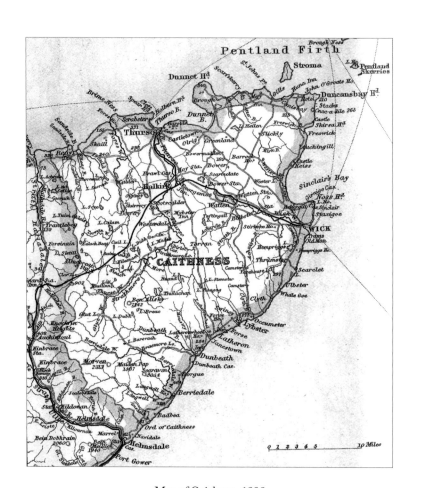

Map of Caithness, 1898

INTRODUCTION

Caithness has a rich history stretching back many thousands of years, but in more recent times many born in the county left to make their mark abroad. Part of the reason for the exodus was the Highland Clearances of the 19th century, while others were looking for adventure or had sampled life abroad during spells in the armed forces. For others still, it was because their parents had taken the decision to leave in search of a better life for themselves and their families. Among these were the first Lady Mayor ever to be elected in the British Empire, the 9th President of the Continental Congress in America during the Revolutionary period, and a pioneering road engineer who moved to South Africa when he was young, to name but a few. Those who stayed at home are credited with great engineering feats and geological discoveries – not only at home but abroad – as well as pioneering work in the arts and sciences. They dedicated, and still dedicate, their whole lives to their work and the impact of these inspirational people has touched the lives of many thousands of individuals worldwide. There are many hundreds of Caithness-born people who had an impact on the world in some way, however there is not enough room in this volume for them all. I have chosen as diverse a group as I could and this book provides an insight into their lives and labours.

ALEXANDER BAIN

At the village hall in Watten stands one of the world's first electric clocks. It was invented by Watten's most famous son, Alexander Bain. It had belonged to Alexander Sutherland, a local teacher, but on his death it was gifted to Wick's Carnegie Library. However, it was not in working order until a local Thurso man (a Mr Purvis) restored it.

Alexander Bain was born on 31 October 1810. His father was John Bain, a native of Watten, and his mother was Isabella Waiter from Halkirk. Bain's twin sister was

Postcard of Watten, early 1900s

1

named Margaret and they were baptised on 22 November 1810. It is believed that the Bains had 13 children, although one of them died in infancy. The couple had married at the turn of the 19th century and John worked a croft at Houstry near the hamlet then known as Achingale – now Watten. Not long after the birth of the twins, the family moved to Leanmore to take over the tenancy of the larger croft, which it is thought was run by John's father, Alexander. At this point the family consisted of their eldest child Elizabeth, followed by Barbara, Peter and William, as well as the new-born babies. By the time Bain went off to the local school at Backlass (aged five), he had been joined by John and George. Between 1816 and 1823, Isabella gave birth to Bessy, Isabella, David and Joseph.

Schooling was important to the Bains. John wanted his children to be educated so they could be successful. However, Bain was not an academic. He would rather sit and daydream than pay attention to the teacher. Growing up on a croft, he enjoyed the outdoor life and during the summer months when the school was closed, he managed to find work on a farm at Bower. He finally left school in 1822. By this time he had become fascinated by clocks and watches and how they worked. On 30 January 1830 he began his apprenticeship with the watch and clockmaker John Sellar in Wick. Ultimately, he spent much less than the required seven years he was tied to Sellar to complete his apprenticeship. He had attended a lecture on electricity and found it a fascinating subject, so after a few years in Wick he managed to break the agreement. Yet it seems Sellar may have been in financial difficulties anyway, because soon after Bain left, Sellar closed the shop and moved on.

Meanwhile, Bain headed for Edinburgh where it is thought he finished his apprenticeship. He managed to secure a position but he was a restless person and soon found himself southbound to London. While at Clerkenwell – the heart of the clock making industry – he attended lectures where he saw electromagnetic apparatus being used. It was while watching this that he wondered if it could be possible to harness electromagnetism in watches and clocks. In 1838 at the house in Wigmore Street where he was staying, he completed an early electric clock and by the end of that year had assembled an electric printing telegraph. It could not have happened at a better moment in his life, as he was beginning to struggle financially. He showed his inventions to his friend Charles McDowell and his clock was later placed in the window of Hunter & Edwards – a clockmaker's in Cornhill in London. He had also managed to devise a small enough device to store the electricity, which later became known as an earth battery.

Bain had faith in his new inventions but he needed backers to support him financially. He was introduced to Professor Charles Wheatstone and decided to take the electric clock and printing telegraph to him. Wheatstone gave him £5 and promised him more money. Instead, Wheatstone had a copy of the clock made and showcased it at the Royal Society, claiming it was his own invention. Needless to say, Bain was furious when he found out. He challenged Wheatstone's allegations, but to no avail. Nevertheless, Bain still had work to do and he approached John Barwise. Barwise was a chronometer maker and between them, they applied for the first electromagnetic clock patent. The process

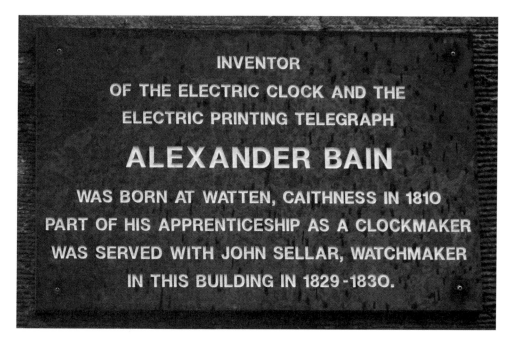

INVENTOR
OF THE ELECTRIC CLOCK AND THE
ELECTRIC PRINTING TELEGRAPH
ALEXANDER BAIN
WAS BORN AT WATTEN, CAITHNESS IN 1810
PART OF HIS APPRENTICESHIP AS A CLOCKMAKER
WAS SERVED WITH JOHN SELLAR, WATCHMAKER
IN THIS BUILDING IN 1829-1830.

Alexander Bain plaque, Wick

took three months and was granted on 11 January 1841. It was the first ever clock of its kind in the United Kingdom.

In March 1841, Bain showed his clock at the Polytechnic Institution and told them he was its inventor. Wheatstone got wind of this and a bitter dispute that was to last their lifetimes ensued. In 1842, as Bain worked on John Finlaison's house (Finlaison was the Actuary of the National Debt), he discovered that the earth could be used as a path for the returning electric current and the following year, having experimented with it, he began working on what was to become the electrochemical telegraph. This machine was the first to be able to send a facsimile message to another place using electricity. It was a remarkable feat of ingenuity, even though he never got the chance to show it publicly, and he never succeeded in gaining the patent for it. This was granted to Frederick Bakewell in 1848.

On 15 May 1844 at the Upper Chelsea Church, Bain married Matilda Bowie, a widow who had a six-year-old daughter. The couple had five children of their own. Their first-born was Elizabeth, followed by Isabella, twins Alexander and Henry, and another daughter named Barbara. Not long after they married, the new family moved north to Edinburgh where he set up his own electric clock and telegraph business. In May 1845, he was awarded a contract to erect the first telegraph line between the capital and Glasgow. During the works, his brother John travelled down from Caithness to aid him, but he returned to Watten in 1852 to take over the croft at Backlass. When the works were complete, he tested it and for the first time, the clock at the Edinburgh railway station controlled the clock at another station. It was a momentous occasion and he saw his dream realised. Later, he was appointed Scottish Manager of the Electric Telegraph Company, but it did not suit him and he soon returned to his love of making his own clocks and telegraphs. He managed to make improvements to the electrochemical telegraph and invented a punched tape sender that sent messages down the telegraph at high speed. In 1846, he demonstrated it in France, to the amazement of the French scientists. A year later, the family left Edinburgh and returned to London.

In 1848, the opportunity arose for Bain to visit the United States, where he was able to show his telegraph to Henry O'Reilly – an Irishman who had emigrated to New York with his family when he was a child. O'Reilly was highly impressed by the invention, and when he formed the New York and New England Telegraph Company with Bain, he engaged Bain to carry out the requisite line building work, which was completed in 1850. The line ran from Boston in Massachusetts to New York. However, the line caused controversy with the Morse Company, who at the time believed it should have the monopoly. Following legal wrangling, the two companies eventually merged to form the New York and New England Union Telegraph Company. The lawsuit cost Bain dearly financially, but in June 1852 following his return to England, the Bain-run New York State Telegraph Company was sold for over $65,000, and by the end of the year, his telegraph lines were no longer operating in America. It was also during his time in the States that he received the news that his mother had passed away, aged 70.

When he returned to England in 1852, Bain returned to clock and watch making. In May he was granted the patent for electric clocks, watches, and all the apparatus needed for them to work. The following year, his wife Matilda became ill. She moved out of the family home at Hammersmith and went to live with her sister Elizabeth (John Finlaison's wife) in Richmond in Surrey. Throughout her stay, her health deteriorated and she died on 14 August 1856. The death hit Bain hard. He seemed to lose interest in his business for a while, but about a year after the death, he resumed his work. However, after a visit to the United States again, he found on his return to England that the telegraph company had been taken over by the Government. Disheartened and without work, he tried to gain employment as a labourer, but his pleadings were ignored, so he returned to Scotland where he met up with John Stephen (from Bower in Caithness), who now resided in Edinburgh. His stay lasted until he recovered from an illness. He then decided to move back to London, probably in the hope of finding work. But his personal life was plagued by loneliness. With his wife gone and his family grown-up and living their own lives, he felt isolated and suffered from bouts of depression.

London did not work out for him and he returned to Edinburgh. By the end of 1871, he had managed to find a job with James Muirhead & Sons in Glasgow and he happened to meet Professor Sir William Thomson who, with the help of the local Member of Parliament for Glasgow (Mr W. Dalgleish) and Mr C. W. Siemens (the first president of the Society of Telegraph Engineers), petitioned William Gladstone – the Prime Minister – calling for Bain to be granted a pension from the State for all the ingenious work he had carried out over the years. The petition was granted, as Gladstone himself knew full well of Bain's work. Bain was granted the sum of £80 per annum. Thomson was delighted for his friend, and he learned a great deal from him watching his demonstrations. This enhanced Thomson's own work with electricity and he later became world-famous as Lord Kelvin.

Meanwhile, Bain found another job, working at an opticians. This supplemented his income and in 1873 he was awarded £150 from the Royal Society. All this money meant he could now live more comfortably, although his health was failing. He returned to the county of his birth for the last time in 1874. When he was younger, he had planned to purchase a farm in the area so he could retire there, but he never found the time. It was something he regretted all his life.

The visit went well, but his health became more of a concern. He returned to the Helensburgh area following the visit north, and worked on clocks until he had a stroke that paralysed him. His friend William Thomson found a place for him at Broomhill Home for Incurables in Kirkintilloch, and it was here he died on 2 January 1877, aged 66. He was buried at the Old Aisle Cemetery in Kirkintilloch.

Shortly after his death, a group of Glasgow electricians had a granite memorial erected. The inscription on the headstone reads:

> Alexander Bain, electrician and telegraph engineer, distinguished for many
> inventions of the greatest value in electric telegraphy &c, &c. Born in the parish
> of Watten, Caithness-shire, October 1810. Died 2 January, 1877, interred here.

In addition to this original inscription, the Town Council of Kirkintilloch added the following:

> On 10 April 1959 the Town Council of the Burgh of Kirkintilloch
> publicly noted the importance of the inventions of Alexander Bain who
> died at Broomhill Home, Kirkintilloch, particularly the electric magnet
> clock, and resolved that this inscription be placed hereon and that this
> tombstone be maintained in perpetuity at public expense. He thought
> above himself and also helped to secure a great and better world.

It was one of the first of many memorials to the Watten-born inventor. At Stafford Place in Wick, where Bain started his apprenticeship with John Sellar, a plaque was also erected. In the village of Watten, Bain Place is named in his honour and just outside the village hall stands a granite memorial which was erected in 1943. It reads:

> Erected in 1943 by public subscription in honour of the
> distinguished Caithnessman, Alexander Bain, inventor of the electric
> clock and the electric printing-telegraph. Born at Leanmore, parish
> of Watten, 1810. Died at Kirkintilloch,1877. He thought above
> himself and so helped to raise a new world industry.

Alexander Bain memorial, Watten

Quite an achievement for a man who daydreamed at school.

In Thurso, at the Enterprise Park, Manpower PLC's building is called 'Alexander Bain House' and the Wetherspoon's pub in Wick is called the 'Alexander Bain'. Glasgow and Edinburgh also have paid homage to him: BT's main building at York Street is called 'Alexander Bain House' while in Edinburgh, a plaque was unveiled at 21 Hanover Street, which was his workshop in the capital in 1941.

During his lifetime Bain also published two books. These were *A Short History of the Electric Clocks with Explanations of their Principles and Mechanism and Instruction for Their Management and Regulation* in 1852, followed almost 20 years later by *A Treatise on Numerous Applications of Electrical Science to the Useful Arts*. He could never have imagined how his work would impact the world, and in his home county he is still revered, especially in Watten.

ANDREW GEDDES BAIN

Andrew Geddes Bain emigrated to South Africa and became one of the country's most renowned engineers and explorers. Not only that, he became heavily involved in geology and archaeology and kept journals of his life and work, which give a good insight to the Caithness man's undertakings in his new homeland.

Geddes Bain was born in May 1797 in Thurso, son of Alexander Wright Bain and his wife Jean Geddes who had married in Thurso in July 1792. Geddes Bain was named after his maternal grandfather, Andrew Geddes (a native of Latheron), and christened in Thurso on 11 June. When he was still very young, both his parents died and he was sent to live near Edinburgh with an aunt. It was here that Geddes Bain was educated. Following his education, Geddes Bain decided to travel with a relative of his mother's who was in the army. Following a trip back to Britain in 1816, Lieutenant Colonel William Geddes took the young Geddes Bain under his wing and enticed him to return with him to South Africa. Geddes Bain accepted the invitation and in October he arrived in Table Bay with the colonel.

Two years later, Geddes Bain married Maria Elizabeth von Backstrom, the 20-year-old daughter of Dutch officer Johan George Frederick von Backstrom and his wife Johanna Georgina Spengler. Johan George Frederick von Backstrom never lived long enough to see his daughter marry, as he died in January 1812. South African-born Johanna however, lived until June 1840. The young couple were married in the *Groote Kerk* (or Great Church) in Adderley Street in Cape Town on 16 November 1818, by well-known English-born Reverend George Hough – the senior Colonial chaplain for the area. Hough had been ordained by the Bishop of Oxford in 1812 and following a brief period of being Curate of St Peter's in Oxford, he was posted to Simon's Town in the Cape Colony in 1813 but was relocated to Cape Town in 1817, the year before Geddes Bain and Maria were married. After 33 years in the Cape, he returned home to England having had a hand in the establishment of the South African College and been on committees that helped slaves and their children to buy their freedom. He took up the post of Rector of

Andrew Geddes Bain
Courtesy the Van Riebeeck Society

Yelford in Oxford where he remained until his death in 1867.

In 1822 the Geddes Bains settled at Graaff-Reinet, where they remained for 13 years. The town had been established by the Dutch East India Company in 1786 on the banks of the Sundays River and is the fourth oldest town in South Africa (following Cape Town, Stellenbosch and Swellendam). It was a great trading centre and today has over 200 historical monuments and buildings of interest. It is surrounded by Camdeboo National Park, which is well-known for its flora and fauna and is the only town in South Africa to be surrounded by a National Park. It was in its early years that Geddes Bain built a house on Napier Street. Here, he worked as a saddler to bring in some money to the household, although he was also known to have been involved in tanning sheepskins. Geddes Bain caused some controversy in the town, especially when he proposed a new road from the town over the Oudeberg, which met with strong opposition from some locals. In 1829 he began work on the pass with the help of some notable locals, including a Mr Murray, Mr Perry and Mr Stretch, who all donated money to the project. This was to be the first of many road-building projects he undertook.

In the mid-1820s Geddes Bain went into partnership with John Biddulph to start trading in ivory over the Orange River. However, the venture into Bechuanaland to the Mines of Mileta was not particularly successful, and to compound matters their trip was cut short. In 1829 the two men set off once more, this time hoping to do some exploration as well. They were met by people from the *Qwabe* tribe and decided to beat a hasty retreat. This time they brought back ivory to sell.

By the end of 1832 Geddes Bain had constructed the Van Ryneveld's Pass, named after the civil commissioner, for which he receive a medal from the local inhabitants. It was inscribed: 'For gratuitously superintending the construction of Van Ryneveld's Pass, 1832'. Two years later he embarked on his last big expedition. He had been commissioned by an American to catch rare, live animals and animal skins, so set off with Dr Andrew Smith – who was given the task of leading the expedition to the Molopo River – and Jan Sauer. Like his earlier expedition with Biddulph, the group was met by the hostile native warriors of Moselekatse – king of the *Matabele* tribe, a branch of the Zulus known today as the *Ndebele*. By December 1834 although Geddes Bain had been given up for lost, he arrived home on 10 December. He had lost his wagons and all they contained. On his way home he had passed through districts that had been devastated during skirmishes between the *Xhosa* and the Government, which inevitably had consequences for the local settlers. As early as 1779 tensions had spilled over to war, and 1834 saw the sixth *Xhosa* war, which became collectively known to Europeans as the Kaffir Wars. The day after he had reached the safety of Graaff-Reinet, a high-ranking chief of the *Xhosa* was killed and his brother sought revenge. With around 10,000 men, he marched into the Kat River Valley where he burned homes and farms and killed those who got in his way. Many locals found a safe haven in Graham's Town, where the women and children hid in a church. The British authorities had little in the way of an army to fight the *Xhosa*, but the Governor Sir Benjamin d'Urban mustered all the men he could and reached Graham's Town to help on 6 January 1835. A few days earlier, Geddes Bain had made it as far as the town, and he described it as a scene of utter devastation and ruin. It transpired that van Ryneveld, commissioner of Graaff-Reinet, had sent him there as part of the Mounted Burghers, where he was given his captaincy. His lieutenant was none other than van Ryneveld's son, Honoratus. Reprisal attacks began against the *Xhosa* from Graham's Town and the war continued for another nine months before the *Xhosa*'s capitulation, but not before 40 farmers lost their lives and over 400 farms were destroyed and pillaged. By July Geddes Bain was in charge of a temporary military post on the Tyumie River. A peace treaty was signed and a vast tract of land was designated British and its

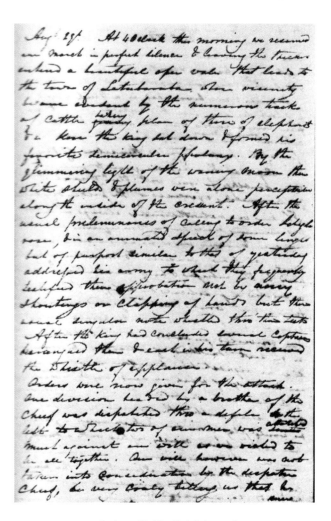

Andrew Geddes Bain's journal
Courtesy the Van Riebeeck Society

inhabitants British citizens. These new citizens were not allowed to cross the boundary unless they received permission and were to remain unarmed. Lord Glenelg blamed the Boers for the uprising, so in turn they took matters into their own hands if they caught anyone rustling their cattle. The *Xhosa*, now feeling trapped, tested this new law and it was Geddes Bain who had to make the decision to counterattack.

On 5 November a skirmish had broken out. A number of *Nqika* had attacked a *kraal* and Geddes Bain had given the order for them to be driven back. In the mayhem that ensued, Ensign Norton asked Geddes Bain's permission to fire at one of the raiders, which he duly did. But the man was killed on the other side of the river, which incensed Maqoma, the new chief. He wrote to Colonel Harry Smith – who was at the newly established seat of Government at King William's Town – threatening all out war again. In response, Geddes Bain was placed under arrest, which was relayed to Maqoma and it was hoped that he would see that justice under the British judicial system was meted out equally, regardless of the colour of a man's skin. What then ensued was a severe war of words between Colonel Smith and the Governor, Sir Benjamin d'Urban. Whilst Smith deeply disapproved of Geddes Bain's actions, d'Urban wholly agreed with his actions and exonerated him. In the end a court martial took place in January 1836, but he was acquitted and he returned to Fort Thomson.

Geddes Bain's woes were not over. In 1835 both he and William Southey had been given farms along the border of the province where they could keep an eye on things, but this was rescinded. Although he had planted crops and built a cottage with proceeds gained by the sale of his house in Graaff-Reinet, he never received compensation for the loss. The land that once briefly belonged to him now lies in part of the town of Alice and the famous Lovedale Mission was built on it.

Geddes Bain was not a man to let these kinds of incidents get the better of him. If anything, it spurred him on and he found the career that was to make his name known throughout the country. In April 1837 he found himself attached to the Royal Engineers with his remit being road building, and from that year until 1845 he became involved in major road construction. The largest of these was the Queen's Road, which ran between Graham's Town and Fort Beaufort. Graham's Town also had a road built to Breakfast Vlei, which was named 'Pluto's Vale Road'. During their construction, Geddes Bain became acutely aware of the geology of the area and this spurred him on to read Sir Charles Lyell's *Principles of Geology*, which he managed to borrow from the civil commissioner, Captain Campbell. Now with a keen eye on what was being lifted from the earth as the roads took shape, he found some fossils and bones of creatures that had not yet been noted, and he was one of the first to write about South African geology. In 1844 he wrote to the London Geological Society and sent a collection of fossils. After some time, he gave up hope of ever hearing back from the society, but finally received a letter from its president, Henry Warburton, who had actually used Geddes Bain's finds and letter to present a paper to his assembled gathering. For sending in the fossils and his descriptions of some of the areas of South Africa he had explored, he was awarded the sum of £20 from the Wollaston Fund. This fund had been set up by the English chemist and physicist William Hyde Wollaston, who had become wealthy when he discovered a way of processing platinum ore in usable quantities. He was also renowned for his discovery of two chemical elements: palladium and rhodium.

In 1845 Geddes Bain received £200 from Lord Peel on behalf of the Government for his scientific work, thanks to a letter received by Mr Warburton from the Earl of Lincoln, who had written about Geddes Bain's fine work in South Africa. This only furthered Geddes Bain's interest in geology and he was soon collaborating with fellow geology enthusiasts, Dr William Guybon Atherstone of Graham's Town and Dr Richard Nathaniel Rubidge of Graaff-Reinet. Both of these men were invaluable to him, as they knew their rocks and rock formation. Dr Atherstone was a medical practitioner who had arrived in South Africa with his parents in the 1820s from England. He was an apprentice with his father, Dr John Atherstone and gained his MD in Heidelberg, Germany. He returned to Graham's Town where he practiced alongside his father. He became famous for being the first surgeon outside Europe and America to carry out an amputation under anaesthetic, and in 1867 was one of three men who discovered a rock named the Eureka Diamond that inadvertently started the diamond rush in the country. But in his leisure time, Geddes Bain had become interested in geology and this interest remained with him for the rest of his life. He collected fossils, plant and mineral samples and later wrote about them.

Dr Rubidge had been born in Wales, the son of Captain Henry Rubidge RN, who had emigrated to South Africa in 1821 with his family. They set up home at Graham's Town but Rubidge went to London to study medicine. On his return, he too apprenticed under John Atherstone and practised in Graaff-Reinet for a few years before moving to Port Elizabeth in 1850. Like Geddes Bain and William Atherstone, Rubidge also collected fossils and botanical samples and became well-known for his geology, especially after a visit to Namaqualand, where he studied copper formations with John Atherstone. It was thanks to them and their enthusiasm that geological societies sprang up in both Graham's Town and Graaff-Reinet.

When Geddes Bain's work on military roads came to an end he was offered the post of Inspector of Roads, which he accepted. Before he took up the post, he went on a trip that encompassed Somerset East, Stormberg, Caledon River, Fort Beaufort and Quathlamba (or Kahlamba) Mountains to make notes of any geological or botanical finds along the way. The Quathlamba Mountains is the native Zulu name for the Drakensberg range, meaning 'the Barrier of Spears' – which is an accurate description of them; some peaks rise over 3000 metres. In October Geddes Bain began his work on Mitchell's Pass. The pass, when completed, ran from the Tulbagh Valley to Ceres, through the Rex River Mountains. There had always been a pass but it was unsuitable for wagons, which had to be dismantled, carried and reassembled at certain sections in order to continue the journey. Before the pass was completed, Andrew had begun what was later named Bain's Kloof Pass, which ended up costing around £55,000. This – as well as other roads in the region, including Mitchell's Pass – was built using convict labour. Around 250 men were engaged on Mitchell and around 100 more on Bain's. Andrew himself taught the convicts' overseers how to build dry stone dykes so they in turn could teach the criminals. Some of these walls still stand today, as testament to his apprentices and his own construction skills.

Bain's Kloof ran from the east of Wellington at the Limietberge to the northern land beyond, following a recce trip he made with Johannes Retief. Mitchell's Pass was opened in 1848 by Sir Harry Smit (the Cape Governor). Bain's Kloof Pass was completed in 1854. For this latter pass, Geddes Bain was presented by the grateful people of the area with a candelabra made in solid silver by the well-known silversmiths Hunt and Roskell in London. It was adorned by Minerva and had three fossils at its base to symbolise his work. He was also presented with a canteen of silver cutlery.

Andrew Geddes Bain
Courtesy the Van Riebeeck Society

Geddes Bain also became involved in the construction of the Katberg Pass, improving the Karoo Poort Pass at Ceres, that runs from the south through the shallow valley, and also the Gydo Pass (which runs between Ceres and Citrusdal, famous for its citrus orchards below the Cederberg Mountians and its cave art). Sometimes, Geddes Bain spent a great deal of time on his roads; inspecting them and making sure things were going to plan. On these trips, he did not miss the opportunity to do some geological digging and theorising. On one occasion he surmised – having found freshwater fossils in the area from the mouth of the Gualana River in the east to Karroo Poort in the west – that it was possible the whole area was once a freshwater lake. He also spent time drawing maps of the vast areas he explored. At his passes where the convicts worked, he also acted as magistrate.

In 1851 Geddes Bain submitted his maps to the London Geological Society. Along with them he sent a memoir of his findings – *The Geology of South Africa* – and a sample of some of his fossil finds. His earlier collection of fossils that had been sent to England in the 1840s had been bought by the British Museum for £150, but these later finds were presented to the aforementioned society. The following year in November, Geddes Bain received a letter stating that his work had been read to the society and had met with approval from Sir Roderick Murchison and Professor Richard Owen. Murchison submitted the map to the colonial secretary and at a meeting of the Royal Geographical Society it was shown to Prince Albert, the Prince Consort. The memoirs Geddes Bain had sent to London were later published in 1856 in *Transactions*. Murchison also instigated Geddes Bain's appointment as geographical surveyor of the Cape of Good Hope, which was supported by Professor Owen (but it never happened due to the fact that Geddes Bain was too busy with his other projects). He did however offer to carry out some geological surveying if he was allowed to take some leave, with only a small amount charged to the State. At first, the idea of a geological surveyor in the area was rejected, but as the copper fields in Namaqualand were being explored and developed, a new urgency to have a surveyor appointed became apparent. Instead of choosing Geddes Bain, the British sent Andrew Wyley to the Cape, as he had a proven track record with his involvement in the Geological Survey of Ireland. Over the coming decades, Wyley's work, although important in recording South Africa's geology, did not add much to the information that Geddes Bain had already submitted.

By 1855 Geddes Bain had returned to the Eastern Province where he began repairing roads that had fallen into disrepair. One of the worst was the Ecca Pass on the Queen's Road, which was described as almost impassable. In order to fix it, Geddes Bain had to call on the military, as local labour was insufficient. During the build, he recommended to the local lieutenant-governor that a bridge be built over the Koonap River.

His workload over the next few years became heavier, instead of getting lighter as he grew older. He inspected and reported on the roads between Worcester and Swellendam, the road over the Tradouw Mountains, and began to suggest further roads out of Graaff-Reinet, such as one to Middelburg, which was over the mountains. His aim was to make travelling for tradesmen easier. In December 1856, he made the arduous journey to Knysna where he surveyed a route from there to the Lange Kloof through the dense forest that clung to the lower parts of the mountains. In doing so, he became overwhelmed with the task and had to rest, but as usual, once he had rested he continued on. When he made his report, he suggested a route from Knysna to the Lange Kloof but also pointed out that it would be very expensive due to the necessity of a bridge.

During his long absences, his wife Maria looked after the children and the family home. They had a long and happy marriage and had 11 children. They were: Jane (born in 1819, died in 1899, unmarried); Johanna (born 1821 and lived until she was 61, having married Frederick Rex and borne six children); Henrietta (born in 1823, married William Southey in 1840, had two children and died in 1842); Elizabeth Alida (born in 1824, married Andries Hartzenberg in October 1843 and had a family); Williamina Robertson (born 1826, married Robert Lavers – a soldier in the Ensign 91st Foot – and had three children); Robert Alexander their first son was born in 1828 (he married Elisabeth Johanna Meintjes in January 1855, they had three children, and he died in 1880); two years later he was joined by another brother, Thomas Charles John (he married Margaret de Smidt, had 11 children – Thomas followed in his father's footsteps and became a road engineer – and died in 1893); Margaret Sophia (born in 1832 and remained unmarried); Andretta Smith (born in 1834, married William Nichol in 1852 and had a family); Victoria Frederica (born in 1837, married Dr James McCarthy and had four children – her husband died in 1874 but she lived until 1923); and finally in 1840, Andrew Geddes was born (he died the following year).

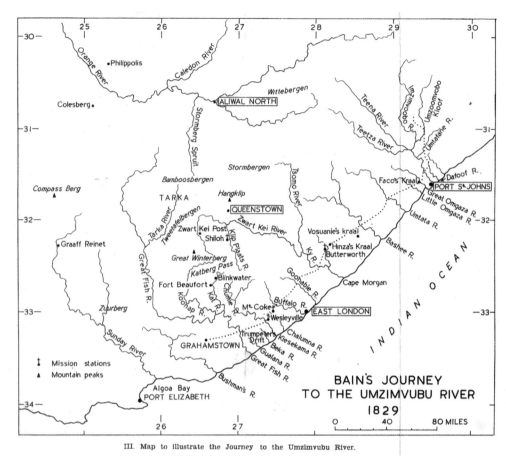

III. Map to illustrate the Journey to the Umzimvubu River.

Andrew Geddes Bain map
Courtesy the Van Riebeeck Society

Tragedy struck again on 19 November 1857, when Geddes Bain's beloved wife died. However, it did not take him long to marry Theodorra Kerr, a widow he knew prior to Maria's death, whom he wed the year after. But this marriage was short-lived and he lived the rest of his life a single man. None of his daughters were ever in favour of the marriage, although they ended up giving their father their blessing.

As mentioned earlier, Geddes Bain became involved in the Katberg Pass when he was aged 63 – a time when he should have been taking things a little easier. The Pass was constructed at an altitude of over 5000 feet in the Great Winterberg Range in order to connect Fort Beaufort and Queenstown and all the men, including Andrew, spent their nights under canvas throughout the year. In the summer the tents were sweltering, and in the winter they were freezing, but he was determined to see the project to its conclusion. However, a few times he sought to leave the mountains, as he had begun to feel unwell with all the climbing that was involved. It came to the point when he was forced to take time off and he decided to travel to England to recover from his heart complaint. The year was 1864 and he was happy to leave, as the Pass was nearly completed. He was granted 12 months leave by the Government and was given full pay for that time. During his time in London, he met some of the people he only knew through letters, and became a member the Athenaeum Club, a private gentlemen's club at Pall Mall. Notable men in the fields of art, science and literature had established it in order to discuss matters of the day in a relaxed atmosphere. It was intellect, not money, that got you membership – something that significantly set it apart from other clubs. As he felt better, he managed to attend dinner parties that he had been invited to, but he never managed to meet Lieutenant Colonel John Geddes, who had by this time returned to Scotland and made his home in Edinburgh, where he had passed away earlier in the year.

At length, Geddes Bain returned to his beloved South Africa, landing at Cape Town. He was too frail and ill to return to Katberg. Instead he stayed with the Honourable W. A. J. de Smidt, who he had known since his early road-building days. He stayed with him and his family, where he was looked after until he passed away on 20 October 1864. He was buried in Somerset Road cemetery in the town. It was later demolished at which point his family had his remains taken to Maitland. South Africa had lost one of her most notable pioneers but his legacy remained and his son, Thomas, carried on his father's profession. Thomas became a well-known road builder and engineer and was appointed Inspector of Roads in 1854. His main achievements were his work on Grey's Pass, Tulbagh Kloof, Prince Alfred's Pass, Cogman's Kloof and Zwartberg's Pass. By 1873 he was in Wellington, where he was appointed District Railway Engineer and in 1888 he was appointed Irrigation and Geological Surveyor.

The Caithness-born Andrew Geddes Bain, like so many others from the county, put his pioneering mark on a land far from home. The roads he constructed to make travel more accessible and the geological work he undertook left their indelible mark on South Africa.

JAMES BREMNER

One of the far north's most notable Victorians is engineer and wreck-raiser James Bremner. Well-known for refloating Isambard Kingdom Brunel's SS *Great Britain*, he also made his mark on his home county of Caithness.

James Bremner was born at Stain, near the coastal village of Keiss, north of Wick, on 25 September 1784. He was baptised on 10 October in Wick, the youngest of nine children to James and Janet Bremner. However, he was one of only three that survived. His father had been in the military and had seen action in the West Indies and the Irish Rebellion, and had taken some of the rebels to Fort George near Inverness at a point when the young James' interest in all things nautical was becoming self-evident. Bremner stayed with his mother and siblings in Caithness where he attended the local school until the age of 15. In the county at that time, like elsewhere in Scotland, there was no proper education system, so all the young James learned was how to read and write – neither of which he excelled at. No formal training was given to teachers, who tended to be women, and the curriculum consisted mainly of passages from the Bible. However, it was seen as important to have an education of any kind, even if it was meagre. The problem for the Bremner family was the cost, but they managed to scrape together enough money to cover the fees. It was his love of the sea that compelled him to soak up as much information about it as he could, and shipbuilding was clearly his intended career from an early age. In one recorded event when he was young, Bremner took it upon himself to launch a tub into Sinclair Bay, where he paddled out into the shallow waters. As the tub drifted further out into the bay, one of his brothers, David, spotted him and raised the alarm and he was duly brought back to shore, yet he showed no sign of being in peril. Perhaps the fact that there was no wind had something to do with it, but he was simply experimenting with the tub, to see how it floated and reacted in the water and was completely at ease with his 'boat'.

When he left school, Bremner became an apprentice at Steele and Carswell in Greenock, where he learned both theory and practice in all aspects of shipbuilding. The company had been formed by Robert Steele and John Carswell, and was fairly new when Bremner took up the position. Steele's father had died so he decided to take over the family business in Saltcoats, which had specialised in building fishing vessels and coasters, when the opportunity arose with Carswell, who had a larger shipyard at Greenock and who had the contacts necessary to make the business a success – which it was until 1815. With the cessation of hostilities from the Napoleonic Wars, there was a glut of vessels and a drop in profits. Many companies on the Clyde faced bankruptcy and partnerships were dissolved. Steele and Carswell dissolved their partnership but Steele formed a new company with his sons Robert and James, and it became the renowned Robert Steele and Sons.

For six and a half years from 1798, Bremner was apprenticed to the original company. At that time, the company was seen as unrivalled in Scotland and the opportunities for learning were varied. Both theory and practical lessons were offered on planning and building ships, as well as raising ships so they could be repaired. Moreover, in 1804, improvements to the harbour at Greenock commenced and at every opportunity, Bremner would watch every aspect of its construction. When his apprenticeship ended he made two trips to North America. He thought long and hard about migrating there and beginning his own business at Pictou in Canada. With arrangements made, his friends back in Scotland managed to dissuade him from going, so instead he returned home to Caithness. On his return he was engaged by James Traill – the Sheriff of Caithness and father of the Caithness flagstone industry – to repair boats at Castletown. It was whilst doing this that he had an innovative idea and went into business. He managed to obtain a life lease of a building yard in the Pulteneytown district, which had just been formed by the British Fishery Society, where for the next 50 years he built 56 vessels. These ranged from 45-ton ships to vessels of around 600 tons, employing workmen from the local community. At one stage he employed 60 men, building ships for markets in the south of Scotland and all over England. Among one of Bremner's most noted achievements was the building of a lifeboat, although in reality it never was put into full use due to problems with its design. In August 1846, this newly-built prototype was launched. It was a fast craft, propelled by two paddle wheels, but when it was tested on breaking surf, it was found that the wheels made it difficult to drive forward. Bremner believed a modification was all that was needed. This notwithstanding, he had designed her to turn sharply in the water, which no other boat had been able to do, and it was claimed she was virtually impossible to capsize. She was never put into full use and the project was dropped.

Shipbuilding was not Bremner's only enterprise. From 1807 he became involved in making surveys and plans for the construction of harbours and piers, which he worked on himself. In all, 19 harbours were planned, built or improved in some way by him. Probably his proudest achievement was the improvement of the Pulteneytown Harbour, and it was this that tested him most. To begin with, he found that in laying the stones on the ordinary seabed, the air got underneath and when the sea struck the stones they tilted so there was no way of getting them to stand up. It was at this point that he tried erecting the stones so that their edges faced outward towards the sea. This meant that the air came between the joints, while the stone kept its place. The original harbour was completed in 1810, but due to the expansion of trade, an outer harbour was required and was completed in 1831 at a cost of £22,000, with the men employed by Bremner working night and day. One night in September 1827, a storm hit the works at the harbour. The gales ripped it apart and eventually more than £5,000 worth of damage was done, as around 100 foot of the pier had been washed away down to the level of the low tide mark. Unperturbed, Bremner gathered together the men and rallied them to try and salvage as much of the work as they could. He was not a man to stand back idly and watch as others struggled. Huge chains were fastened down over the space of two tides to prevent any more substantial destruction from occurring. After the storm subsided, Bremner inspected the considerable damage and work began to repair it immediately. This was not the only disaster to hit the harbour project though. A few years following its completion, sand began to build up within its confines and an engineer was sent out to inspect it. This was going to be a continuous problem: the sand washed up from the shoreline and deposited there, so something had to be done as a preventative measure. This came in the form of a breakwater.

Even with Bremner's significant improvement to the harbour, he and the others involved failed to take in to account the fishing boom. As early as 1840, it was reckoned the harbour was too small and two years later Bremner knew it would have to be extended further to accommodate the steamships that now ferried the herring to other seaports. A plan of works was submitted to the British Fishery Society, in which Bremner proposed a low water harbour with its entrance in the deeper waters but away from the Wick River – which would also be free of sand by means of breakwater heads in order to deflect the sand away from the harbour. It was to be usable regardless of the tide, with a minimum depth at all times of 18 feet. At the South Harbour, work was to begin on removing the sand and also making it deeper, to accommodate the rising number of vessels using the port.

The British Fishery Society introduced a levy that each boat in the harbour had to pay. This was used for repairs and maintenance. Otherwise no contingency money for repairs was available – who better to ask than those who were actually using the harbour?

James Bremner's harbours were unique in that the heavy slate slabs were placed like books on a bookshelf. Bremner built the Castlehill Harbour in the village of Castletown around 1820 in this unique way, using the vertical slabs at a cost of around £1,500. The quay was triangulated in order to facilitate the transportation of the flagstones for which Castletown was famous in the 19th century. Between 700,000 and 800,000 foot of stone was transported from his harbour each year and it was said the industry was worth around £30,000 per annum. During its construction, Bremner also placed boom gates at the entrance, which could be 'shipped or unshipped at pleasure'. Ten years later, he designed the harbour at Sandside, Reay, which was built by Major William Innes for the local fishing industry and for exporting his surplus grain to the key markets in the south. Again, this is a fine example of the vertically-laid stone for which Bremner was famous. Other harbours included one at Sarclet and at Keiss, where he had been born. Work began on the Keiss one in 1818 but was suspended in 1821. Work recommenced,

James Bremner

thanks in the main to a government grant of £5,000. It was finally completed in 1834. At Sarclet, James had his work cut out for him. Twice the breakwater had been destroyed by the high seas. In 1834 an inspection of the harbour took place with Mr Gibb from Aberdeen and Mr Mitchell of Inverness, who drew up plans and consulted with Thomas Telford. The following year, Bremner got the work underway, using jib cranes which were placed high enough up to avoid the ferocity of the sea during the winter storms. The materials used for the sea wall was quarried in Wick and the whole breakwater was completed during the summer of 1836. His final harbour was built at Sandhaven near Fraserburgh, at a cost of £4,000. The local fishermen had forwarded a petition to the commissioners of the Herring Fishery in Edinburgh in 1835 and permission was granted for the 14-acre harbour to be built. By the year of Bremner's death, the harbour was considered a complete success with 46 boats fishing out of it.

This notwithstanding, Bremner had a growing reputation as a wreck-raiser. He is attributed to raising over 230 sunken or wrecked ships. When notified of an incident, he would go to the vessel to ascertain her position, her size and her cargo. What was vital for him was to know on what she lay – whether it was on rocks, sand or shingle – as this dictated how he would proceed. One ship that ran into trouble was the *Orion* of Pillau, Russia, which sank at Watersound in Orkney in 1825. The ship had been carrying timber and using this, plus some of the wreckage from the ship itself, he constructed a raft. On the raft paddles were attached, and five poles upon which he rigged the courses and topsails of the ship. He managed to refloat the vessel and guide it across the treacherous Pentland Firth to Pulteneytown Harbour at a speed of just over three miles an hour. Another ship, the *Lord Suffield*, ran aground off Canisbay and was totally written off. He salvaged her cargo of logs and eventually took the almost-new ship apart, towing her to the harbour in Wick. There, he totally rebuilt her. Another ship worth mentioning is the *Isabella* of Sunderland, which ran aground at Dunnet Bay during a storm. This ship posed a problem that perplexed Bremner, but not for long. She was wedged in sand and every time trenches were dug, the sea would come in and destroy them. Being a man of ingenious mind, he used locals to place heather around the trenches, which did a remarkably good job and eventually the ship floated on this heather seabed and was pulled back out into the bay and went on her way.

In 1828 the *St Nicholas* of St Petersburg in Russia became stranded on sand at Sinclair's Bay, a well-known place in Caithness that a ship might encounter danger and become wedged in the sands. She had stuck fast in 7 feet of quicksand and as the sea lashed her, she broke apart, losing her cargo of iron. Bremner, as always, rose to the challenge magnificently, but only after Mr William Harrison – who had been sent by the owners of the iron (Messrs Jevens & Sons of Liverpool) – had tried to salvage the cargo. Harrison had failed to raise a single bar, even though the exercise involved many men and cost the company upwards of £200. Bremner was then engaged. He surveyed the ship and came up with the idea of a triangulated machine made of timber with 'a floatation in the centre' and a scraping device beneath to remove the sand. The ship was eventually re-floated and 57 tons, out of 60, was salvaged. Jevens were very impressed by his efforts and in a letter to Lloyds of London as a reference for Bremner (who had applied for a position as surveyor in Wick), concluded that 'a more fitting person could not be found to undertake the charge of shipwrecked vessels' than him. A final salvage worth mentioning was a six-month-old ship called the *Uncertain*, which sank off Lewis in 1841 with over 700 tons of coal in her cargo. For two years she had laid in the sand, and although three other people tried to raise her, it was Bremner who succeeded. He used five boats and 12 floating casks attached to two pairs of boats, so that these took some of the weight of the ship when the tide was right. She made it to shore, had a temporary repair done to a hole using cowhide, and she eventually made her way to Stornoway for proper repairs.

In 1845 Bremner published his *Treatise on the Planning and Construction of Harbours in Deep Water on Submarine Pile-Driving, the Preservation of Ships Stranded and Raising of those Sunk at Sea on Principles of Lately Patented Inventions*. This pamphlet detailed some of his inventions that he used to aid in the construction of harbours, as well as those used to raise sunken wrecks. It also outlined his use of, and his misgivings about, the diving bell. His main gripe was that the bell could only be used at certain times of the year, and in his opinion, as far as sub-sea construction was concerned, it was a complete waste of time and money: it was, and still is, a very expensive business. Added to that was the fact that any work done using it was left exposed as the weather deteriorated. The other main problem was the 'limited dimensions' of the bell, which was 'barely sufficient for building a single stone at one time'. His other papers included: *An Apparatus for Floating Large Stones for Harbour Works*; *Pulteney Town Harbour*; and *A New Piling Engine*. However, most credit is given to him for the raising of the SS *Great Britain* off the coast of Ireland in August 1847. The *Great Britain*, which had been designed initially for the luxury passenger trade, had been launched in 1843 and had a 1,000 horsepower steam engine. On her maiden voyage to America she managed to break the previous speed record. The 3,500-ton ship was at that time the largest in the world, and the first iron-hulled vessel to be built, but she had run aground the previous year whilst on her way from Liverpool to New York. The ship's captain, James Hoskin, made an error in his calculation of the ship's speed and to compound matters, the charts available to him were poor, so when he saw the lighthouse at St John's Point, he mistook it for the Chicken Rock lighthouse off the Isle of Man. Some of the United Kingdom's most eminent engineers had tried to move the *Great Britain* but to no avail. It is said that Brunel himself believed that only one man would be able to move her and that was none other than James Bremner. Bremner took his eldest surviving son Alexander with him to raise the stricken vessel.

Alexander had been born in 1817 and had followed in his father's footsteps. After many years of aiding him on numerous projects, he worked for six years as assistant engineer on the harbours at Lossiemouth, Garnish and Calicott before becoming his brother David's assistant on work at the West Hartlepool Dockworks under James Simpson. For the next six years he practised as an engineer in his own right. His father chose him to aid him on the *Great Britain* project.

In October 1846 Bremner and Alexander travelled to Dundrum Bay in County Down to have a look at the stuck ship. She lay on mountain limestone covered with sand, but the damage that they could see was minimal. Following their inspection, they reported back to the directors of the Great Western Steamship Company in Bristol, who owned her, on how best to protect the vessel over the winter, with a view to moving her when conditions were favourable. However, on 19 November that year, a gale caused the ship to move and she ended up being suspended on a projecting rock. This storm caused severe damage to the engines. In a letter, Bremner wrote that he had left the vessel in the hands of Captain Claxton who was stuffing her larboard with 'faggots, brushwood, sandbags, and chains and bolts' as Brunel had ordered, but he was unconvinced of its effect. In order to move her, he claimed that she would have to be raised '13 feet perpendicular height, then her bottom patched' and finally launched so she could be repaired properly in England. He hoped to return to her in April the following year in order to raise her, and hoped that she would not be in danger over the winter months. It was on 13 May the following year that Bremner finally went back to the ship for an inspection. He noted that attempts had already been made to move her. But it was not until August that she was finally moved with the aid of the HMS *Birkenhead*, which had arrived with 50 riggers from the dockyards at Portsmouth and Plymouth. The *Great Britain* was moved astern at high water and was laid on a sandbank until she was ready to be moved to a place of safety. At first, she was supposed to go to Ardglass (an historic fishing port 30 miles south of Belfast), but a thick fog had descended, so she went instead to the Ulster capital. Here she was placed on a mud bank at Belfast Lough. Unfortunately, the mud seeped into her damaged base but after labourers freed her, she was taken to Liverpool to undergo repairs.

Yet Bremner never saw the raising of the *Great Britain* as his greatest achievement in this capacity. When he died in 1856, the obituary in the local newspaper claimed that Bremner felt the recovery of a ship fully laden with coal off the West Highland coast was a much greater personal triumph to him.

Not only was he involved in harbour building and wreck-raising, but James Bremner also worked with the Aberdeen, Clyde and Leith Steam Shipping Company as their agent in Wick. For 12 years, he ferried passengers and goods out of Wick to the ships in the bay, and although these waters can be dangerous, not once was there a loss of life or a loss of goods during this time. He was a natural seaman. The eminent geologist Hugh Miller met Bremner in Wick and later wrote that he had a feeling that he was a rather melancholy and sad individual. He could not understand how a man of genius like him could be working for a steamship company as an agent, when he had been so gifted in his earlier years. He wrote: 'Napoleon … could have estimated more adequately than our British rulers the value of such a man', and that if he had indeed been French, Bremner would not be working 'as a mere agent'. During the visit, Miller was perplexed by Bremner's use of stone in his harbours vertically rather than horizontally. Received wisdom had dictated that they should in fact be laid horizontally, but his reply was very simple: there was one rule for the land and a different one for the sea. As he pointed out, his stones, set on end, were wedged together 'like staves in an anker' and after many, many years were still wedged, regardless of what the sea threw at them. Bremner of course, was no stranger to the might of the seas.

On one occasion while he was heading to Orkney, Bremner was on board the steamer *Queen*. The boat had left Ackergill Bay at 7.00 a.m. on 30 March 1850 in heavy seas and as time passed, the weather worsened. In fact, Bremner likened it to a hurricane. The *Queen* was a 700-ton boat but with the heavy seas, he reckoned there was 30 tons of water on the deck at times, such were the horrendous conditions. By the following morning, there was no change but later, in the early afternoon, the wind subsided and the sea calmed. In notes he made, he wrote that: 'hardly has it ever been known that so heavy a gale continued so long'. The reason for this was that it happened to be the spring equinox.

In 1851 he contributed to the Great Exhibition of the Works of Industry of All Nations in London, which was the largest showcase industry had ever seen in Victorian Britain and the brainchild of Prince Albert. Exhibitors came from all over the Empire and beyond, and it lasted for 141 days with over 6 million visitors entering the Crystal Palace. In all, around £186,000 was raised and this was used to fund, amongst other things, the Victoria and Albert Museum. Tickets ranged in price from a shilling for the day for the working classes to 3 guineas for the upper classes. Needless to say, more shillings were gathered than guineas. Among the exhibits was a precursor to the fax machine, kitchen appliances, and, from America, a reaping machine. It was here in the Crystal Palace that Bremner received the public recognition he more than deserved for his work. Models of the apparatus he used in the salvage of the SS *Great Britain* had been put on display which had demonstrated their use in the treacherous conditions that the sea could muster.

Bremner was married on 24 May 1811 to the very amiable Christian Sinclair and had numerous children, some of whom died in infancy. His life was marred immeasurably by the death of one of his sons, David, who had followed in his father's footsteps and had become a chief engineer for the Clyde Trustees in Glasgow. He was Bremner's second son, born in Wick in 1819, and showed his interest in engineering from a very early age. He had helped his father with the building of the harbour at Lossiemouth in Moray then had trained as a civil engineer with John Gibb of Aberdeen. After a stint in London, he had returned to Scotland in 1844 and took up the position of chief engineer on the Clyde in February 1846, but all those years of working in water took its toll and on 14 March 1852, he passed away, unmarried, aged 33. His body was brought back to his hometown by both rail and steamer, where he was interred in the family plot. This affected Bremner deeply and he never fully recovered. In 1856, tragedy hit the family once more when his wife died on 14 May. Only a few months later, in August 1856, Bremner himself passed away. On the morning of his death, he had been at work as usual but everyone had noticed that since Christian's death, he had not been a well man. Many said it was as if he had given up on life without her. On his return home to the Round House in Harbour Place, he fell ill and by the evening Wick had lost a remarkable son. As a mark of respect, when the news spread, all the ships in the port lowered their flags to half mast. The local newspaper, *The John O'Groat Journal* ran the obituary for him, expressing profound regret at the loss of the man who had been 'so long and honourably associated with that of the town'. The paper also expressed its disbelief at the death, noting that although people knew he was old and failing 'in physical strength ... he had shown no signs of such a speedy dissolution'. In fact, he had been an incredibly healthy man throughout his adult life. He was known to have stood in water for upwards of two tides, dripping wet, and still manage to bark orders without any hesitation or any hoarseness in his voice. He was interred at Wick Old Parish Churchyard. The funeral was a large affair, with many ordinary townsfolk paying their respects. Among the other mourners were the Honourable Captain Dunbar of Latheronwheel, the Sheriff, Mr Russell and numerous ministers including the Reverend Mackay of Inverness, the Reverend Gunn of Watten and the Reverend Lillie of Wick. The Pulteney Improvement Commissioners – as well as many merchants, fish curers, local farmers and tradesmen – also attended in great numbers to pay their respects.

In 1833, Bremner had become a member of the Institution of Civil Engineers and in 1844 he was awarded the highest honour given to British engineers: the Telford Medal, in memory of Thomas Telford who was its first president until his death in 1834. This award was bestowed on Bremner for his important papers on the work he had done on the construction of harbours and for the raising of wrecks. This is remarkable for a man who had no mathematical talent, but was simply a naturally gifted engineer. He was also known not be an articulate man, and often his mind would drift off when someone was talking to him. One thing he did possess was a fiery temper, although it has to be said that his outbursts were short, sharp, to the point and over just as quickly as they began. There was another side to him too. On seeing disaster unfold in front of him, his first action was to help the sailors to safety, but if he were unable to do so, he would shed tears for them. Often he would allow the men he saved, especially the ships' captains, to stay with him and offer them hospitality until they were able to go home. His generosity under these circumstances became legendary. There are stories of him helping a widow who owed money and was having her goods sold on the street, and of him handing out food and money to the poor of Wick and its environs from his home.

Wick honoured James Bremner with a portrait that was gifted by the people of Wick to his family by Provost William Bruce. The subscribers, who were in fact local townspeople as well as acquaintances of Bremner himself, presented Bremner and his wife with it on 7 April 1833 as a 'token of their esteem and admiration in which he is held by all who know him'. The dedication goes on to mention his daring rescues of so many men who were in peril on the sea and how he so often placed his own life in danger to help them. On several occasions, the dedication calls him a 'genius'. Long after he died, the Wick Town Council appealed for money to have a lasting memorial erected in his honour. An obelisk was constructed at South Head above the harbour in 1903 following the appeal. It is inscribed on three sides. To the north, facing his beloved Pulteneytown Harbour it reads:

> Fellow Caithness men and kinsfolk at home and abroad raised this
> memorial in 1903 to the resourceful, fearless and beneficent genius of
> JAMES BREMNER C.E Naval Architect and Harbour Builder.

On the east-facing plaque, which faces the Moray Firth and North Sea, the inscription reads:

> Wick Harbour is sheltered by one of 18 yet efficient breakwaters on this coast
> by his skill. He saved scores of wrecked mariners' lives at the risk of his own. He
> refloated 236 stranded or sunken vessels including the Great Britain.

The third plaque, facing the west, gives a short account of his life and death.

> In life, James Bremner had been an impulsive man, although some also
> thought he was rather impetuous too, but nothing in his harbour-building
> or shipbuilding career daunted him. He was once described as 'Herculean',
> and he had been described as being a handsome man who was fair, kind and
> benevolent. In death, his loss was a tragedy for not only the people of Wick
> but also the civil engineering fraternity as a whole.

The SS *Great Britain* was sold on to Gibbs Bright &Co to take emigrants to Australia during the Gold Rush of the 1850s. She continued to sail until 1886, when she became a floating warehouse in the Falkland Islands until 1937. Thereafter, she was abandoned. She now lies in dry dock in Bristol, having been salvaged in 1970, and is both a museum and a venue for functions. As for Alexander Bremner – who had helped his father raise the great ship – he was involved in the building of several piers and improvements to harbours such as Rothesay and Gourock. He emigrated to Australia but returned to England. He became involved in the construction of a steamer that was to take him to China where he was to raise submerged vessels. However, he caught cholera there and died at Shanghi on 20 October 1862. The disease killed him in less than eight hours. Only a year earlier, he had become an associate of the Institution of Civil Engineers.

James Bremner memorial, Wick

Of their 11 children only three daughters and two sons survived their parents, including Alexander Bremner. James, born in 1820, served an apprenticeship under his father but he decided to leave Caithness and eventually set up a shipbuilding business in Hull, where he died in 1876. As for his daughters: Christian married James Bell, captain of a ship with the Cunard Line and died in Liverpool aged 86; Jessie left the county too and worked in Glasgow where she died in 1884 aged 70; and finally Sarah married a doctor and settled in England, where she died in 1913 aged 82. Bremner's grandson James Bell, son of Christian and James, carried on the family tradition of engineering, although his work centred on railway construction.

The portrait of James Bremner given to the family by the Wick Town Council in the 1830s was returned to Wick by his great-great grandson, James, where it now hangs in the Town Hall in tribute to the engineering brilliance of a Wick family.

ROBERT BROWN

When Dr Robert Brown died in 1895, Scotland lost one of her foremost scientists and explorers. He was also author of the books *Manual of Botany* in 1874, *The World, Its Cities and Peoples* 1882–1885 and the four-volume *The Story of Africa and Its Explorers,* published between 1892 and 1895. He also wrote many articles and scientific papers during his lifetime and is not to be confused with Robert Brown of Montrose, the eminent botanist who died in 1858. To make this distinction, Brown called himself *Camsterianus* after his birthplace.

Robert Brown was born at Camster on 23 March 1842. He was christened at Bower on 20 April that year. He was the son of Thomas Brown – a farmer – and his wife Ann Stewart. The harsh Caithness climate forced the family to move when Brown was still a youngster, because his father's health could not withstand the weather in the north. The family moved to Coldstream in Berwickshire.

While Brown was studying at the University of Edinburgh, his interest in botany grew. He won prizes for essays that he wrote on plants such as marine algae, and he knew this was the path he wished to pursue. Before taking his final exams he embarked on a journey in order to study natural history. Upon his return from this trip in the far reaching areas of the North Sea and North Atlantic, he gained passage on the ship *Narwhal* having been appointed the ship's surgeon. As far as Brown was concenred, although the role of surgeon was important, it was simply a means to an end. On this expedition he managed to participate in the seal and whale hunts in the waters around northern Greenland. He returned to the port of Dundee in October 1861 and travelled back to Edinburgh to complete his studies.

During the following summer Brown's thoughts once again turned to travel. His timing was perfect. The British Columbia Botanical Association of Edinburgh had proposed some years earlier that they wished to do some research in Oregon in the United States, but having appointed John Jeffrey as their lead collector, the actual expedition failed to get off the ground because Jeffrey was dismissed from his post due to lack of attention.

At the 1862 meeting Brown was approached to see if he would be interested in such an expedition, this time to Canada. When he replied in the affirmative, the association approved but thought it would be best if the whole idea was put on hold until enough money had been raised by means of subscription. The following spring was favoured, if the subscriptions were forthcoming.

On 23 February 1863 Brown was appointed to the post. His remit was to collect seeds and plant specimens over a three-year period, in which time he would be paid £80 in the first year, rising to £120 in the third and final year of the expedition. In March he set sail from Southampton, bound for the West Indies, where he landed safely. He then took the train overland before catching a ship to San Francisco, where he changed ships again – although he had to wait over a week before the next one sailed for Canada. On 6 May 1863 he set foot on Canadian soil for the first time, arriving at Victoria. Here he met many prominent locals, such as Governor James Douglas, and he managed to secure passage on a ship owned by a local sawmill owner, which took him to Alberni. He arrived in the town on 25 May and left on his expedition the following morning. As he travelled, he discovered a lake that was not reflected on his map, so he called it Sproat Lake. As he travelled down the Alberni Inlet, he collected samples of the local flora and fauna. Surprisingly, he found many of the plants were not indigenous, so therefore believed that the local settlers had introduced them. He stayed for three weeks before returning to Alberni, and then travelling on to Victoria, where the local press interviewed him. His blossoming reputation had begun.

At the end of July, Brown waved goodbye to the fine citizens of Victoria and headed to the United States. At one stage during his travels, he took a canoe up the Snohomish River and travelled with Native American Indians to Seattle using an old Indian trail. One of the most frustrating episodes happened when he had to cross a river on his horse and all his seeds that he had collected so carefully were soaked. All of them were ruined and his hard work had been for nothing. From Seattle, Brown returned to Victoria and arrived in the town at the end of August. Only two days later, on 1 September 1863, he began his next expedition. He made his way to the mainland by way of the Fraser River, stopping off at New Westminster for a week. Here he collected a number of samples before heading off to Lillooet, where he spent another week taking samples of the local plants. On his return to Victoria he had all his seeds packed up carefully and shipped back to Scotland. Not content for this to be the last outing of the year, he decided to return to Alberni, in order to see if the Great Central Lake was indeed the 40 or 50 miles long it was said to be. On 22 October, when he arrived at the head of it, he measured it to be a great deal less: it was only about 18 miles long. He returned to Alberni again but only for a week, due to the incessant rain. He left and returned to Victoria in order to spend the winter there. But it seems the rain followed him for he wrote that during these winter months, it simply rained and rained.

He managed to spend this time at the local theatres and having dinner with prominent men such as the former chief factor of the Hudson's Bay Company, John Todd; and the trader Captain William McNeill. It was also during this period that his thoughts turned towards his funding. The trips he had taken so far had cost more than anticipated and he feared that if he did not write to the Botanical Association about it, the money would simply run out. He explained that the Hudson Bay Company could not foot the bill incurred from staying in their properties nor could the company give him passage – be it at reduced cost or free indefinitely. He also explained to the association that he was not only gathering seeds and plant samples, but he was also involved in cataloguing the indigenous languages of the Native American Indians. The reply he received was that he was only there in the first place to collect seeds – not to write about his findings of new languages. Brown was unimpressed by this. He did not see himself as merely a seed collector: he thought of himself as an explorer, geologist, and botanist. By the late spring the association had become disillusioned with him: he had promised to send over seeds but none had arrived. They even contemplated relieving him of his duties. In turn, Brown had become disillusioned with them and, due to lack of funds being forthcoming to continue, he found himself a new sponsor in the form of the Vancouver Island Exploring Expedition.

Vancouver Island had been explored before, but not exhaustively and there was renewed interest following the demise of the gold rushes of 1858 and 1861. If there was gold on the island, the economic benefits would be overwhelming and the only way to find it was to set up an expedition. Gold had been found at Goldstream near Victoria in 1863, so it was hoped by the sponsors of the new expedition that more would be found. This was the primary reason why it was given the go-ahead. An official sponsor came in the form of Governor Arthur Kennedy who had taken office in March 1864. On 20 April Kennedy promised two dollars from the federal reserves for every one dollar raised by the public. In May the local newspaper the *Evening Express* published a glowing report about Brown's 1863 expedition that had been delivered to the Botanical Association of Edinburgh the year before. It also reported that Brown had already applied for the position of head of the forthcoming mission, citing that he was ready and able to undertake the task, being not just a botanist but also a zoologist, aptly capable of taking notes on the topography and ethnology to be found in the various parts of the island. On 1 June he was formally appointed expedition leader.

In order to placate his sponsors back in Edinburgh, Brown wrote to them explaining his new position and told them they would have no extra costs because of it. Back in Edinburgh, the association was furious. They felt that he could no longer do the job he had been sent out there to do. The situation was left hanging in the air as the expedition got underway.

Brown was joined by the artist Frederick Whymper, the son of an English wood engraver. Whymper had narrowly escaped massacre by the Chilcotin Indians when he decided to leave the road builders he had been working with on the Bute Inlet. John Meade, a former soldier, was another to join the group and Lieutenant Peter Leach was appointed second-in-command. Also joining them were two university students: botanist John Buttle and John Foley – who was knowledgeable on bushcraft and knew about copper mining and gold digging. Lastly there was Ranald Macdonald, having been involved in the Australian gold fields and who, by all accounts, was a lively person (even though he was the oldest of them all) and well-liked within the group. On 7 June 1864 the men embarked on the gunboat *HMS Grappler* at Victoria, bound for Cowichan. When the party arrived, Brown employed Tomo Antione – a one-armed hunter, trapper and farmer who was among the 200 settlers in the town. He was notorious for having been accused of killing his wife, but was acquitted on the grounds of lack of evidence. Brown chose him to join them because of both his hunting skills and the fact that he was a good linguist. Antione's mother had been Chinook, which meant he could negotiate with other natives in the area and that he knew the region well. Later, Brown attributed the success of mapping Vancouver Island to Antione.

By the time the expedition, which had split into land and water groups, reached Lake Cowichan, they had been joined by yet another man, Kakalatza, the joint chief of the Somenos. During this time, gold had been discovered locally and quartz, copper and iron ore had also been detected in the surrounding mountains. It was also here that Brown noted the beauty of the forests and the myriad of wildlife that had made the area home; such as hummingbirds and eagles. The group was then split up once more, with half heading towards the south side of the lake to Port San Juan under the command of Leech, and Brown leading the other group to the west end of the lake, then following the Nitinat River in order to meet up with Leech and his party at Port San Juan. At the port they would receive new supplies from the Vancouver Island Exploring Expedition Committee.

When the two groups met up, they exchanged notes. Leech and his men had been forced to chop down bush and trees in order to make it through the terrain and mark it on the map. They were exhausted when they arrived and had been disappointed to find that in fact no supplies were waiting for them. Brown and his team had a fairly easy passage, but they too were deflated at the lack of food and equipment. However, the supplies did arrive a few days later. Upon his arrival, Brown picked up his mail. The Botanical Association in Edinburgh had written demanding that he send back his journals. They urged in most pressing terms that he concentrate on seed collection. This was neither what Brown wanted nor what he was doing. The Botanical Association saw him as a seed collector and his new patrons saw him as the leader of a gold prospecting party. It did not help matters when he later discovered that Leech had made a gold discovery during an absence that saw Brown back in Victoria. This brought a new gold rush and jeopardized the whole expedition.

Whilst Brown was in Victoria, Leech and his men made their way for Cowichan again. It was on a tributary of the Sooke River that they discovered the gold and it was only when Brown joined them in late July that he was told. Leech's men were ecstatic with the find but Brown knew the whole expedition was in peril: it was human nature to prospect gold when it was found, rather than continue on an expedition that could involve very little reward. In order to protect the mission, he wrote to the Vancouver Island Exploring Committee, requesting that they withhold pay from anyone who had no certificate of service.

In August, the two groups once more headed off in different directions and again it was Leech's group who had the more arduous journey. They ran out of food and were grateful when they reached Sarita Lake, where they fished. Brown's group had a more pleasant journey in canoes along the coast to Comox. He discovered coal, much to the delight of the settlers. On 24 September, Brown, Leech and their men arrived back in Alberni, tired of living in the wilderness and fearful of their lives due to the troubled relationship with the local native Indians. In October, Brown received word that the explorers were to be picked up by the ship *Grappler* a week later. In the meantime, the group explored what had been termed a well-established route – in reality they found it to be anything but. The journey took them from Alberni to the Qualicum River, but it was not as beautiful as had been recorded. On 21 October, they boarded the ship and returned to Victoria. A heroes' welcome awaited them, with Brown being the most highly praised. A very successful exhibition was held for all the drawings that Whymper had done.

In April 1865, Brown's account of the expedition was published. The 27-page *Vancouver Island Exploration 1864* included the route that had been taken, the mineral deposits found and an outline of the potential agricultural benefits of the region. He also listed the place names that they had given to various settlements he had established. The publication met with a great deal of success, but due to lack of support from Edinburgh, Brown sent a resignation letter along with the seed samples that he had found. A little later, Brown received word that his resignation would not be accepted.

Shortly after its publication, Brown set out on another expedition – this time to Washington and Oregon. Over the course of the trip he collected numerous plants and seeds and travelled through the Cascade Mountains and the Sierra Nevada mountains, which led him to San Francisco. From here he returned to Victoria in Canada, in October. In March 1866, following his hibernation over the winter, he headed out to the Queen Charlotte Islands with a group of coal miners. He travelled along the east coast of Vancouver Island and stopped off at Fort Rupert. Here he came across whisky-drinking natives and Indian prostitutes, which he later wrote about. It was a sight that disgusted him. It was not the fact that they were involved in drinking and prostitution, but that they had been encouraged into it by traders who wanted simply to make money out of them. By May, he had returned to Victoria, having discovered one last group of natives: the Koskeemo Indians. It was here that he received his dismissal from the Botanical Association back in Edinburgh. The seeds he had sent over had rotted during the journey and he was told the results from his explorations were less than satisfactory, therefore his services were no longer required.

A result of his dismissal was the option for one final expedition, although it never achieved its objective, due to hostile natives. In July, along with the writer and artist E. T. Coleman, he decided to try and climb Mount Baker; a mountain which had previously never been climbed. However, after travelling along the Skagit River in order to reach their destination, they met a bunch of hostile natives and promptly abandoned the climb.

Before returning home in 1866, Brown visited Leechtown where a burgeoning community was established. The town could boast shops and hotels and many smaller settlements had begun to spring up for the prospecting miners. Gold had brought prosperity, although many miners were now turning their thoughts to Big Bend where the gold was more easily extracted in greater quantities. Brown enjoyed his stay, but it was time for him to return home to Britain. Instead of taking a direct route though, he travelled through California, Nicaragua and the West Indies. When he arrived back in Edinburgh, he divided his time between the capital, Kew Gardens in London and the British Museum where he took notes. In April 1867, he headed for Greenland on an expedition with Edward Whymper, where he observed the wildlife as well as collecting botanical specimens.

A year later, Brown applied for the Chair of Botany at the Royal College of Science in Ireland. Even though he had glowing testimonials, he was not elected. Disappointed, he turned to lecturing instead at Heriot-Watt (which was then a college), and the Andersonian Institute in Glasgow. In 1873 he applied for the Chair of Botany at the University of Edinburgh, but was again unsuccessful. So too was his foray into British mainstream publishing: he had hoped his memoirs on his journeying in Canada would be published in the United Kingdom, but instead he opted for a niche in the German market and was awarded a doctorate by the University of Rostock because of it. He submitted articles to various British publications however, and these were printed. His scientific publications (specifically those for the scientific societies) included work on ethnology, ornithology and geology, as well as botany. For the more mainstream publications, he commented on Canadian society and wrote of the indigenous peoples he met – although these tended to be unsympathetic, as he often referred to them as being untrustworthy. He also contributed to H. W. Bates' *Illustrated Travels: A Record of Discovery, Geography and Adventure* (1869–1875). In this he wrote an account of his expedition to Port San Juan in precise detail. Later in *The Races of Mankind* (1873–1876), he wrote an account of Native American life as he saw it from his observations. All of this published material helped him financially, especially after 1875 when he married Kristiane Rudmose in Copenhagen on 3 August of that year. She was the daughter of a Danish schoolteacher. He managed to secure a position with *The Echo* in 1876 and moved to London. Two years later he found a position with *The Standard* where he became a member of the editorial staff and he continued to write articles until his death in Streatham, south London in 1895. The couple had two sons.

Brown looked back on his days in Canada with a great deal of nostalgia. For example, in *Countries of the World* (1876–1881) he wrote extensively on his travels between Sooke and Victoria, and wrote roughly the same amount for his travels in Washington, Idaho and California. A year after he died, his final work was published. Although it was only an introduction to a book entitled *The Adventures of John Jewitt* (1896) with notes, he wrote of his own experiences, even though this happened almost a century after Jewitt's captivity there.

Throughout his life, Brown was firm friends with Robert Dick, the baker and geologist of Thurso. They corresponded with each other and in his *Remarks on the Flora of Caithness,*

Brown referred to Dick's find of *Luzula forsteri* near Thurso (usually only found south of the Thames) and how he had gone to the locality to see it for himself. He never forgot his Caithness roots, even though he had left the county at such a young age.

ANSTRUTHER DAVIDSON

In 1923, the definitive book of the flora of southern California hit the bookshops. This was the culmination of over three decades of study by the dermatology professor and keen amateur botanist Anstruther Davidson, who had been born in the village of Watten in Caithness in 1860.

Davidson was the eighth of ten children born to George Davidson and Ann McAdam. Before him had come Isabella, Charles, Peter, Jane, George, William and Thomas, later joined by Ann and Robert. George was from the county town of Wick and Ann was the daughter of Peter McAdam, (who had been born in Anstruther in Fife) and Jane Gunn of Watten, and it is through this connection with his Fife-born grandfather that he was given the name 'Anstruther'. McAdam's father Peter (Davidson's great-grandfather) had moved to Caithness following the purchase of the Watten estate and Bridgend by Sir Robert Anstruther of Balcaskie, 3rd Baronet, around 1780 – for whom he had worked in Fife as a miller. He bought the Caithness property from Sinclair Manson, who had lost his money due to the failure of Douglas Heron & Co, the Ayr bank that collapsed in 1773.

McAdam Senior had apprenticed in Leith but had been thrown in jail for refusing to work on the Sabbath Day. However, after a year languishing in the cell, he gave in and finished the apprenticeship, finding work in Anstruther in Fife once he had completed the course. The move to Caithness had its problems and all the children were sent to Fife for their schooling. Later, Peter and his son (Davidson's grandfather) went down to Balcaskie with the proceeds from Watten Mill. However, when McAdam Senior died, his son Peter took over the tenancy of the Mill and that of Bridgend Farm with his wife Jane Gunn.

George Davidson (Davidson's father) made his living as a farmer, working 100 acres. In the 1850s he employed five labourers and a domestic servant at the 142-acre arable farm at Cogle. By the 1861 census, he employed just two servants and two ploughmen to help on the farm.

Davidson's early education came from the local school and following that, he attended Pulteneytown Academy under the tutelage of Mr Dick. However, when he was just nine years old, tragedy struck the young family. His father was diagnosed with stomach cancer and died on 25 September 1869, leaving Ann to bring up the ten children. Davidson's older brother Charles took over the running of the farm, employing three men and two women to help him. The death of his father spurred Davidson on to do well at school and he threw all his energies into studying. In 1876, along with his brother Thomas, he passed his university entrance exam and left Caithness to study medicine at the University of Glasgow, where his interest in botany was stimulated further. He graduated as a medical practitioner in 1887, and left his native Scotland for the United States of America two years later, where his chosen field of medicine was dermatology. He spent some time at the University of California, rising to assistant professor of dermatology. He also spent time at the Good Samaritan Hospital in Los Angeles, where he became consultant dermatologist right up until the end of his life.

Davidson found he had a keen interest in the flora and fauna of California: something that had stayed with him since his time back in Scotland. He had written about the flora and fauna of Sanquhar in southern Scotland as an appendage to James Brown's *A History of Sanquhar ... To which is added The Flora and Fauna of the District by Dr Anstruther Davidson* which was duly published two years after his emigration to the States. In the Sanquhar book, he wrote that in 'the interests of the botanist', he had closely followed the classification that had been given in the *London Catalogue of Flora* in its 8th edition, to which he added the more 'familiar English name, the locality where found and its comparative rarity' for each of the specimens he found in Sanquhar's vicinity. Like elsewhere, he found that 'the geological formation exercises an important influence on the floral distribution'. Altitude too had its part to play: it had 'likewise an interesting and, to the close observer, quite as marked an influence on the distribution of the various species' in a region. During his years of research he found that Sanquhar district had no less than 40 species, which had until that time been unrecorded in any other part of Dumfriesshire. Two of these species: the yellow pond lily (*Nuphar intermedium*); and the floating rush (*Juncus fluitans*), were found to be exceptionally rare, 'having previously been reported from – with the possible exception of Thornhill – but three or four other places in Britain'. He went on to list hundreds of plants and mosses, recording where he found them and their rarity. These included: goldilocks; marsh marigold; creeping crowfoot; smooth-headed poppy; yellow rocket; marsh violet; shepherd's purse; marsh cinquefoil; catsfoot; burdock; common comfrey; black willow; marsh horse tail; and moonwort. Each of these had the Latin name listed alongside the common English name.

Of the numerous birds nesting in the district, he noted that 'the songsters rank first, both in numbers and importance'. Of these, the missel thursh and the blackbird were very common. He also noted that the wheatear was the most regular migrant to the area, 'usually arriving on the 2nd of April' and was most commonly found on the upland pastures. He observed the dipper (or water craw), which was 'one of the few birds hardy enough to withstand the winter's snows': it could be 'found along almost all the water courses year after year in the same locality'. His diligence led to an interesting observation of black-headed gulls. In the spring of 1884 a few pairs of these gulls had nested on the island in the Black Loch, but over the next few seasons 'their numbers so increased that the eggs literally covered the island' and some of them were unable to find space for a nest, so they built themselves 'nests like little boats on the floating leaves of the bog-bean and water-lilies that abound in the lake'. Among the many birds he managed to list were sandpipers, curlews, starlings, swifts, magpies, cuckoos, tawny owls, ducks, and herons. He concluded that the list he had produced was simply the 'fruits of but a few years' observation on the part of the writer', and was 'probably far from complete'.

Lastly he turned his attention to the animals of the district. Almost all of these that he observed were common and well-known species. The rarest he saw were the 'pole cat – now very seldom seen and probably limited to the Memmock Glen – and the otter, of which but a few exist on this section of the Nith'. In the outlying areas or in quiet glens that very few people disturbed, a few foxes were found and every year they produced cubs. Among the other animals he recorded were hares, rabbits and mountain hares, which were abundant. He noted that these animals were not 'indigenous, having been introduced on Hartfell, and subsequently on Cairntable, some fifty or sixty years ago, from which they have spread over all the higher ground'. Among the small rodents he found brown rats, voles, field mice, harvest mice, moles, weasels, squirrels, hedgehogs and the common rat. As with the plants, he had listed their Latin name and where he had found them.

It is his work on botany in America for which most credit is given. For over 40 years Davidson made expeditions all over southern California in search of new species of plants or rare ones, which he began cataloguing. He travelled thousands of miles, examining the seashore, mountains, wetlands and prairies of the area, but during that time many species of plants were lost due to the industrialisation of the district and the influx of an ever-increasing population. In the early part of the 20th century for example, he found that the tubers of the *Helianthus*, commonly known as sunflowers, were being burned to make way for human habitation. Swampland too was beginning to disappear – with its various plants to boot – to make way for railways stations and other engineering projects, all of which deeply concerned Davidson.

Over the course of his travels he submitted numerous articles detailing his finds to the *Bulletin* of Southern California's Academy of Sciences (he was also a founding member of the academy in 1891). These articles included field notes from 1894, botanical records of new or noteworthy species in 1911, new Californian plants in 1923, and numerous pieces on specific plants he found, such as *Delphinium* in 1908 and *Opuntia rubriflora* in 1911. By 1922 he had discovered new botanical species in the area and a year later he published his seminal work: the *Flora of Southern California* with G. L. Moxley. He continued writing articles about the plants he found until his untimely death.

In May 1906, Davidson and Dr Herman Hasse, a German-born lichenologist, went to Shoemakers' Ranch on Big Rock Creek to discover what plants or animal life lived there. Dr Hasse had published *Lichens of Southern California* in 1898 but knew there were species still to be found. The area lies at the desert foothills, some 30 miles east of Palmdale. The desert itself had no life, but 4,000 feet above the foothills some wild flowers were to be found. From the ranch, a wagon was able to take the men up to 7,000 feet where the Lowell Mine had been established. En route they discovered two new varieties and some that had not been catalogued for California. These included a woolly-fruited form of *Layia heterotricha*: a herb native to and endemic in California, usually found below 5,000 feet in both wetlands and non-wetlands. Nearer to the mine, he found what he named *Phacelia davidsonii*: an annual herb commonly known today as Davidson's phacelia; as well as small-flowered *Phacelia*, which had not been identified.

It was while he was on holiday in Meadows Bear Valley in the San Bernadino Mountains in July 1909 that Davidson discovered a new species of mariposa lily; one of the most beautiful wild flowers to be found in California and member of the *Liliaceae* family. The flower was named 'mariposa' by the Spanish who had settled in the area – they thought it closely resembled the wings of a butterfly because of its beautiful and varied colours. It was found in the foothills and the ravines of the mountains during the early spring, before the moisture evaporated from the heat of the sun as summer drew closer, near to the streams and pastures bordering the southern side of the Bear Valley dam. He named his new botanical find *Calochortus paludicola*. It was also in the Bear Valley that he took measurements of some trees such as the western juniper, which was scattered in patches around the dam. He noted that the white fir and the yellow pines were the largest trees he came across. These trees were soon to be lost when the dam was raised by another 12 feet. Others he noted were firs that were anything up to 100 feet high when they grew in the wetter soils. At Buff Lake Meadow he measured a circumference of one that was 22 feet at a point just 5 feet from the ground. Of all the trees he looked at he found the oldest one to have 255 rings. The rings also showed that its growth had slowed from its 18-inch diameter over the first 45 years to only 4 inches in the 90 years prior to when he took his measurements.

Davidson had travelled to the Bear Valley by stage on the old road by the Squirrel Inn. This took him through a fir and pine forest that he thoroughly enjoyed. He noted on the journey how some of the dead trees had spiral trunks, usually running left to right but occasionally right to left. He thought this unusual and asked his driver why this should be. Allegedly knowing about trees, the man replied that the trees with the twists were all female. Davidson was sceptical. A few years later he visited Redondo, where he actually saw the twisting occurring. He noted that the branches on the sunny side of the tree were much better developed and covered with foliage rather than those on the shaded side. Also, the prevailing winds seemed to be coming from the west, so on that particular side the tree was under pressure because of the weight of the branches and the natural grain of the wood became twisted. It depended on the position of the heavier branches whether the grain twisted to the left or right. The twisted pines were no use to the local lumberjacks, so he concluded that was the reason they had survived in the area.

In April 1910 on the banks of the Haiwee Reservoir in Inyo County he discovered the *Acrolasia tridentata*: a small plant with prickly leaves that has a flower loosely resembling a buttercup. He described it as short – roughly two inches – with a flower measuring roughly five inches. A month later he discovered *Lepidium perfoliatum*: a member of the mustard family and commonly known as clasping pepperweed, which he found in Drumholly Tract in Hollywood. Another botanist, Mr Amos Heller, also found it growing in Oregon and Salt Lake City. At the bluff at Del Mar in Orange County, Davidson found *Plantago bigelovii*: a herb that had also been recorded at Inglewood, Los Angeles, but which he believed was probably growing on many of the sea cliffs of California. Heller's son Ronald also discovered plants, such as *Phyllospadix torreyi*: a perennial herb that he collected at Balboa from a wreck. Later, this was found all the way from Santa Barbara to Catalina Island and is also known as surf grass.

In July 1912, Davidson went on holiday to Andrew's Camp on Bishop's Creek, some 8,000 feet above ground level. The valley was around 12 miles long with a small stream running through it, the icy cold water stocked with fish. Near to the camp was a dam full of very large trout. All over this area there was an abundance of plants for the botanist to write about. There were birch trees and willow as well as aspen and cottonwood. He collected samples of *Erigeron concinnus aphanactis*: a small yellow herb commonly known as basin rayless daisy; and *Castilleja montana congdon*: a member of the figwort family. The animals and birds he saw included grey squirrels, chipmunks, deer, sheep, robins, white crowned sparrows and grouse. A flock of Belding's blackbirds stayed close to the camp. There was also a myriad of insects including bees, beetles and ants.

As far as his medical work was concerned, Davidson wrote many papers on dermatology and presented them to the local medical society. In one such paper he talked of the growth of cancer on the face. 'Rodent ulcers' as he called them, were known to be the most common form of cancer on the face. No reason had been fully established as to why this should be the case. Davidson put forward his own theory to the Los Angeles County Medical Society in 1913, that the parts of the face which were less mobile than others – and therefore not nourished as much as the more mobile parts – gave causation for the growths. He found that women who applied creams and applications to keep their skin soft and supple had fewer incidences of these cancerous ulcers than men. He also stated that because women had an 'extra layer of adipose', it helped prevent the growths to some extent. Yet one of the most striking points he made was that the sun and the weather in general caused higher incidents of cancerous skin if people were outdoors for any length of time. His studies proved that people who were exposed to the sun through their work had a much greater risk of contracting cancer than those who worked indoors. In one case, he had seen a man who had been a locomotive driver all his life and on one side of his face he had five rodent cancers. He concluded that these were due to the man's face being exposed out of the side of the engine, as well as being bombarded by the smoke and dust from the coal. It was the California climate that gave him greatest concern, for although some diseases were almost unheard of in the county, such as bronchitis, the rodent ulcers were 'entirely out of the normal proportion to all other skin diseases'. Yet, he conceded that the sun alone was not the only factor, as it could not explain all the rodent cancers. Certain glands in the face also played a part. The lachrymal glands, as pointed out by the London physician Dr Evans, corresponded closely 'to the distribution of rodent ulcers on the face'.

In 1915, Davidson received news that Herman Hasse – his close friend and colleague from the 1906 expedition to Big Rock Creek – had died on 29 October. The whole botanical community was saddened by the loss of such a well-known scientist. All of his journals on his lichen work are now held at Harvard University, along with many of his samples, but his death came as a bitter blow to Davidson as the two had shared such a great devotion in botanical work throughout their time together.

Davidson himself died on 3 April 1932, three months after he was hit by a car. His internal injuries were not thought to be life threatening at the time, but consequently they resulted in his death at the age of 72. He is buried in the Hollywood Forever Cemetery, Los Angeles.

Shortly before his death he was visited by Joseph Ewan, who described Davidson in *Madrono*, Volume 2 as an interesting man who was not cynical but had a melancholy about him, although above all, he came across as a wise old man. He had slender face with what was described as having sharp features and a goatee but his eyes were bright and he was full of life. Ewan described how Davidson sat in a rocking chair, in which he made up his cigarettes and talked of the old days when he would go on expeditions all over the south of California. Davidson spoke enthusiastically of the Californian botany in which he had immersed himself for many decades.

Davidson married Alice Merrit of Michigan and the couple had two children: Ronald Anstruther Davidson (born in July 1899); and Merrit Thomas Davidson (born in early 1902).

Davidson's mother, Ann, outlived her husband by over 40 years and died on 28 December 1912 in Caithness. She is buried in Watten.

ROBERT DICK

On 24 December 1866, Thurso went into mourning for the loss of baker and geologist Robert Dick, who although not Caithnessian by birth, lived most of his life there and became well-known to the local populace. Mr James Mill, the chief magistrate of Thurso, issued a statement that summed up the sentiment. He asked the people of the town to hold a public funeral and they should assemble at 1.00 p.m. on Thursday 27 December to 'accompany his remains to the New Burial Ground of Thurso'. Duly, many people – not only from Thurso, but Wick and far beyond – came and paid their final respects to him. It was a sombre procession through the town with the band of the Thurso Rifles playing at the head of it. All the shops

Robert Dick

and businesses closed as a mark of respect. Yet Dick was a private man and would have been astounded that so many people came out for him in such a public way. That was the measure of the man who had adopted Thurso as his home.

Robert Dick was born in the small village of Tullibody near Alloa in Clackmannanshire in January 1811, son of Thomas Dick, an excise officer, and his wife Margaret Gilchrist, whom he had married in 1807 at Cupar in Fife. He was one of four children born

Robert Dick's birthplace

to the couple, however his mother died shortly after giving birth to her fourth child, James. When Dick reached the age of five he went to the local school, where he learned reading, writing, arithmetic and a little Latin. He had an aptitude for learning and as he grew in confidence, it was suggested by his teacher Mr Macintyre that Dick should go to college and study for a profession, such was his enthusiasm for learning. However, school was not always plain sailing for him. Like so many boys, he managed to get himself into bother and by way of punishment Mr Macintyre would hand out exercises such as learning verses off by heart, which Dick committed to memory exceedingly quickly. When he realised Dick enjoyed learning the verses, he resorted to more physical methods: the strap.

Dick never went to college, due in part to his father re-marrying. In 1821 Thomas Dick married Margaret Knox, the daughter of the owner of the local Cambus brewery, Robert Knox. But, owing to a conflict of interests in that no relative of the owner of a distillery or brewery could inspect it under excise regulations, Thomas Dick was moved to the distillery at Glenochil. The family moved house, so Dick and his brother and two sisters had to move school, now attending Menstrie parish school. Here, Dick did not do as well as he had at Tullibody because the teacher was not so enthusiastic. After the school day was over, Dick would wander up the glen and into the Ochil Hills.

The Ochils run between Fife in the east to Stirling in the west, and the area where the villages of Menstrie, Alva, Tillicoultry, Dollar and Muckhart lie are locally known as 'the Hillfoots', because that is exactly where they are situated. In fact, nowadays these small towns and villages have begun to encroach onto the hills themselves. But in Dick's time, they sat at the bottom, nestled between the hills and the River Devon. There was an abundance of plants and flowers not seen at lower levels and above Menstrie lies Dumyat, an extinct volcano. There are two summits to the hill: one called Castle Law (on which are the ruins of an old hill fort); and the other is Dumyat itself. A gulley that is the result of a fault was the easiest way of reaching the summit, but another easier route is Menstrie Glen. The young Dick, who would have become aware of the rock formations at this very early age, would have used either of these routes. He found numerous stones on the hills and began a collection, although it is not certain if he ever discovered the famous Ochil Eye. This was onyx that was worked locally into ornaments for those who could afford to buy them. Dick's enquiring mind would have also been aware of the silver and copper mines in the hills, as well as the veins of lead that had been discovered there.

It was not only geology and botany that young Dick became interested in. The hills were abundant with wildlife too. The rare *Falco peregrinus*, a type of hawk, had a nest nearby in Alva at Craigleith, and as a breeding pair, every year they hatched their young and could be seen soaring in the skies above the villages. Eagles too nested in the area. Other birds included finches, blackbirds and skylarks. On the ground, the hills were home to many other creatures ranging from deer, foxes, rabbits and badgers, to fish in the flowing rivers, and otters, as well as an abundance of insects and the odd adder. Occasionally, if Dick were out when darkness had descended, he would have seen owls and bats too.

Robert Dick's house in Thurso

These hills soon became an escape for him. The new Mrs Dick had begun to bear children, which eventually caused friction within the family unit. Dick's father tended to favour his children from his first marriage and try as she might, Mrs Dick just could not get on with her husband's children. As Dick grew up, he stayed out of the house as much as he possibly could. There is a story that he wore out his shoes due to his wandering in the hills and his stepmother took to hiding them, forbidding him to climb the hills anymore. Dick paid no heed and went out anyway. Thrashings soon became commonplace in the house. His stepmother would hit Dick with a stick when he disobeyed her: he took it without complaining, although in later life he spoke of how it had a profound effect on him. On the other hand, his brother James did complain: he would hit back and as soon as he could, he left home and went to sea. Dick could not wait to leave the family home either.

His time came when he became an apprentice baker in Tullibody. It was a move that delighted him, although it was tinged with some sadness for he knew that had his own mother survived, he would have been off to college to study for a profession. However, it was not to be. Mr William Aikman took the 13-year-old Dick under his wing in the bakery. He had a thriving business that supplied all the local villages and beyond. Dick's first job in the mornings was to get up at 3.00 a.m., kindle the fire in the ovens and begin preparing the bread. It was a hard life, and he sometimes did not finish until 8.00 p.m. – sometimes later. He was paid no wages, but he did get a bed and his meals and became much like a part of the family. As he grew stronger, he was able to diversify and would go out delivering the bread, rolls and cakes to Menstrie, Blairlogie, and Bridge of Allan: he enjoyed doing it.

The apprenticeship with Mr Aikman lasted around three and a half years and in that time he made no friends; only the Aikmans. On his day off, he would wander in the hills – even go up Ben Cleuch if the weather was fine and look at the flora and fauna surrounding him. The views that he saw over the Devon Valley and beyond captivated him. He could see the Firth of Forth and the meandering Devon, as well as the landmark of Stirling Castle and on a very clear day, Edinburgh. Below him sprawled the villages and he could see Alloa and Falkirk. However, his attention was always more closely drawn to what was immediately around him. He would gather up some flowers and if the season was right, take hazelnuts back to the Aikman children. It also gave him the chance to look at specimens of various plants to see how they differed. The hills provided him with almost every moss of the Cryptogamia family. He was curious about everything in nature and the hills provided him with a platform from which to engage his young mind.

Throughout his life, Dick kept in touch with the Aikmans. In 1846 Mr Aikman wrote to his former charge to inform him he was retiring from his Tullibody business and that although he had not yet put it up for sale, it was his firm intention. In the letter he strongly hinted that Dick should take over, but by then Dick was established in his own business, far away from Tullibody. However, things had not gone smoothly for him in the intervening years.

When Dick left the Aikmans, aged 17, he headed out to Leith to try and find work as a journeyman, which he did. He would rise early, do the baking and deliver his bread to his customers. He did this for six months before moving to Glasgow then Greenock where he stayed for the next three years.

In 1826, Dick's father was promoted to supervisor within excise and moved to Thurso. Dick had been writing to him, and told him that he felt his career in Greenock was stagnant. This led to a life-changing proposition from his father. During his time in Thurso, Thomas Dick had found bakers lacking. In fact, he counted only three in the whole of the county – so there was obviously an opportunity for his son to fill in this gap. Fresh bread at that time was not a staple of the Caithness diet. Instead, the people lived on oatmeal, using it to make bannocks, porridge and even oatmeal cakes for everyday living and only had fresh baker's bread on Sundays.

Dick gave the matter some thought and it did not take him long to decide the move would be a good one. In the summer of 1830 he arrived in Thurso. During his first few weeks, he spent time at the seafront watching the Pentland Firth as it lapped Thurso Bay. As time went by, he frequently walked along the beach and on numerous occasions found items such as driftwood, nuts or shells that had travelled from faraway places such as the West Indies or the Gulf of Mexico, furthering his curiosity as to why they had landed in Caithness. However, his main priority when he arrived was to establish a business premises. He found what he was looking for in Wilson's Lane and had to purchase an oven. The only other baker in Thurso was a Mr Mackay.

Business was fairly slow but at least Dick made enough money to live on. His sister Jane also lived in Thurso with the other family members and when she minded the shop for him, he would go out for walks along the beach or along the rocks on the shore, even as far as Dunnet on occasion. Two years after his arrival, his father was moved again, this time to Haddington in East Lothian. The rest of the family moved with him, leaving Dick in Caithness alone, with the exception of his housekeeper Annie Mackay from Reay. But he never felt completely alone, for he had his beloved nature all around him and it fascinated him. He began collecting insects, from bees to beetles and managed to enlist the help of some local boys to collect butterflies. He was teaching himself about these creatures and in 1835, he attended lectures on geology and astronomy. He borrowed books on the subjects and learned a great deal. Because he only had himself and his housekeeper to provide for, he had some spare cash. There was never a Mrs Robert Dick: he had once asked a woman to marry him but she refused. He never again proposed and died a bachelor.

As time went on and he travelled more extensively throughout the county, his insect collection (which he began when he was 25 years old) grew. What he desired was more books on the subject, although in retrospect, he himself probably knew more than was written in the books. Many of them were sent from Leith via a flour merchant he used. The books were wrapped up carefully and packed in the flour bags. When the goods arrived in Thurso, Dick would read the books as the bread baked.

During the summer months, he would wander over the moorland and make notes on the different plants he found. Being from the central belt, he knew that with Caithness

Scrabster Harbour and Dunnet Head, Thurso.

Postcard of Scrabster, early 1900s

being so far north the flora and fauna would be very different from that in the Hillfoots. He found that this was not the case. It simply blossomed later. One plant that did intrigue him was the *Juncus balticus*, which he found growing on the riverside. Usually found by the sea, one day he found it six miles inland for the first time. Finding plants and taking specimens took up much of Dick's free time, and occasionally he would be out at night or in the very early hours of the morning collecting samples. On one occasion, just an hour before dawn, he was down by the Thurso River (famous for its salmon), gathering some plants and herbs. Suddenly from behind, a man shouted at Dick: 'Now I have caught you poaching!' Dick simply turned round and said to the man: 'No, sir. I am not poaching; I am only gathering some specimens of plants.'

Over time, Dick gained a growing reputation for his knowledge of botany. He was the man to go and see if you found a plant you did not recognise. However, he is most famed for discovering the northern holy grass on the banks of the river at Thurso. A young botanist friend of Dick's sent a sample to the professor of botany at the University of Edinburgh, who at first doubted very much that it was indeed this plant. Dick, as requested, sent information on it to Edinburgh in July 1854. It was 20 years after its initial discovery that Dick submitted a paper on it and was finally thanked by the Royal Botanical Society for his find and the information he gave.

Throughout his wanderings, Dick was forever learning about the world around him. Nature was a wonder to him and not only did he collect insects and plants, but he was becoming ever more interested in the geology of Caithness. At Dunnet Bay the rock is exposed to the sea. He later wrote that he spent time at the western face of Dunnet Head.

He found the sandstone had fallen from the cliff high above him and using a hammer to break the sandstone apart, he discovered elements of quartz within it, as well as 'clay pebbles of a reddish brown and ... balls of yellow sulphur clay'. In these same notes he surmises that Dunnet Bay 'has been literally hammered out by the force of the Atlantic waves.' Geology became a subject he threw himself into.

When Dick was out gathering his plants, he would sometimes come across fossilised fish in the rocks. This delighted him, for he knew that eminent geologists had believed that these fossils did not exist in the Highlands, so he studied them closely. When Hugh Miller published *The Old Red Sandstone*, Dick read with enthusiasm that was unsurpassable. He immediately began investigating the geology of Caithness and found that the Thurso area bore the best findings along its shore. He sent some of the examples that he found to Miller, who wrote back to Dick congratulating him on his find of the *Holoptychius*. Miller later wrote of how grateful he was to Dick for sending him these as yet undiscovered fossils. Although Dick was not the only one in Caithness interested in fossils, he was the only one that would roll up his trousers, get wet and dirty and really look for them. From 1845 onwards, Dick sent Miller all the new fossils he found, although he kept copies of them for himself too, and as a consequence Miller had to edit his *Old Red Sandstone* to accommodate these new findings. In the third edition of that book, he wrote: 'The remains of one of the largest fish found anywhere in the system have been discovered in its lowest formation near Thurso by Mr Robert Dick, who, by devoting his leisure hours to the study of geology, in a singularly rich locality, has been enabled to add not a few interesting facts ... and who has kindly placed at my disposal his collection of fossils'.

The Clett

On 8 April 1845 Dick implored Miller to come to Caithness for a visit so that Dick could 'lead the way'. He described the route between Scrabster and Dunnet Head in quite some detail. He mentioned the Bishop's Palace and 'the old kirk; and there almost beneath our feet, is the bed of the river'. Further on, he mentioned Thurso East Castle and the beds clearly visible because the sea pounded away at the upper layers so that 'the underlying strata do not dip in the same direction as the overlying'. He described the abundance of fossils, and him being 'among the tombs of deceased millions of living creatures'. By the time the desription had reached Dunnet Bay, he had told Miller of the ravages of the sea on the cliffs and the exposure of the rock where fossil fish and plants could be seen. At one stage he retold the story of a piper that had gone into Pudding Gyoe – a cave that looked like 'the entrails of a cow, or cow's pudding' (hence the name) – and had never been seen again, although his music was heard. At Murkle Bay, Dick had discovered a fault line and told Miller of the twisted strata 'dipping in various directions', which was unusual.

A month later, Dick wrote to Miller again, this time describing the shore to the west of Thurso where the strata twisted and contorted just like at Dunnet. He pointed out that at this side of Thurso is its most famous landmark, the Clett. 'This' he wrote, 'is an oblong rock of calcareous slate of about 100 feet high', which at some stage had been separated by the sea from the mainland and now housed a myriad of seabirds, who flocked there to nest during the summer months. Dick used the power of persuasion well when he described Brims to Miller: 'The strata west of Brims are well worthy the inspections of a geologist, on account of the very extraordinary position many of them assume'. However, it was Holborn Head that held Dick's interest most of all, because it was here that he found fossils which impressed him so much that he returned time and time again.

Finally, after many, many letters and much persuasion, Hugh Miller agreed to visit Dick in Thurso. Dick let Miller stay at his house and from there they visited much of what Dick had described so vividly in his letters. Unfortunately, the stay was short due to Miller's commitments elsewhere. They had a dig at Thurso East and walked out towards Dunnet, checking for fossils and looking at the strata along the way. Later Miller wrote: 'how many marvels we have witnessed ... There is no lack of life along the shores'. At Dunnet Bay they inspected the cliffs, hoping to find fossils, but their chiselling found nothing that day.

Miller was invited by the Town Council to breakfast with them at one of the hotels in Thurso and Dick was also expected to attend, but he was absent. The assembled company were disappointed, as they had hoped for a lively and informative conversation with the two eminent geologists. During the discussions, it was suggested that Dick should become custodian of a geological museum in the town and the idea was put forward to him some time after the meeting had broken up. Earnest as always, he refused, citing that the extra hours of labouring to find specimens for the museum would fall on his shoulders: those who were willing to help would probably give up after a while and he would have it all to do himself. He had neither the time nor the inclination for the venture.

Later that day, the pair headed out towards Scrabster where they climbed Holborn Head and Miller chiselled out a fossil fish at the Clett. The days spent together were enjoyed enormously by both men but Miller had to leave and return to his work.

During his short stay, Miller discovered boulder clay and during research asked Dick to investigate, which he did willingly. He visited everywhere in the county and looked at the clay, from Thurso, Mey, Canisbay, and John o'Groats, down as far south as Dunbeath on the eastern seaboard, but most of his visits were by night. In *Elements of Geology*, Sir Charles Lyell had firmly stated that very few organic remains had been found in boulder clay anywhere in Scotland, but Dick discovered that this statement was in fact wrong, communicating this to his friend. He sent Miller samples of the shells he found in the clay in the burn at Freswick. He also described the village of Castletown as being built on boulder clay, which he had found evidence of in the form of blue boulder clay 'at the bottom of the bay ... it can be seen right off Castlehill Harbour'. He returned to the Freswick area again and what he found there astonished him. He found pieces of flint, chalk, granite, quartz and a small but significant fragment of belemnite, which he drew a picture of and sent to Miller. All these findings meant one thing to him: that the weather had changed the face of the earth. Only water could have brought some of these things to Caithness and deposited them there, such as a large boulder he had discovered at Weydale, which had once belonged to Morven.

In 1846 Dick received the news that his father had died at Tullibody. It came as no surprise to him as his father had written, explaining that he had a heart condition and that there was no recovery from it. Dick had no savings to travel down to Clackmannanshire. If he ever had any spare money, it went on books and in addition to this, since more bakers had begun trading in Thurso, business had lately suffered. Dick also had the problem that he worked on his own: he did all the baking without help and to take time off would have meant even less income. After the funeral, he wrote to his sister Jane, sending her his condolences and comforting her as much as he could.

Ten years later, in late 1856, Dick received the news that Hugh Miller – his friend with whom he had corresponded for so long – had committed suicide just before Christmas. It was yet another devastating blow for him. Miller had been suffering from terrible headaches and after he had checked the printer's proof for *Testimony of the Rocks*, he had put a gun to his head. Shortly after this, a local man named David Stephen went to see Dick to express his condolences. Dick told him that if he had known his friend had been in so much pain, he would have invited him up to Caithness where they could have walked and Dick could have pointed out things of interest in order to distract him from his illness. It is thought that Miller suffered from depression and some historians believe that when his work began to cause problems with his faith, it was this that caused him to take his own life.

Earlier that same year, 1856, two more bakers set up business in Thurso and Dick's business began to fail. Not only that, but his health was beginning to deteriorate. In May that year, he contemplated all kinds of work but none were suited to him. He thought about joining the coastguards or even leaving Thurso for the central belt to set up another bakery, possibly in the tiny hamlet of Muckhart near Dollar. But he did not really wish to return to where he had come from. It was becoming an industrial area with many woollen mills starting up and was no longer for him, so he decided to stay put. Yet more bakers set up in Thurso, and some began selling other items such as groceries and whisky. By 1862, Thurso had no less than six master bakers and 13 apprentices and Dick was the oldest of them all. On hearing her brother was in difficulty, Dick's sister Jane offered to send him money, but he refused. He thought at one stage, with the influx of people to the town, he could survive, but the incomers did not flock to his shop. His honesty, it was said, also cost him dear, because he would not cheat with his measures like some of the new bakers in the town.

Even when business was this bad, Dick still got up at 4.00 a.m. every morning. In a letter to Jane, he mentioned a baker who rose at 7.00 a.m. but worked until well into the evening, which would never have suited him when he had other things to do, such as his fossil digging. In the same letter, he said: 'any real happiness in this world is out of the question'. Dick was now feeling the weight of the world on his shoulders, from his business, to his health and his lack of money. His eyesight was also beginning to fail and rheumatism troubled him. Yet the one thing he did have was his belief. He was not a church-goer and it is thought that this was reflected in his struggling business. He believed that many sermons were simply old ones being repeated and this did not hold his interest when he sat in the pews, but he had attended the kirk faithfully before the Disruption of 1843. At this time, many deserted to follow the Reverend Walter Ross Taylor who left St Peter's Church in the heart of Thurso to work for the Free Church, but Dick was not at all interested in the politics of the church so he stayed with the established Church. On one occasion Dick was speaking to a local barber about a sermon they had both attended, when Dick suggested that the minister had used a couple of books to do the sermon rather than write it himself. The barber spread the news and it soon reached the minister's ears. The minister was enraged and would have his revenge on him. Dick would often go for a walk on a Sunday morning during the summer months, so in a sermon the minister pointed out that it was wrong to go out in pursuit of 'science' on the Sabbath day. Dick knew it was aimed at him. Whether it was or not is debatable, but it was a turning point for him. He swore he would never be preached at again and decided to stay at home and read the Bible himself. He had numerous copies of it and other religious works among his collection of books and he took to doing that rather than attending church.

Dick's book collection was vast. He acquired 33 volumes of the *Naturalist's Library*, and had 27 books on geology alone. He had 19 books on entomology, 18 books on botany and 27 volumes of the *Penny Cyclopaedia*. This notwithstanding, he had over 200 other books which were mainly made up of scientific subjects. This was where any spare money went, rather than it being spent on clothes.

In 1862 the eminent Professor Wyville Thomson spent a few hours with Dick. He heard of Dick through their mutual acquaintance with Charles Peach, a native of Northamptonshire, who moved to Wick in 1853 through his work, having been promoted in the coastguard service. Peach had been doing similar work to Dick in Cornwall and had become an honorary member of all the scientific societies there before his promotion. His work included looking for wrecks in the Pentland Firth and of course from his vantage point in the boat, saw the rugged coastline. It was on 19 October 1862 that he met Dick for the first time and a firm friendship developed between them. Thomson only met Dick this one time, although they kept in touch with each other, and Dick sent the professor the results of his many findings.

Dick was now about to face one of the biggest challenges of his life. The bakery business was still failing but Dick tried his best to keep it going. This he did all by himself, which meant every penny counted. In March 1863, he had ordered flour from his usual supplier and it was put on board the *Prince Consort*. During a stop in Aberdeen, the ship struck a platform and although all the passengers were safely removed, the damage done caused it to split in half. Dick lost his consignment of flour, and although the ship was insured, Dick's flour was not. What made it worse was that the flour had yet to be paid for and he had to order more, but he had no money. Not a man to ever ask for money, he was forced to write to his sister, who forwarded him £20. He hated doing it and knew at the same time it was not enough. He had received 12 bags of salvaged flour out of his 23, but when he opened them sand had managed to seep inside, so it was useless. There was only one thing he could do. He would have to sell some of his beloved fossils. Luckily, Mr John Miller, formerly of Thurso and a good friend of Dick's, agreed to buy the fossils, for which he paid £46.

The loss of his fossils was devastating, but he continued his searches for both fossils and plants and began a new collection. On one occasion he headed off to a quarry and by the time he had finished excavating, he had 'so many heads, jaws, coccosteus bones and such like', that he 'nearly killed' himself carrying his finds home. He also made a discovery of a fossil fish that had been buried beneath some red sandstone conglomerate, which his friend Hugh Miller had once thought impossible. Dick blew that theory out of the water, following this find.

Out at Murkle Bay in 1863, Dick found a huge fossil that took him several weeks to dislodge. It was one of the biggest finds he ever made, but working with it took a great deal of effort and during the excavation he cut his hands and little finger badly. Even during December when the weather had turned, he could be found digging and in January 1864 he continued still, despite it being freezing. And during all this time, he still awoke at 4.00 a.m., baking his bread and biscuits before walking the many miles to where he wished to dig.

Even though his health was worsening, Dick still managed to climb Caithness' highest peak, Morven, where he discovered pebbles at its summit. It amazed him that the sea could have been so high up, forming either a small island or wholly engulfing the mountain.

He was continualy looking for new plants too, and to no one's real surprise, he found them. He discovered bullrush, holy grass and the very rare Lapland reed in the county, and many botanists wrote to him for information. These included Dr L. Lindsay of Perth, a lichenologist; and Mr Roy, a botanist from Aberdeen, as well as many from London and abroad. The Reverend Mr Brodie, a geologist, asked Dick to send him some fossils and George Roberts, secretary of the London Geological Society asked him to send some oil-bearing shales for analysis. But it was with Charles Peach that Dick kept up his correspondence most, following the death of his friend Hugh Miller in 1856. Peach and Dick shared everything they found but due to age and illness, Peach retired from the coastguard, aged 61, and left Wick in 1865, moving to Leith Walk, Edinburgh.

Another acquaintance of Dick's was Sir Roderick Murchison, the one-time Director General of the Geological Survey. He was an eminent geologist from Muir of Ord in Ross and Cromarty and had travelled extensively in Europe with his wife Charlotte. He joined the Geological Society of London, which had as members his friend Sir Charles Lyell and Charles Darwin. However, it was his work on the Silurian System on the Welsh/English border in the 1830s that propelled him into prominence, cemented by his work in Russia, especially in the Urals, which culminated in a monograph in 1845. Ten years later (in 1855), Murchison travelled to Sutherland but no new discoveries were found, and he travelled on to Thurso, where his friend Professor Nichol established a meeting with Dick. Murchison had heard of Dick but this was the first time they actually met. As usual, Dick was working in his shop in Wilson's Lane and time was against both parties, so it was a few years later before Dick could show him his collection of fossils and talk to him about his findings in Caithness. When Murchison arrived at the bake house, Dick once more was busy preparing his wares, but Charles Peach had come along too and so the conversation flowed. It was also at this time that Dick devised his own map for Caithness: he made it out of flour on his workbench and included all the main points of geological interest for Murchison's perusal. Dick spoke enthusiastically about his findings and took Murchison to see his collection of fossils and plants. This astounded Murchison because he thought Dick was simply a geologist; not a botanist as well. He was amazed at the number of plant specimens Dick had and knew that he had almost a complete catalogue of the Caithness vegetation. Before he left, Roderick Murchison wrote to Dick expressing his gratitude for all the information he had received. Following the visit, Murchison gave a speech in Leeds Town Hall in late September 1858, a report of which was printed in a newspaper. Charles Peach sent Dick the cutting and in reply, Dick sat and wrote a poem that was later printed in the local paper, under the title 'Song of a Geologist'. So impressed was Murchison that he implored Dick to take up a position with the London Geological Museum, where he would have received a good salary instead of living on the meagre wages he allowed himself from his bakery. Of course, Dick refused. It was then suggested to him that he could travel and speak to people about his geological discoveries, but again he refused, stating that he was more suited to his own profession, and besides, he enjoyed baking despite the fact that it was hard work and not financially rewarding.

Throughout his life, Dick penned a number of poems; the 'Song of the Geologist' being one of his most famous efforts. In this poem, he refers to the tools of his trade: 'Hammers and chisels an' a"; and of how 'the deeper we go, the more we shall know'. But it was his reference to 'Sir Rory' that delighted both Roderick Murchison and Charles

Peach alike. However, the more Dick heard about Murchison's speech, the less thrilled he was with it and with the resultant attention. In 1859, Peach proposed that Dick visit Aberdeen to attend a meeting of the British Association or at the very least let his friends speak of his work. Dick refused on the grounds that: 'People bothered me so much last year after Sir Roderick's speech at Leeds that I have no desire for any repetition'. He also asked Peach to say to another geologist, Mr Cleghorn of Wick, not to speak of him. This being the case, when Peach left, he sat down and wrote a poem for his friend. In it he described how 'When Charlie spak, the great were dumb', and wrote of the bag of stones he took with him as well as 'His pouches fu' o' fossil bones'.

In 1863 Dick penned a long poem about his time of his great struggle to survive in business. He wrote of 'fruitless toil', that 'my heart is sick', and referred to his 'weary struggle'. In December of that year, Dick found peri ferns. They enchanted him, as they were luscious green, which was completely unexpected, although he had seen sea spleenwort at Dunnet Head, which was green all year round. He looked for new mosses on the hills and new ferns but by 1866, he had exhausted the flora and fauna of Caithness.

Throughout his years of fossil digging and botany exploring, he continuously wrote to his sister Jane about his finds. Towards the end of 1863, she became very ill and in order to keep her spirits up, he wrote a detailed letter of a recent dig. She died early in 1864 and her death affected Dick deeply, as although they lived many miles apart, they were very close.

From that time on, Dick never fully recovered. He became a melancholy soul with few friends, although he did have many correspondents. When he first arrived in Thurso, he simply lived to work and took his greatest pleasure from his fossils and plants and his collection of books that he built up over time. He could be seen by the locals going out in his swallow tail coat with chisels and a hammer, but he never explained to them what he was doing. He was invited by Sir George Sinclair to be his guest at dinner once and did not show up, for he disliked being in company, and when someone once suggested he write about his findings, his modesty forced him to refuse. He spent a lifetime trying to make his business a success, but the growth of competition in the town meant he seldom had any extra income and he became embittered with some of the Thurso merchants. Yet, as his closest friends knew, privately he could be a cheerful soul and had a sense of humour that was appreciated by those around him. His housekeeper of 33 years, Annie Mackay, said after his death she had never heard him angry nor had he said anything in haste, which he could have regretted later. He was an independent man to the end and his morals were never brought into question, with the exception of the minister who frowned upon his Sabbath scientific walks. He was honest and moreover was an extremely knowledgeable man, happy to share that knowledge with whoever asked. He rarely, if at all, drank and was willing to help anyone.

In 1866, Dick's health was worse than ever, even though he still went on laborious walks. His eyesight was poor and the rheumatism was bad. He began to have a shortage of breath and he found it difficult to eat. On one occasion he was out in the countryside and took ill. He had a burning sensation in his chest and was violently sick many times

Plaque on Robert Dick's house, Thurso

before he managed to stagger home. The burning pain left him but he remained light-headed, yet he continued to work in the bakery as best he could. Sleep no longer came easily to him as he had coughing fits and slowly became weaker. He soon realised that he had the same heart condition that killed both his father and his sister Jane and realised the end was not far away. His housekeeper pleaded with him to call a doctor, but he refused, as he did not like them. However, when his friend John Miller visited and saw how poorly he was, he called for Dr James Mill to come and see him. Four months after his symptoms began on that fateful walk, Dick died peacefully. Shortly before he died, he wrote in a letter to Peach some poetic verses about his physical condition: 'See the wretch, who long has tossed, On the thorny bed of pain'. By this stage, his writing was shaky and his letters had become short as the disease took its toll.

Among those attending his funeral were James Mill the chief magistrate, Sir George Sinclair, Bart. Office bearers from the Thurso Scientific Society were also on attendance. In the weeks following; Dick's beloved collection of books was sold off to pay a debt of £72 that he owed for flour and much of his furniture was also sold so that his debts were paid in full. His housekeeper Annie was allowed to stay in the house at Wilson Lane with one furnished room and a broken heart.

A number of years later, Samuel Smiles wrote a biography of Dick. The eminent publisher John Murray approached him and asked him if he could write a volume about

Dick's life and work. Smiles, a former surgeon in Haddington, had met Dick in the town when he had been visiting his family, but had been involved in an accident. It was Smiles who patched him up and having now abandoned medicine and turned to literature, he had the opportunity to write about the man he had treated. Smiles was no stranger to writing biography. He had already written about George Stevenson and the lives of the engineers Thomas Telford, Mathew Boulton and James Watt. Preceding the publication of Robert Dick, in 1875 he had written about another Scottish naturalist: Thomas Edward from Banff, who studied animals and collected animal specimens, which he stuffed. Smiles also wrote numerous self-help books such as *Self Help* (1859), *Character* (1871) and *Thrift* (1875).

By the time Smiles had written about Edward, Dick was already well-known in many areas, but none more so than in the north of Scotland, so a plea went out via newspapers for the locals to come forward with their anecdotes and memories of him. Smiles had the added bonus of finding a treasure trove of letters left by Dick, which included both personal details and diligent notes on the local flora, fauna and fossils he found. He also found his communications with Murchison and Miller, amongst others. This culminated in the 1878 publication *Robert Dick, Baker of Thurso, Geologist and Botanist.*

Before the book was published, many people wanted to learn about Dick, as over the years they had read about him in newspapers, not only in the United Kingdom, but throughout the English-speaking world. This notwithstanding, Hugh Miller and Sir Roderick Murchison had mentioned him in their works, which shot him to a fame that he never enjoyed. When he died in 1866, a brief biography of him appeared in an Alloa newspaper, which was copied and sent to international papers. However, after he died his fame diminished for a time until the book was proposed. His nephew and heir, Mr Alexander of Dumfermline, gifted all of Dick's botanical, geological and other specimens to Thurso, but a number of years passed during which time they were simply abandoned and neglected. However, in 1879 the keeper of Thurso Museum managed to gather them up and they were eventually placed in proper order and finally cared for. This was because of the publication of the book and the many people who had a renewed interest in the baker of Thurso.

Such was the impact of Dick's work on the county, in the 1870s it was agreed to erect a monument to Dick in the New Cemetery in Thurso. It was paid for by public subscription from people in Thurso, Tullibody and elsewhere. It was many years later that Tullibody too recognised its most famous son. At the house that had been the family home on Main Street, a plaque was erected in 1918. It was wholly funded by public subscription and read:

<blockquote>
In this house was born, January 1811
Robert Dick
Baker, Thurso, botanist and geologist
Whose life, spent in the pursuit
Of science, amid many difficulties,
Is an inspiration and example.
</blockquote>

The house was demolished in 1958 but the plaque was salvaged and has been placed in the local museum at the Speirs Centre in Alloa. His home in Thurso also had a plaque erected in his memory. This had been done under the auspices of Marwick Sutherland, a Halkirk journalist. It reads:

Robert Dick
Geologist and Botanist
Lived here 1830 to 1866
Earning His Daily Bread By His
Hard Work, Obliged to Read and Study
By Night and Yet Able to
Instruct The Director General
Of The Geographical Society.

In May 1950 Robert Mackay wrote to the local newspaper *The Caithness Courier*, asking for Dick's name to be added to the Memorial Seat Fund, as he believed the people of Thurso – and in fact all of the county of Caithness – would see it as fitting gesture and tribute to a man so much revered in the area. A month later, Mackay was informed that a seat would be forthcoming. The Thurso Memorial Seats Committee had met in the intervening weeks and they too decided Dick was worthy of such an accolade for his work. Mr Mackay pointed out in another letter to the *Courier* that it was also rather sad that it took such a long time after his death for him to be recognised as one of the greatest botanist and geologists the county – and indeed Scotland – had ever seen, but was delighted by the decision.

More recently, Thurso has once again honoured him by naming a street after him near to his Wilson's Lane home and a bust adorns the entrance to Sir Archibald Road. In 1956 Major P. W. Murray-Threipland discovered a well-preserved articulated fossil of around half a metre long at Spittal Quarry, which he named after Robert Dick: *Dickosteous threiplandi*. Charles Peach found a fragment of a *Pterichthys* in 1863 and decided to name it after Dick. At a meeting of the British Association in Dundee in 1868, he gave a description of the *Pterichthys Dicki*. These small acts for Dick are testimony to his impact on not only the places he lived or the people he met, but also the work he did during his lifetime.

Some years after Dick's death, David Stephen of Bower wrote about Dick and the memories he had of him. He recalled hearing the stories of his honesty with the weight of the bread he made and his regular customers thought very highly of him for it. On one occasion though, his honesty was rewarded by greed. A young man had gone out with him and showed a great deal of interest in fossilised specimens, so Dick showed him where the best ones were to be found. The unscrupulous young man then embarked on an expedition himself, dug out the fossils and sent them to the market in England where he made quite a sum of money. This was not in the vein of Dick's work at all. He never did it for money;

simply for the pleasure of safeguarding his love of science and all it could reveal to others who could study it further. Never again did Dick take the young man out and he was always happy to tell anyone who would listen about the incident.

Stephen also recalled a time when Dick went traipsing over land at a farm at Murkle. Captain David Henderson of Stemster had found that people had been damaging his fences and when he saw a man walking through his farm, he called out to him that he would fine him. The man called back: 'Go ahead'. Furious at this response, he asked his farm manager who the man was, and when the reply came that it was Dick out on a field trip, the captain felt rather sheepish and said that Dick could pass freely in future, should he wish to pass through the farm on his way to a geological dig.

One of the strangest things that Dick had in his collection was a genuine cast of the skull of Robert Burns. He had an interest in phrenology: a branch of science concerned with the function of the human brain, especially in regards to determining the strength of the faculties by looking at the shape and strength of the skull lying over those parts of the brain which were thought to be responsible for them. In his estimation, he believed Burns 'was not void of firmness, but it must have been diseased', from what he had deduced from his cast of the Bard. He believed that Burns may have had 'a sore struggle between good and evil', and this is borne out by some of Burns' work.

Robert Dick was a self-taught geologist and botanist and although he was born in Clackmannanshire, where his love of nature grew, it is his legacy in Caithness that today makes him one of the greatest Scotsmen of all time. Some of his surviving collection can be viewed at Caithness Horizons in the Old Town Hall in Thurso.

NEIL MILLER GUNN

Neil Gunn was the Far North's most prolific and successful writers. His final novel *The Other Landscape* was published in 1954, and his career had seen him write numerous novels, essays, articles and biographical accounts, some of which he based around the beautiful landscape of his birthplace and its environs. Dunbeath, its strath and Caithness as a whole, were immortalised in his work, and his love and deep knowledge of the county's Norse and Pictish heritage comes through in his vivid descriptions.

Neil Miller Gunn was born on 8 November 1891 to James Gunn and his second wife Isabella Miller, who had married in 1878 in Dunbeath on the rugged east coast of Caithness. At that time Dunbeath, in the parish of Latheron, was owned by William Sinclair Thomson-Sinclair of Freswick, who had purchased the estate lands in 1876. Population decline had begun in the area and many families who were left behind worked in the fishing industry or as crofters on the land, or both. Some had moved closer to the coast as the land was stripped bare of its grasses and heathers by the sheep and was no longer of any use. Others left for employment in the larger towns and cities, which offered a different way of life. By the time Gunn was born, the population of the whole parish stood at just under 6,000: a drop of around 2,500 in 30 years; and by the time he left, aged 13, it had dropped further to just over 5,000 inhabitants.

Neil Gunn

Cottages by the shore, Dunbeath

James Gunn, his father, was a skipper on a herring boat. In 1850 a small pier was built in Dunbeath to accommodate the local fishermen, but the larger vessels went to nearby Lybster because it was a tidal harbour. An ice-house had been built to provide ice for the catch, preserving it until it was sold, and a small warehouse for salmon was also established – the Dunbeath River had a good supply of salmon for fishermen. Isabella Gunn brought up her stepsons, William and Donald – who had been born to James and his first wife Isabella Budge (she died in September 1873) – and their own children. Their eldest daughter Janet was born at Ballacladdich in the cottage the couple lived in, right by the sea and which duly flooded when the fierce storms came. When James had enough money to build the family home they moved into the village itself. At this point the village was improving and growing, with new houses being built and a school recently established for the education of the local children. After Janet's birth (or Jessie as she was known) came Mary, who was born 1882. James followed a year later, then twins Donald and David, born in 1885, and Benjamin who arrived three years later. Neil was next, later John, who was born in 1897, and Alexander followed in 1901. Family life suited Isabella Gunn well but she always feared for her husband as he set out to sea, for the loss of life was, and still is, a danger all fishermen faced, none more so than in the harsh winter seas. The Caithness coast, especially the Pentland Firth on its northern edge, is treacherous and many boats have been wrecked there. When his father returned home from his trips, Gunn, and many villagers who came to the family home, would sit and listen to his father as he told tales of his adventures at sea. Isabella would simply be thankful he was home safe and sound.

When Gunn turned five, he attended the local school. Although he was a very good scholar, his love of the sea had him more captivated than sitting in a classroom doing sums. Whenever he could, he would go to the harbour and ask the fishermen about their work. He was curious as to how they knew where to fish exactly and how they managed to catch so many. Hours would pass as he listened to them explain their trade, but it was their stories of life at sea and the legends they told that held his attention. He had been born in an area rich in folklore, from both the sea and the land, and he always remembered the stories he had been told all his life. One day a dream came true for Gunn. His father offered to take him out on his boat. It was an experience he was never to forget. He loved being out at sea, but his mother had already spoken of her fear of her sons becoming fishermen and tried desperately to dissuade them from following in their father's footsteps.

While still young, Gunn and his friends made model boats and took them to sail on the river that flowed from Dunbeath Strath to the sea beyond. Here was the young boys' playground. They sailed their boats in the pools and pretended to be their fathers on their fishing vessels. The river was not the only source of fascination for Gunn. The kittiwakes, black-backed gulls, herring gulls and terns made their presence felt as they squawked and swooped over the boys, and they captivated Gunn.

By the time he was 13, Gunn left school and moved away from Dunbeath. His elder sister Mary had married Dr Keiler and the couple had settled at Dalry in the south of Scotland. Gunn was to stay with them: it was thought the move would be good for him. During his stay, he would spend time practising his fiddle playing, and when he returned home to Dunbeath for visits, he would play at concerts held in the Dunbeath Hall. The locals truly appreciated the fiddler as he marched across the stage, lost in the music. It became something he did for many years when he returned to the village during holidays or family get-togethers.

Two years later, Gunn moved to London to join the civil service where his brother James worked. He stayed there for two years, then was transferred Edinburgh where he was allocated work in the income tax department. This he found interesting and as such he decided to study for the entrance exam to begin his career properly. Of course, he passed the exam and so began his training in Customs and Excise. He was sent to Inverness where he was given responsibility for a vast area of the Highlands. This meant he had to invest in transport to get him to the more outlying areas and so he bought himself a motorbike. His work took him all over the area and as he made his way around, he soaked up the beauty of the hills and mountains, as well as the rivers and sea. He had never lost his love of nature.

In the course of his work he had to occasionally deputise for various distillery officers. It was while doing this that he made the acquaintance of Maurice Walsh, an excise officer who worked at a distillery in Forres in Moray. It was the beginning of a lifelong friendship between the men.

By the early 1920s Gunn had met and married Jessie Dallas Frew, the daughter of Provost John Frew of Dingwall. Before the marriage Gunn had been transferred once more; this time to the impoverished industrial town of Wigan in northern England. Here they were married in the local registry office. The couple spent a year in the area before he was transferred to Lybster, a small village around 8 miles from his birthplace. During his year-long stint in the county, he travelled all over it on his motorbike, learning more about his home county from the older generation who would take time to talk with him and tell him about the old days and yet more folk tales. The couple settled well into the village, living in a house on the main thoroughfare. It was during this time in Lybster that he began to write. Initially he wrote small articles then moved on to short stories, which were published in magazines. It was to be another three years before his first novel appeared.

Before long the time came again for Gunn to be transferred. In 1923 the Gunns moved to Inverness where Gunn was appointed Excise Officer at the Glen Mhor Distillery, which had acquired the Glen Albyn Distillery in 1920. Initially the two companies were rivals but the partnership put an end to competition between them. During his spare time Gunn continued to write. This culminated in his first novel, *The Grey Coast*, which was published in 1926. The book was a success. The royalties from its publication meant the young couple could build their own home, which they did at Dochfour Drive in Inverness. More success followed with *Morning Tide* (published in 1931), *Sun Circle* (1933), *Butcher's*

Neil Gunn memorial, Dunbeath

Neil Gunn house, Dunbeath

Broom (1934), and *Highland River* (1937). This latter novel won the James Tait Black Memorial Prize and this led to Gunn being offered to lecture at the English Department at the University of Edinburgh. He declined, not keen on being on public show.

That same year Gunn began to dedicate his time writing his beloved novels, so he left Customs and Excise to concentrate on his new chosen career path. With the money he had made, he and his wife bought a boat and they embarked on a journey through the Hebrides. Of course, these travels found themselves into a book: *Off on a Boat* (1938).

Not content to be living in Inverness any more, the Gunns decided to sell their house and moved into a rented farmhouse at Braefarm on the road between Dingwall and Strathpeffer. Here, he used one of the rooms as a study. It had wonderful views over the countryside towards Dingwall and the Cromarty Firth, which he found inspirational as he worked. This was his most prolific writing period and one that was never achieved again, especially after the couple moved again in 1950. Gunn managed to get himself into a routine of writing in the mornings and walking in the afternoons, where he would meet the local crofters and spend time talking with them about their lives. He continued his love affair with his roots, staying with his sister Jessie and her husband John Sutherland, a retired Metropolitan Police officer, at their home at Knockglass House, Dunbeath. He spent time catching up with old friends too and continued to gather tales from the local crofters and fishermen, which he weaved into his work. During the summer, the couple would spend a fortnight sleeping rough up in Dunbeath Strath at Leas of Achnacly. Here Gunn could be seen by the local shepherd taking a walk at dawn, whilst he would write during the day, before taking a walk with his wife up the hills or sitting by the river, simply enjoying being there.

Over the 11 years he and Daisy (as he affectionately called his wife) lived at Braefarm, Gunn wrote over ten novels, including his most famous ones *The Silver Darlings* and *The Silver Bough*. But the time came when they had to leave and life was never the same for them again. They bought Kincraig: a house near Evanton; but the stay was short lived. In 1951 they sold Kincraig and bought Kerrow House in Glen Cannich, with a stretch of salmon river. While here, Gunn was appointed to a commission set up by the Secretary of State for Scotland that looked into crofting in the Highlands and Islands. But he still had time for his writing and wrote *Bloodhunt* (1952), *The Other Landscape* (1954), and *The Atom of Delight* (1956) – his final novel.

In 1959, the Gunns sold up yet again and moved to Dalcraig: a house situated in North Kessock, just north of Inverness. This was the couple's final home.

On the occasion of his 70th birthday, Gunn was presented with a portrait that had been commissioned by the Caithness County Council at Mackays Hotel in Wick. On his birthday itself a group of his friends in Edinburgh threw a party, which although both he and Daisy enjoyed, neither of them were in the best of health. A few weeks later Gunn had to go into hospital for an operation on his prostate and later that year Daisy also had to go into hospital for a bowel operation. She never fully recovered: the operation took its toll and within 18 months she was dead.

Following her death, Gunn lost his zeal for writing. Daisy had been the one to transfer all his handwriting to typewritten work, which was then submitted to his publishers. With her gone, he no longer had his writing companion to help him. Her death hit him hard and it took a long time for him to come to terms with it.

During the years that followed, Gunn visited his brother Alexander in Castletown in Caithness and his other brother John who had moved to Edinburgh. But so much had changed and slowly his health began to worsen. In 1972, just a year before his death, the Scottish Arts Council decided to set up the Neil Gunn International Fellowship, which would enable an international novelist to come to Scotland bi-yearly to talk about their work and hopefully be inspired by Scotland.

By January 1973, Gunn was gravely ill in hospital in Inverness. He died on 15 January 1973, and was buried alongside his beloved Daisy in Dingwall Cemetery.

In 1986, the Neil Gunn Trust was founded and a monument dedicated to him was unveiled at the Heights of Brae, Strathpeffer on 31 October 1987 by the Scottish poet Sorley Maclean and writer Jessie Kesson. The Neil Gunn Trust, along with Ross and Cromarty Council, also launched a bi-yearly writing competition, which is still run today by the Highland Council, but now allows entries from writers worldwide. In June 2009, a plaque was unveiled on the former Customs and Excise building in Inverness. It commemorated his work there during the years 1921–1937. There was an earlier commemorative plaque, but it had mysteriously disappeared a few years earlier. In Dunbeath itself, the house in the village where the family lived is now known as 'Neil Gunn House' and by the harbour is a bronze statue of a young boy with a fish draped over his back. It is taken from the book *Highland River*, and the boy is Ken – the main character who poaches a salmon from the local river. It was erected by the Neil Gunn Society and unveiled on 8 November 1991 to commemorate Gunn's birth exactly 100 years before. The sculptor was Alex Main from Halkirk in Caithness.

JAMES MCKAY

Many Caithness-born people emigrated to the far-flung corners of the world, and most of them became citizens of those countries. However, the 6th Mayor of Tampa in Florida was one of those who never took out citizenship in the country he made home and he remained a British national all his life.

On 17th May 1808, James McKay was born in Thurso. Following his schooling, he went to sea. His love of the sea was due to the established fishing industry in the area. When he returned to shore, he would spend time with his family in the town. Much of his work took him south to the port at Edinburgh where the catch would be sold. It was during one of these trips he met, and later married, Matilda Alexander in Edinburgh in 1837. By the time they emigrated to America, they had four children: George, Sarah, James, and John. In 1846, McKay took his family to Tampa in Florida where they settled.

At that time Tampa was only a fledgling community of around 200 souls. A small amount of this population were freed slaves, and McKay and his family brought one of them – an eight-year-old boy called Isaac Howard – to the town. In Tampa there was a hotel, a store, a post office and churches for worship. Following the Great Gale of '48 (a devastating hurricane that hit Tampa Bay in September that year and destroyed almost everything in its path), McKay built the family home from wood that he had ordered from Mobile in Alabama. The hurricane had lasted three days, caused the coastline to alter dramatically, and overwhelmed the town. Only five properties were left standing and rising water levels added to the destruction. At Fort Brooke, the commanding officer reported the obliteration of public buildings, warehouses and the local wharves. Not only that, the hospital too was ruined in the storm. Even the lighthouse succumbed to the hurricane, although the keeper survived. Only the tops of trees were seen in some areas thanks to the high water in the bay. Land had simply disappeared beneath it. Remarkably there was no loss of life.

In the days following the storm, the settlers searched the rubble for their possessions. Many had lost everything apart from the clothes on their backs. The captain of a marooned ship named the *Sprague* delivered hard bread and coffee to them, but when the soldiers of the fort heard of this a detachment was sent out to divide it between the storekeeper, Mr Ferris, and the soldiers. Major Wade and his men helped the Tampa folk in any way they could. But his services were not required when a few barrels of whisky appeared in Hillsborough Bay and some bottles of wine were found amongst the rubble on the shore.

Instead of working for someone else, as he had always done back in Scotland, McKay opened a general store and a saw-mill. His businesses went from strength to strength and soon he had bought a great deal of land and a couple of schooners in order to trade with Cuba and Central and South America, as these were vital trading places. He also traded with the sugar plantations in the area and acquired herds of cattle that he transported to the Cuban market, making himself one of the wealthiest men in the region at that time. In addition to his work, his family expanded as well. The couple had another four children. They were Donald, Marion, Matilda and Almeria. As for the ever-expanding Tampa, he built a courthouse there in 1858, by which time it had officially become a town.

During the 1850s McKay became involved in local politics. Being a businessman, he saw the complications with licensing and paperwork when dealing with trade, so upon his election as Mayor on 12th February 1859, he changed the procedures, making it easier and less bureaucratic. Standard forms were introduced for legal notices and licences and he introduced the regulation of the local Jackson Street ferry service, which was to ensure the safety of passengers. Being a former seaman himself, he knew of the dangers involved and he wanted to provide as safe a service as possible.

At the outbreak of the Civil War in 1861, McKay ran the gauntlet with the north. He used his ships to break the blockade, transporting goods into the town and surrounding areas, and managed to smuggle guns and munitions in for the Confederate Army. Every time he did this he ran the risk of being caught, but he felt he needed to protect the citizens of the town.

Blockade running was done out of both loyalty and necessity. All the runs were done at night in the cover of darkness, so the vessels had less chance of being spotted. McKay instructed his crews to keep lanterns in darkness and there was to be no smoking of cigars or pipes, as this could cause the vessel to give away its position. In all, McKay risked six runs, bringing the guns, munitions, highly-prized Cuban cigars and fine wines into the port as well as food and other supplies.

However, after months of success and good fortune, his luck ran out in October 1861. On the 14th of that month, the Union ships captured his vessel and he was imprisoned in Key West. A brief account of what happened that night is as follows. The Unionists had discovered the runs and began firing at Fort Brooke, a military post in Tampa that McKay had tried to purchase in 1859 but instead only rented when his offer was refused. The firing was a ruse for the gunboats USS *Adela* and *Tahoma* to put their plans into action. They knew the townsfolk would be distracted by the firing, and while that was the case around one hundred Union troops landed on the shore six miles away and began firing on the *Kate Dale*, a schooner belonging to McKay that was well-known for her speed.

The troops set fire to her and she burned to the waterline before she sank. The Unionists attacked another of McKay's vessels – the *Scottish Chief* – that same night. She was towed down the Hillsborough River where the 124-foot oak and pine steamship was stripped of any working components before being left to the mercy of the water. The local militia had been mustered and a skirmish ensued, but they were unable to prevent the invaders from returning to their ships. McKay was caught and taken to Key West.

Languishing in jail gave McKay time to think and in March he finally decided to pledge allegiance to the Union so that he could be freed. He was released later that month and in April he wrote to the Adjutant General, declaring his wish that the Union be restored. As the war dragged on, the Confederate Major Pleasant White appointed McKay as Commissary Agent for the Fifth District of Florida. True to his newfound loyalty and his word to the Unionists, he began making up excuses for the lack of supply of beef to the Confederate Army. These excuses ranged from bad weather to poor health. Being no fools, the Confederates realised where his new allegiances lay.

When the war ended in 1865, McKay returned to his cattle trading and shipping until his death. Tampa had suffered economically during the war and afterwards it was in need of repair. It was heavily depopulated too. Yellow fever had a devastating effect on the population and it returned frequently due to the swamplands in the surrounding area. Another factor was the lack of a good road system for the transportation of goods overland. As time passed, the shipping industry began to pick up again, but there were no rail links and the roads were dusty and sandy. By the time of McKay's death on 11 November 1877, the population had dropped from around 880 in 1861 to somewhere in the region of 750.

Today a plaque has been placed at the site of his home in Tampa, telling the people who visit of his Scottish roots and his time as 'one of Florida's most active blockade runners'.

Late in 2009, the remains of the *Scottish Chief* were discovered. Perhaps surprisingly, she is still pretty much intact, but there are no plans to raise her.

In 1883, not long after McKay's death, phosphate was discovered in a region to the southwest of Tampa. This began a reversal Tampa's fortunes and today it is the phosphate capital of the world, shipping hundreds of tons overseas and to domestic markets in the United States. The railway came in 1884, making transportation of goods easier.

ELIZABETH OMAN YATES

History was made in the British Empire on 29 November 1893 when the first woman mayor was elected in New Zealand. It was the same year that the Electoral Act was formally ratified and women were allowed the vote in New Zealand. The first woman to do so was Caithness-born Elizabeth Oman Yates. She had emigrated with her parents as a child and was closely involved with women's suffrage.

Elizabeth Oman Yates was the eldest of two daughters born to George Oman and his wife Eleanor Lannigan in Caithness in the 1840s. In late 1853 George decided to take his family to New Zealand for a better life. They arrived at Auckland near Christmas that year. Following schooling, Oman Yates took a keen interest in women's rights, no doubt inspired by the feminist and social reformer Mary Ann Colclough. Born Mary Ann Barnes, she was a Londoner who had emigrated to New Zealand in 1859 aged 23. Two years later she married Thomas Colclough – a man more than 30 years her senior – and had two children. Following his death in July 1867, she opened her own girls' school in 1871–72 in order to support her young family. Colclough then took a teaching post at Tuakau for a year then another one the following year before moving to Melbourne in Australia in 1874. It was her prolific writing to the local press and her lectures on women's issues that she is best remembered and revered for, and it was while reading the articles that Oman

Elizabeth Oman Yates
Courtesy Auckland Museum

Elizabeth Oman Yates and husband
Courtesy Auckland Museum

Yates began to take an interest in what Colclough had to say. She sought to improve conditions for women prisoners and prostitutes and advocated practical measures that would help them. She had issues with the legal rights of married women, due to her own bitter experiences: her husband wasted the money that she earned as breadwinner, only for the bailiffs to strip her home bare when they tried to recoup it. She pointed out that women should have a right to education; not simply be a wife and mother but to have a career on the same level as any man. Her most contentious view was that women should not be subjected to laws of which they had no say in their making. Colclough returned to New Zealand after only a short stay in Melbourne, where her radical views, especially on marriage, were hotly challenged. She disappeared from public view and died following an accident in 1855. But her impact on the young Oman Yates, and many other young New Zealand women, was profound.

In December 1875 Oman Yates married Michael Yates, a well-known local master mariner, at St Peter's Church in Onehunga, a suburb of Auckland. Fate was to deal them a blow when they could not have children. Her sister Eleanor had married Thomas Henshaw in the same church four years earlier, and Oman Yates doted on her sister's children instead.

Onehunga became an important port in New Zealand in the 19th century, as shipping from the United Kingdom could dock there without travelling the few extra days round the North Cape. It also became the hub for shipping heading south. In the days of early settlement the harbour grew in importance: it was a strategic point during the Maori Wars for raiding enemy settlements. By the time Oman Yates had married, Onehunga had access to a railway. This was the beginning of the demise of trade to the harbour and it did not help that the waters were shallow. Incidentally, some years earlier in February 1863, HMS *Orpheus* ran aground with the loss of 189 lives out of a total of 259. It was and still is to date the worst maritime disaster in New Zealand water. The corvette had left Sydney, Australia, the week before and although the sailing master William Strong had up-to-date and revised charts, the commodore overruled him and told him to use the out-of-date 1856 chart, which did not show where the dangerous sand bars were that had been discovered seven years earlier. The ship was warned as it approached the harbour and efforts were made at the last minute to change her course, but she hit the bar. As she swung round, she exposed her port side to the relentless strong waves and she sustained fatal damage. Many of the mariners were swept away to their deaths as they were told to abandon ship.

Ten years after their marriage, Michael Yates became a member of the Onehunga Borough Council and in 1888 he stood for mayor. He won the election and with his wife by his side, remained in the position until ill health forced him to resign in 1892. His days

---

C 28,191

DU 402.2

C 28, 192.

ELIZABETH YATES WHO MARRIED
CAPT YATES IN ST PETERS CHURCH
ONEHUNGA DEC 15, 1875.
THE OBLONG BROACH IS GOLD AND
SET WITH DIAMONDS AND THERE
ARE MATCHING EARINGS. I HAVE
THEM NOW 4 JULY 1976.
E. MARY THOMSON 36A CLONBURN RD
REMUERA.
ELIZABETH YATES NEE OMAN.
[FIRST WOMAN IN BRITISH EMPIRE TO BE
MAYOR IN HER OWN RIGHT]
COPIED FROM CABINET CARD LENT
BY MRS E.M THOMSON 1993.

CAPTAIN MICHAEL YATES
MASTER MARINER, MARRIED
ELIZABETH OMAN AT ST PETER'S
CHURCH ONEHUNGA, AUCKLAND IN
DEC 1875.
MRS YATES WAS ELECTED MAYOR OF
ONEHUNGA IN NOV 1893. (1ST LADY IN
THE BRITISH EMPIRE TO BE MAYOR IN
HER OWN RIGHT). MICHAEL YATES WAS
A FORMER MAYOR OF ONEHUNGA (1888-
1892) THE YATES WERE THE AUNT &
UNCLE OF E E M HENSHAW WHO MARRIED
S.B.IL HAMLIN IN 1903. AT ST PETERS
CHURCH ONEHUNGA.
E.E.M. HENSHAW WAS MY MOTHER. SIGNED
E.MARY THOMSON. (NEE HAMLIN),
COPIED FROM CABINET CARD LENT
BY MRS E.M. THOMSON. 1993.

Handwritten card about Elizabeth Oman Yates copied from a Cabinet
Card by Mrs E.M Thomson. Courtesy Auckland Museum.

in local politics were over, but Oman Yates had learned a lot during his time as mayor. She had assisted him in all matters that he dealt with, and one of the most politically hot subjects that mattered to her was women's suffrage.

In 1893 the Electoral Act came into force, giving women the right to vote in New Zealand. It was a pioneering move and the following day Oman Yates became the first female mayor in the Empire. She had accepted the nomination, but winning went far beyond her wildest dreams. Her opponent for the position was F. W. Court. Her win caused an outpouring of feelings. Queen Victoria and Richard Snedden, the premier of New Zealand, congratulated her, but some council members could not stomach the fact that a woman was mayor and a justice of the peace to boot, which was part of the mayor's civic duty. Four councillors and the town clerk resigned immediately and the male-dominated council opposed many proposals put forward by Oman Yates. The reason was that she was a woman doing a man's job. It did not help the situation that she was a strong-willed woman, often lacking in tact, and also disregarding some of the established rules and regulations laid down by councillors long before she came on the scene. Sometimes the public would enter the gallery and cause disruption to proceedings and she was jeered outside. She had been sworn in by Edward Conolly on 16 January 1894 and was duly ousted on 24 November that same year. New Zealand, it seemed, was not yet ready to have a woman in power.

However, in that short space of time Oman Yates had left her mark. She had liquidated the borough debts, improved roads, footpaths and sanitation. She had also established a sinking fund and had pestered the Government regarding the re-opening of the Waikaraka Cemetery.

Five years later, Oman Yates returned to the chamber. Although, again, she had only a relatively short term of around 18 months, she let the whole chamber know what she was thinking of the proposed policies. In April 1901 she lost her seat.

Oman Yates lost her husband in 1902 due to ill health. In 1909 she was admitted to the Auckland Mental Hospital. She died within its confines on 6 September 1918 and was buried beside her husband in St Peter's churchyard in Onehunga.

ALEXANDER HENRY RHIND

Archaeology is a popular pastime in Caithness due to its array of prehistoric remains. For centuries people have excavated the area, and it has always been of great interest to the locals as they learn more about the people who settled there thousands of years ago. In the 19th century local man Alexander Henry Rhind took an avid interest in the remains at Sibster. This early interest, combined with ill health requiring a change of climate, led him to journey to Egypt where he undertook the excavation of ancient tombs and became one of the most renowned Scottish archaeologists of his time.

Alexander Henry Rhind was born on 26 July 1833, the younger son of Josiah Rhind, a banker in Wick, and his wife Henrietta Sinclair. He studied at Pulteney Academy under the instruction of Mr Andrew Scott, who went on to lecture at the University of Aberdeen as professor of oriental languages. Upon leaving school, Rhind applied for, and was accepted at, the University of Edinburgh, where he studied Natural History and Natural Philosophy.

In March 1851, Henry Rhind, as he preferred to be called, returned to his native Caithness and undertook work at the cairns of Yarrows, to the south of Wick. The county is littered with ancient stones and cairns – such as the Hill o' Many Stanes and the chambered cairns of Camster – that show how long the area has been inhabited by peoples who settled there. Later that year, Rhind attended the Great Exhibition in London before setting off for Europe, visiting the many and varied museums of Switzerland, Austria, Italy and Denmark. This merely reinforced his love of antiquity.

Upon his return, Rhind began to correspond with John Stuart who later became the secretary of the Society of Antiquaries of Scotland. In early 1852, Rhind sent a rubbing to Stuart of a slab at Ulbster. It took Rhind a couple of days to scrape away the mosses and vegetation which covered it, but he was determined to send it to Stuart, of whom he had only just lately become aware. Stuart was delighted with the rubbing and so began an enduring friendship between the two men. By the end of the year, Rhind had been elected a Fellow of the society and began delivering papers to it.

Rhind's love of Caithness was unwavering, and in 1853, the year his father bought the estate of Sibster, Rhind began work on the remains of a Pictish house, or broch, at Kettleburn near Wick. Today nothing remains of it, not even the mound where it once stood, as it is grazing land, but when Rhind came across it, his team of workmen managed to excavate it. They collected a range of artefacts, although he regretted that the 'ruins were not in a more perfect condition'. It took the team almost three months to excavate and in that time the group measured the diameter of the mound on which the ancient structure stood at 120 feet, but only fragments of the actual broch were found, as a small cottage nearby had been built entirely from what had been left of it. It was one of the largest of its type in the Far North. Inside was a drain and some steps, which were catalogued, and there was a well that was used by the cottars in the cottage. Among the items found were a comb made from what is thought to be whale-bone, some bronze tweezers, some pottery and some human remains. The bronze tweezers were of 'extraordinary size' compared to the small tweezers that had so far been found, and it was also the 'most remarkable' workmanship that drew the assembled group's attention to them. Some broken querns or stone hand mills for grinding corn were also found, as well as several stones that had circular cavities hollowed out of them. Rhind believed these had been produced by the action of polishing other stones on them. He had found a similar stone at Lynegar near Watten. Numerous discs were found too, ranging in size from two inches to nine inches, which he surmised children had possibly made. A 'dagger-shaped bone' was also found, tapered to a point and 'fixed securely to a handle', and half of a stone cup. Charles Peach and his son discovered these among the rubbish pile at the site.

By the end of 1853 Rhind began to realise his heath was becoming poor. He had been keen on walking to find the ancient remains, as well as shooting and boating, but he found even walking up the slightest incline was becoming difficult, especially in the colder weather. In a letter to his friend Dr Davis, which he wrote from his Clifton home in Bristol in April 1854, he commented that 'the ascent of a gentle acclivity has now more terrors for me than climbing to a point in the Mont Blanc range 10,000 feet above the sea-level had two or three years ago'. He came to realise that he would have to spend the winters away from his native Caithness in a warmer climate. During the winter of 1853/54 while he was staying at Clifton, he received news that his older brother Josiah had died. It was also during that winter that he decided not to continue studying for the bar and become a barrister. He was simply too ill. Instead he spent his time writing about antiquities. He told John Stuart that he would 'write something for the Antiquaries' because he believed it was a 'necessary duty to do so on the part of everyone who professes to take an interest in national antiquities and in the society'. During a spell the following winter at Ventnor, a Victorian health resort with an almost Mediterranean climate on the Isle of Wight, he wrote *Bronze Swords Occasionally Attributed to the Romans*, which he sent to Stuart.

During 1854 Rhind submitted an article to the *Ulster Journal of Archaeology* on the results of an excavation in the north of Scotland that he compared it to an Irish cairn on the banks of the River Boyne. However, in a letter he wrote in early summer 1854 to Dr Davis, he realised that his excavation work may be limited due to his failing health. He still had hope, although he would need a great deal of help if he were to carry the work out himself.

For the winter of 1855/56, Rhind made the journey to Egypt, which became a life-changing decision. The warmer climate suited him and he became interested in the culture and ancient antiquities of the country. He began to research the tombs at Thebes and found many interesting and rare artefacts, including a set of bilingual papyri, which later became known as the Rhind Papyrus. In a letter to John Stuart, Rhind explained how he wished to add Egyptian antiquities to the British museums: these extraordinary people were so near to the beginning of civilisation and should be compared to other civilisations. With this in mind, he proclaimed that where he could, he would 'gladly purchase ... objects suitable for my purpose, which any of the peasantry around may possess, with the view of supplementing where the results of my own excavations may be wanting'. By November 1856, Rhind had completed a small book entitled *Egypt: Its Climate, Character and Resources as a Winter Resort*, in which he enthused about its weather as an aid to those afflicted with illness. In the preface, he wrote: 'Although I am not without hope that its contents may have some interest for those desirous only to increase their acquaintance with the realities of eastern travel, the whole design has acquired its colour from having been undertaken chiefly with a view to those who have to think of countries with reference to the sanative influence of their climates.' Not only did the book contain Rhind's experiences in the country but also had thermometrical notes, which had been submitted by the likes of the late Lord Haddo of Aberdeen and Sir Gardner Wilkinson.

As was the norm, Rhind returned to Sibster in Caithness for some of the summer months. When his health allowed, he again spent time out and about on trips excavating various places. Among the excavations he undertook were the tumuli on the Sibster Estate, which he later wrote a paper on and delivered to the Society of Antiquaries. None of the four mounds were taller than five feet but he investigated them because two of the mounds 'rose as green-swarded hillocks from a swampy strath', while the others were raised up on elevated undulations that bounded the river. One of these tumuli contained burned matter and a few incinerated bones near its centre, but the most interesting point was the fact that stones had been placed about four feet above the deposit and were only just beneath the surface of the tumulus. In the other similar mound, Rhind discovered a pile of stones at its very centre, two upright slabs at either end, and fragments of slabs on what would have been the other walls. This led him to believe that there once would have been a cist or small vault. Two feet from the west end of the vault he found a skull but it was in very poor condition, and a cup. In 1680 a fierce battle had ensued in the area and became known as the Battle of Altimarlach. Campbell of Glenorchy had laid claim to the earldom of Caithness, and Sinclair of Keiss knew that Campbell would be coming to the county. He mustered hundreds of men and waited for Campbell and his men. They met at Stirkoke, but the Highlanders were tired from their march and Campbell refused to fight. Sinclair thought he had won and the men headed off to Wick, where they drank freely under the influence of a man who it was later said was an agent for Campbell. While the Sinclairs and their followers revelled, Campbell rested his men and the following day led them across the Wick River at Sibster. They prepared for battle. Having over-indulged the night before, the Sinclairs had problems rounding up their 800 or so followers. Eventually they were gathered and the opposing groups readied for battle at the burn. The signal to attack was given by Campbell and his men advanced. Although the battle lasted only a few minutes, between 80 and 200 of those fighting for the Sinclairs were slaughtered, although Sinclair of Keiss escaped injury as he was on horseback. It was a humiliating defeat for the Sinclairs and was the last great battle in the Far North. Following the battle, legend stated that the mound where Rhind excavated the skull was known as Campbell's Mount: it was thought that a number of bodies of higher ranking men that had lost their lives in the battle had been buried there. Instead, Rhind found a skull that dated much further back in time than 1680.

The two small mounds were also measured and excavated. The third mound had a diameter, which measured around 65 feet with two rows of large stones fixed to the edge. Rhind found these to be 'superficial', because none of the stones penetrated the ground more than two and a half feet. The sepulchre was fully two feet below this. Here he found burnt earth with charred wood and some incinerated bones. The fourth and final mound measured 35 feet in diameter and was the smallest of all. Here too was evidence of fire, as some of the stones had a 'dull red appearance', and when touched they fractured easily, which proved they had been subject to intense heat. Rhind also found traces of charcoal and burnt bones. But its design was different from the other three mounds. Half of its mass had been made up of these red stones before it was covered with earth.

With at least two of the tumuli near the river, Rhind concluded that in days gone by, it would have been likely that they would have been surrounded with water during the winter when the water levels would rise or during the summer if flooding occurred. The land was swampy, and although the river's course had been straightened since the ancient days when the burials had taken place, it did seem a likely scenario.

In July Rhind travelled down to Edinburgh to attend a meeting of the Archaeological Institute, where he read a paper on the megalithic remains of Malta to the assembled company. It was during this meeting that he also read *On the History of Systematic Classification of Primeval Relics*, in which he pointed out that the Scots had been the first to classify ancient relics in fixed progressive periods; long before archaeologists had done so in Scandinavian countries.

A few months later, Rhind was back in Egypt for the winter. He simply took up where he had left off at the tombs at Thebes. This time, he had been granted permission by the British authorities to excavate wherever he pleased. But he was not a man to abuse this privilege. In a letter to Dr Davis dated 9 January 1857, he explained that the governors had also said to him that all he had to do was ask: whatever he needed would

Alexander Henry Rhind

be provided. On 8 January, his team of workers found eight mummy cases and the next day another six had been found, much to everyone's delight. The following Monday, according to the letter, he and his men were to head out to the 'valley of the splendid tombs of the kings'. He had already gone 'diligently over the ground' and had 'marked off several spots' that seemed promising to him. In addition, about 150 miles up the river from where Rhind was working, Lord Henry Scott and his team had begun excavating on the Island of Elephantine and he promised to send for Rhind should they find it a promising site.

All this work took its toll on Rhind's health. He had to give up on the idea of a series of investigations in the Western Valley as it meant long daily treks travelling on horseback and he just was not well enough to do it. Instead, he worked in proximity to his base near Thebes and he was rewarded by finding a 'remarkable tomb', which had been untouched. In early April he left Egypt for Malta. The island was an inspiration to him. The scenery was breathtaking and instead of going directly on to Rome, he stayed there as long as he could, before setting off back to Scotland. He described the island as 'a delicious place' and one that 'the eye may be constantly intoxicated with the exquisite landscape'.

Again, the summer of 1857 was spent at Sibster, before Rhind stayed for a time in Edinburgh. Whilst there, he became very ill. He had been on his way to church when he suddenly felt blood flow into his chest and began coughing it up. He spent many weeks in bed before being able to travel to Malaga to recuperate. Here he spent time working on a pamphlet called *The Law of the Treasure Trove – How can it be best adapted to accomplish useful results?* In this pamphlet he described how the law currently worked and how some discovered treasure was being disposed of, or was being concealed if it was of any significant value. When an artefact was found, it should be reported to the local procurator fiscal who acted on behalf of the Crown, but much of what was reported was not always preserved. He advocated a system that was followed in Denmark, which gathered all its antiquities in one national store. In order to stop people throwing away any finds, he suggested that by allowing the finder to be paid the value of the objects he found, more items could be preserved for the nation. On St Andrew's Day, he was elected an Honorary Member of the Society at its anniversary meeting.

It was while in Malaga in February 1858 that Rhind received news of his father's death. It was another devastating blow to him. Josiah, who had worked for the Commercial Bank and had been Provost of Wick on two separate occasions, was 64 years old. Because Malaga reminded him of his loss too much, Rhind decided to leave Malaga and head off to Algiers. While there he composed a letter to Dr Davis and told him of the death. He wrote of his 'great grief' at the unexpected demise of his 'most affectionate father' and that the 'affliction was the more severe, that the stroke, by snapping the last tie of near relationship, leaves me as it were alone'.

Rhind found Algiers pleasant. The weather suited him. He described the air to his friend John Stuart as 'soft and balmy' but noted that the local doctors believed that the 'air being somewhat stimulant, does not always suit those who are nervously excitable'. He stayed in the hustle and bustle of Algiers until the beginning of May, as it was too lively for him to stay any longer, and moved to Avignon in the south of France, before heading to Sibster once more for part of the summer and autumn. But even on home ground, he kept working and corresponded with those who had questions for him. By late October he was back in the south of France, where he intended to stay until January when the spring winds came and either move down the Spanish coast or go to Italy.

This year also saw the publication of his work *British Archaeology: Its Progress and Demands*. In this book he took a swipe at the establishment in their treatment of archaeological finds. He wrote: 'it would appear that the sole cause why British remains are so entirely overlooked is to be sought in the inadequate perception of their value and interest by the Trustees, or rather by those of them who attend the meetings and transact the business'. What he advocated was the British Museum having a department for British antiquity, with a view to Scotland and Ireland having the same. If this happened, he was certain that larger deposits would be made that would be of great national interest and they would all be collected under the one roof. He pointed out in the book that already in Scotland, the Society of Antiquaries had a reasonable collection, which would be more beneficial in the national museum where it would be nourished, but it was funding that prevented the museum from purchasing the remains. This was because Scotland received no Government help in their fund for the acquisition of historical artefacts, whereas in

England the British Museum was 'at liberty... to purchase native relics', and in Ireland the Royal Irish Academy received a grant to purchase relics. Rhind proposed the Government take charge on the basis of what he had seen in Denmark and other European countries and put forward the idea of an Ordnance Survey map of all the remains to Lord Duncan, 'the Scotch Lord of the Treasury', which received a positive response. He appealed to landowners to allow excavations and to preserve the past by ensuring the preservation of the remains by bailiffs, gamekeepers and ground officers. In this way, archaeological finds would be saved. He hoped the book would bring to the attention of Members of Parliament the problems facing archaeological finds and that they in turn would be able to do something about it and raise the matter with a view to finding an acceptable solution.

By March 1859 Rhind was in Rome, where he marvelled at the ancient Roman remains. Ancient Rome provided him with a myriad of ruins, which he examined over the course of a week and he decided to devote most of his time in the city to 'the study of Etruscan antiquities'. He was then in Naples and was again enchanted by the antiquity. However, as always, he over-exerted himself in these two great cities and retreated to Capri to recuperate, but had to leave the island due to hostilities that had broken out. He returned to his house at Clifton in England.

During this time, he took an active role in helping the National Museum of Scotland to proceed with its classification of archaeological finds. Having visited many of the finest museums in Europe and noting their displays, he wrote his *Memorandum on the Arrangement of the National Museum of Scottish Antiquities*, in which he outlined how the displays should fall naturally with the relics. He wrote the collection 'should be arranged with respect to its instructive capabilities, and not merely in a manner most convenient for generic adjustment or reference', and that the collection 'should not, as far as possible, be classified to any conclusion that may be doubtful ... instead of being allowed ... to evolve whatever shades of meaning they may bear'. Over the coming months he corresponded with the keeper of the museum, Mr McCulloch, but as he was unable to visit the museum in person, the difficulty arose that he could not see how the displays were being mounted. Rhind therefore asked John Stuart to keep an eye on things.

Towards the end of the year, illness once again took hold of Rhind. A severe cold laid him low. He had caught it on the boat as he made his way to France for the winter. Just as he recovered, his heart complaint returned and he was bedridden for over a month. While he was laid up, he read what he termed a 'remarkable' book, and one that he believed had opened a whole new chapter in science. The book was Charles Darwin's *On the Origin of Species*. He thought it was 'a great performance, from the evident and continuous thought with which it has been elaborated', and although he had not had the time to fully consider what Darwin proposed, he thought that Darwin had 'done more than has ever been done formerly to show cause for believing that species are not necessarily fixed elemental points'. He hoped that the issues raised in the book would allow debate between zoologists and physiologists, although when he wrote this in March 1860, neither of these professions had commented to any great extent.

Over the next few months, Rhind spent him time at Hyères in France, where he continued writing. As usual, in the spring he made the journey back to his rented home Down House at Clifton near Bristol. He stopped at Nismes for a few weeks, 'as there is a good deal of antiquarian interest there and close by at Arles', before reaching England in early June. It was during this time at home that he began his work on his book on Thebes. His health was good, even though the weather was unseasonably wet, and he managed to catch up with his friends. In October he and his friend Mr Palmer headed off to Madeira, where they began excavating on 1 January 1861. He continued to work on his book while out there. When the two men returned to England in May, the book was complete and ready to be published. However, tragedy struck once more. In September, Mr Palmer was visiting Rhind when he suddenly took ill. In the middle of the night Mr Palmer began coughing up blood. A surgeon was called for while Rhind did all he could for his friend. On 19 September 1861 Mr Palmer died.

The winter months were spent in Madeira once more, where he stayed in the same rooms, met the same people and worked on the final edition of his book _Thebes, its Tombs and their Tenants_, which was finally published in 1862. Rhind hoped at the very least that it would 'meet with some degree of success', as he had worked on it so hard for so long. In it, he included chapters on the general history of Thebes, the tomb of a Theban notable that had not been ransacked and the finds he made there, notes on the excavations at the tombs of the kings, a chapter on the Necropolis, and one on the ancient use of metallurgy. In the preface to the book he explained the circumstances for the delay being his 'lengthened annual absence abroad' and how he had spent time going through the book checking the proofs some 'fifteen hundred miles from England'. But it was also down to his bouts of severe illness, which stopped him from working at all.

In the spring of 1862, Rhind spent time in Tenerife. Here he found the climate favourable and hoped to revisit the Canary Islands the following year, and then Gibraltar and Morocco, before returning to his Bristol home. He decided that for the coming winter he would return to Egypt, where he would spend time investigating and observing the River Nile and its deposits. He left England on a steamer on 4 October 1862 bound for the Nile. He travelled 1,000 miles and had decided to write another book, but the work again took its toll. While healthy, he made notes on 'the operations of the river and the growth of the alluvium, with reference to monuments'. He measured the depth of the water, the rate of the current and took samples of the sediment. It could then be calculated why the monuments along its course had been built in that particular area, and how the course of the river had altered during that time.

When Rhind reached Cairo, he was 'prostrated by a sharp attack of haemorrhage from the lung'. The heat of Egypt did not help matters and although still very ill, Rhind made the journey to Corfu, which did not suit him, before settling at Lake Como. His spirits were raised there when he received some letters. One of these was from his good friend John Stuart, and despite the severity of his illness, Rhind wrote back to him. He wrote that he was unable to write very much about himself, for his 'condition ... hangs in the balance'. He continued: 'It is for me to bow to the will of the Father, whether His hand leads me into sunshine, or into the valley of the shadow'. He stayed at Lake Como until he felt well enough to begin his journeying again, but knew he would have to break it up into small sections if he was to make it back to England. At the end of June he made the four-day journey to Zurich, even though he was not fully recovered.

On 2 July 1863, Rhind had gone out for a drive, but the weather was too hot for him and he was exhausted by the time he arrived back at his accommodation. On his return, he complained of being worn-out and decided to go to bed. His servant, James Fisher, checked on him several times, but in the morning when his master still had not moved from his sleeping position, Fisher found that Rhind had died in his sleep. Rhind's body was brought from Switzerland back to Wick where he was buried on 13 July.

Over his lifetime, Rhind had amassed a huge library of 1,600 books, which he left to the Society of Antiquaries. He also bequeathed £400 for archaeological excavations to take place 'in the north-eastern portion of Scotland', especially, but not exclusively, Caithness, Sutherland and Ross, and left an endowment for an institution at Wick for the industrial training of young orphan girls from some of the Caithness parishes. He left the copyright of his seminal work on Thebes to the Society of Antiquities and bequeathed the profits to them. He also wanted two scholarships funded at the University of Edinburgh, for which he left the sum of £5,000. He left the residue of the Sibster estate 'for the endowment of a professor of, or lecturer on, archaeology' in connection with the Society of Antiquities. However, the money from the estate could not be freed up until Mr Bremner, who had lifelong rent at Sibster, passed away. In total it was thought to be worth £7,000.

Rhind's memory would also be continued thanks to a purchase he made in Luxor. In 1858, he bought a papyrus scroll that had been found at a tomb in Thebes and thanks to this single act, history enshrined his name on that scroll. It is widely known as the 'Rhind Papyrus'. The scroll explains that the scribe Ahmes was writing it in around 1600 BC but that he had copied some of it from an even earlier time. It is a mathematical treatise, which included calculations for accounting, building and surveying as well as some 87 mathematical problems, including the volume of cylinders and areas of circles. A table has also been included, which made it easy for the person using the papyrus to look up the solution to commonly asked arithmetical questions. There are also exercises on determining the height of the pyramids. It is one of the oldest mathematical documents in existence today. At the same market, he also acquired what became known as 'the Leather Roll'. This too was a mathematical treatise and pre-dates the Rhind Papyrus by two hundred years, thought to have been written during the Egyptian Middle Kingdom. It was not unrolled until 1927, when it was discovered that it consisted of 26 listed rational numbers followed by the equivalent Egyptian fraction for each of the rational numbers. Both of these were much more advanced than had previously been thought. Money from his estate was also made available for a volume containing a facsimile of two bilingual papyri that he found at Thebes. This was published in 1863.

A final lasting legacy of Alexander Henry Rhind is the prestigious Rhind Lectures, which take place annually. They began in 1874 and consist of a series of six lectures, usually presented by a single academic over a weekend. The first lecture was given by Arthur Mitchell: it was called 'The Past in the Present'. Joseph Anderson gave his first talk in 1878, entitled: 'Scotland in Early Christian Times'. Other talks included: 'Egyptian Science' by Professor W. M. Flinders Petrie in 1921; 'The History of the Broch' by Reginald A. Smith in 1929; and 'Death and Wealth in Viking Scotland', by Professor James Graham Campbell in 1995.

WILLIAM ROSS

Known simply as Ross of Cowcaddens, William Ross came from humble origins in Caithness and went on to become one of the most well-known ministers in the west of Scotland.

On 11th June 1836, William Ross was born on the shores of Loch Rangag on the road between Latheron and Thurso. He was the third son to Murdoch Ross, a miller who worked at the Allt-a-Chliabhan mill on the shores of the loch, and Christian Mackay. The family lived in the miller's cottage nearby.

Murdoch Ross became a lay preacher, holding services in his home throughout the month when the minister could not attend. Once every three weeks the minister would come to the area and take the service from a meetinghouse not far from Murdoch's home. In the minister's absence, although Murdoch did not preach as such, he read in Gaelic to the assembled congregation from religious books. In his duties, Murdoch visited the ill and sick of the local parish and would spend time with them in contemplation and prayer. If he was called out in the parish he would go, especially to the dying who needed comfort in their last hours, and their families who could take comfort from his words. In the family home, religion played a huge part of daily family life and Mrs Ross would keep books on a bookcase, with the Bible and Psalm Book in pride of place in the middle. Other reading material included poetry but there was only one book of fiction, *Robinson Crusoe*.

It was in this atmosphere that William Ross came into the world. In all, the Rosses had six children. However, the only daughter and one of their sons died young, leaving them with four boys, three of whom eventually went into the church ministry, much to their mother's delight. Ross was christened on 7 July 1839 at Latheron and later attended school in a rundown ramshackle building with a thatched roof at Rangag. The school was only open during the winter months and all the students would sit round the peat fire and listen to the teacher as he taught them their lessons. The family then moved to Latheron, which meant no more fishing on Loch Rangag for the Ross boys, but the new Free Church School had opened (in much better condition than their old school) and fishing was to be had down at the harbour. Later, Ross attended Wick. At school, he learned English grammar, some Greek and Latin as well as elementary mathematics, but his core enthusiasm was for competitions and the lure of a prize aided his thirst for educational knowledge.

In 1852, Ross decided to take the Temperance Pledge and joined the Scottish Temperance League. He and his elder brother John formed a temperance society of their own in Lybster. Five years later Ross won a scholarship to Moray House in Edinburgh and in 1859 completed his course. He gained his certificate with special added qualification, which allowed him to teach Gaelic. From there he entered the University of Edinburgh, where he won the Macpherson Scholarship and the sum of £88 towards the fees of his fourth year of study. The Macpherson Bursary was 'intended for the benefit of students from the Highlands. It is bestowed on a student in the fourth year of his course in Arts, who has attended all classes for M.A.' The founder of the bursary was Sir John Macpherson, the late Governor-General of India, following his death in 1821.

After Ross finished his course at Edinburgh, he read divinity, which took another four years of study. He finally finished his education in 1867. During his studies, he had been offered the position of professor of mathematics at Nagpore in India, and also the rectorship of a New Zealand grammar school, but his calling to the ministry outweighed these and he chose the Church. Notwithstanding his studies, Ross also became involved in several different ventures. These included becoming secretary of the Highland Committee of the Free Church and he was appointed inspector of Gaelic schools in 1865. He was later to work on a revised version of the Gaelic Bible. He began conducting meetings and services at St Columba's in Edinburgh and became a firm friend of Dr Thomas Maclauchlan of that church. Maclauchlan later published *The Dean of Lismore Book*, which contained ancient Gaelic poetry that both he and the historian William Forbes Skene managed to transcribe and translate in 1861. Ross and Maclauchlan both had a great love of their native tongue and it never left them, and Maclauchlan never forgave the landowners who had cleared the Highlands to make way for sheep.

Ross was ordained at the Chapelhill Gaelic Church in Rothesay in November 1867. During his time preaching there, he met his wife, Jane Wood Mein, a Kelso girl who had moved to the town with her family. However, tragedy hit the couple. In October 1870, Jane gave birth to a son, John Murdoch Ebenezer, but complications set in and aged only 23, she died. Her sister moved into the manse to look after the baby, but she too died after only nine months. Ross threw himself into his work, but many said he never was the same again.

As well as his work for the Church, Ross gave lectures. Sometimes these would be on religious matters but he was interested in Celtic studies and history. He travelled to the Gaelic-speaking communities, and at Wick at the height of the herring season he would bless the fishermen and the sea. But all this work and travelling took its toll, leading to a nervous breakdown. Even this breakdown did not stop him. He went to Ireland to recruit men from Killarney and in 1878 he made his first trip to North America to lecture on temperance in Canada to the Presbyterian Church in Hamilton. In the same year he also visited Wales for the first time. His ministry in Rothesay came to an end in 1883, when he was elected by the congregation of Cowcaddens in Glasgow to become their minister. On 2 October he accepted the proposition and was inducted on the 18th of the month.

In Glasgow, there was no manse for Ross to live in, due to lack of funds. When he decided to take up the post, many of his friends wondered if the city would kill him, as he suffered badly from headaches during his time at Rothesay. The Cowcaddens church was also heavily in debt to the sum of £3,300. At first he would go round the parishioners and ask for money, but he soon realised what a poor parish he was working in so he turned to the post office for help, where he opened a savings account. Every extra penny went into the account and the generosity of parishioners can be summed up in the story of one gentleman who placed £5 in Ross' hand after his business flourished. An American gentleman also donated £100. Yet even the poor helped. An old woman saved ten shillings and gave it to Ross: she had heard a story of a coloured lady who had kept a handful of rice aside every day 'for God's cause' and she had taken this as inspiration. In 1887, £2,000 of the debt was paid and by 1889 the church debt was paid in full. He was lucky that two wealthy Glasgow men – Mr John Campbell White and Mr James Stevenson – gave large donations to help the church with its work.

Campbell White was an eminent Glaswegian who in 1867 became a partner in his father's chemical business – the Shawfield Chemical Works, which was one of the largest of its kind in the world. With the money he made, he helped his employees by founding an institute in Rutherglen. This had a gymnasium and swimming pool that the workers could use. He was also heavily involved in church matters and formed the Glasgow United Evangelistic Association which raised thousands of pounds over the years to help Glasgow's needy. In 1893 he was made a peer and became Lord Overtoun. He died in February 1908 aged 65. Ross was grateful to receive any money, whether from the wealthy or the poor in society, but Campbell White's donation was especially well received.

At first, Ross lived in Hill Street, Garnethill then he moved to 42 Windsor Terrace. According to people who occasionally stayed with him, this house was like a surgery, especially since Ross distributed medicines, that were generally homeopathic, while his servants said it was more like a hotel. His home was full of medical books that he referred to when someone came with a malady for him to treat. Tea and coffee were offered to those who came to talk about their partners or to students who wished to discuss entering the ministry. He had a special place in his heart for those who visited from the Highlands.

In Glasgow, Ross' wages were low and the workload heavy. Not long after his arrival he wrote: 'The burden of work requiring to be done seemed intolerable'. He felt the Church was spending too much time abroad and not paying attention to the problems he could see for himself at home. What the people of Cowcaddens needed was 'a genuine Christian mission'. It was not a case of giving to the deserving poor, but one in which God had to be seen as righteous; the people would benefit from that. One of the first things Ross decided when he arrived in the city was not to pay fines for people who had been arrested or who had been in trouble with the police. People did come begging to him, and with the exception of a few cases, he kept to his word. He also believed that the church should be the centre of the community and of the district, in order to have any lasting affect on the people. The Cowcaddens church lay in the centre of a triangulated street pattern. Ross wanted to know about his parishioners, whether they were church goers or not, what their works was and so on, so that he had a better idea of how to deal with them and bring them into the fold. Every evening Ross held an evangelical meeting in the church and if they would not come to him in the church, he would go out to them, promoting his aggressive form of evangelicalism and his temperance beliefs.

All of his life, Ross believed in total abstinence from alcohol. Moreover he believed the Government of the day should enforce prohibition in the whole country, from Kent to Caithness. When he was in Rothesay, he spoke at public meetings in favour of a reduction in the granting of alcohol licences and asked that the locals help magistrates by giving their opinion on those who were or were not worthy of it. The reason that he was so against alcohol was because he saw what happened when it was all too easily abused. At one particular meeting he held the audience's attention by telling them of a man who had promised to love his wife and protect her on their wedding day, only to be seen beating her and their children and wilfully neglecting their needs, all thanks to drinking. In another instance, a family appeared at one of his Sunday morning 'Free Breakfasts' that he set up during the winter months in Rothesay. Both the mother and father were alcoholics and the children were destitute. In later life these children made Ross aware that his sermon that morning on 'The Lost Sheep' had changed their lives forever.

In 1876 the Free Church revived its Total Abstinence Society with Ross as its secretary. In 1880 he became a founding member of the Highland Temperance League. A year later he was appointed as its director and remained so until his death. However, he was most well-known for his work with the Independent Order of Good Temperance, which he joined in the early 1870s. This order had been established in Rothesay in 1870, had two lodges with around 600 members, and soon came to the fore with its good works. Ross was made chaplain of the Scottish Lodge in 1876, then 'Right Worthy Grand Templar' a year later:

William Ross of Cowcaddens

the highest position in Scotland within the order. It was a worldwide organisation, and out of 400,000 adult members, he was finally appointed 'Grand Worthy Chief Templar' for the world. As such, Ross travelled extensively. He visited America on numerous occasions, and went to Norway and Sweden. In 1892 he headed out to Australia and New Zealand to gather information on temperance in the Empire. However, the Church alone could not do all the work.

Ross was a strong supporter of Sir Charles Cameron, who, according to Ross, was trying to 'awaken Parliament to its duty' on temperance. Cameron believed that legislation would curb the consumption of alcohol – having this as law would command respect from almost every quarter. Ross' enthusiasm for the temperance movement was infectious to those around him. He was forever optimistic as far as it was concerned and had an absolute and unwavering belief that he had been put on this earth to do this work in the name of God.

Within a minute walk from the church in Glasgow from which Ross preached, there were 22 public houses and licensed grocers. The former (reliable sources told him) took an average of £40 a day, although others put that figure at £60. It was no wonder then that in Ross' sphere of influence, the people were so poor and had so little money left over for food and clothing. It was his intention to cut the takings of £40 a day to £20. What also irked him was the presence of the theatre and music hall in close proximity to his church. At a meeting of the Glasgow Housing Commission, he was asked what he would replace the theatres and music halls of Cowcaddens with, 'for the amusement of the people'. He replied that people had said to him, that although they had frequented the public houses, theatres and music halls, they no longer wished to do so and were able to find 'recreation and enjoyment elsewhere which were quite adequate to their circumstances'. The problem was that he never understood that ordinary people did not want to spend their days at church meetings or sermons.

At this same meeting he pointed out that many people were borrowing money to pay for their alcohol. Some men were borrowing £1 from a moneylender and having to pay back £1 plus a shilling interest – if this was not paid it would be added to the debt until the borrowed money was costing them dear. In order to pay back the money, some would turn to stealing, whilst women often turned to prostitution. One writer that visited the area, described a Saturday night as demonstrating 'social evil'. Men and women huddled in groups, all at varying stages of being drunk, surrounded by absolute squalor and destitution, but it was the despair that most saddened him. Ross blamed this situation entirely on the Church.

Ross set to work. First of all he recognised the need for the Church to take responsibility for its failings in the area, then put it to rights using the office bearers and church-members, rather than any outside organisation. He also recognised that although the church was doing its good work in Africa, India and China, it needed to change its focus to its own back yard. Scotland needed help just as much as these other countries, and although he never wanted to take the overseas work away from the ministry, he did want a new focus at home. This was to be done spiritually.

Ross decided to help the people not with money or soup kitchens, but by preaching to them and getting them to help themselves as much as possible with church support. He believed that if they changed their heart and life, all else would follow. He once wrote to a friend: 'To give the working classes a new heart and a right spirit is one of the best ways, if not the only way, of giving them new houses, better surroundings and a more elevated social status'. This stemmed from his belief that they should be dealt with 'on the highest grounds because it is there the greatest change is required'. The church building itself played a vital role in the community in addressing this.

It was a long held belief of Ross that the actual physical church building was essential in nurturing the locals and uniting them in their beliefs. It was a focal point where they could gather and where work was carried out for the betterment of their lives. He was against the use of a hall and believed that such places be avoided if at all possible, so that the church itself became the spiritual home. It had to be the centre of the missionary operations and if necessary, it would have to adapt. As Ross later pointed out, the public houses were open every night, as were the theatres, so why not the church too? People passing by could simply drop in. He managed to entice enough people from his congregation to spend time at night in the church, either singing as part of the choir, working, or simply providing a sympathetic ear. For all the years of Ross' ministry, the church opened at night, whether there were many people in attendance or only one. It never mattered. It was something that he felt was the right thing to do and in a report to the Presbytery he made it clear that although many years ago he would have taken a night or two off, he now saw the benefit of what he was doing. He was convinced that 'the nightly meeting is not only warranted, but absolutely required, when we take into consideration the history, home life, surroundings, and temptations, of those whom we desire to reach and bless'. Ross firmly believed that Christian service had to be a daily occurrence and not spasmodic if it was to do any good. But it had to be done by the whole congregation: not just by the minister and a few office bearers and workers. This was the main thrust of his work. He wanted the whole congregation to become involved in spreading the Word of God and if they felt they did not have the knowledge they needed to be successful, they were offered training. He was simply embodying the old Highland saying: 'Better to plough a small field than scratch a whole acre'. In other words, his allocated parish – although small within the city of Glasgow as a whole – was his small field.

During his early years in Glasgow, Ross managed to attract 450 new members to his church and steadily the numbers rose. By December 1886 over 1,000 people had joined since he took up his calling three years earlier. On occasion, his sermons would suffer due to his heavy workload, but he was a knowledgeable man who was widely read and when he stood in the pulpit, people listened to his oratory. He put emotion into his sermons and when he realised he was being too subjective, he switched tack and 'lead his hearers to look away from themselves to the great truths and facts of the Christian faith'. He would often use analogies between the spiritual world and the natural one and, as he was interested in the subject, even introduced science into his sermons. At the centre of his preaching and teaching was Jesus Christ, especially the Crucifixion, but he was a Presbyterian through and through. According to his son, Ross had a strong dislike for episcopacy and if he was on holiday and had to attend an Anglican service, he would never truly be at ease. He was also intolerant of Baptists, who he believed hung 'on the outskirts of good work' that others were doing and not going out to find those who had lapsed themselves in order to bring them back into the fold.

Ross' church not only reached out to adults in the district, but the children too. Ross enjoyed nothing more than to hear children sing – he introduced Bible classes, and due to the enthusiasm for Sunday school, the numbers increased so dramatically that the big hall had to be used and the class split into two. It was run by Alexander Fraser and under his direction it swelled to having 400 students. Fraser believed that children had an eye to the soul and he had a special way with them. Once, on a ferry, a young baby was crying – he took it in his arms and it stopped. On another occasion, his parishioners saw him become emotional when he was baptising babies in his church. In his journal, he wrote that 'the little ones are the dew of the morning' such was their innocence. Ross also founded the Medical Mission within the church and his willing helper was Dr Muir Smith, who gave up his time for free. Over ten years it is thought the mission helped over 40,000 people. The Boys' Brigade and the Boys' and Girls' Industrial Societies, which taught woodwork and sewing, were also set up, as were a Mothers' Meeting group and a Home Improvement Society. In Ross' own home in 1889, he formed the Glasgow Free Church Minsters' Evangelistic Union and it is known that he was deeply interested in Irish Home Rule and acted as secretary for the Scottish Association for Irish Missions.

Of course, over and above all this work were christenings, weddings and funerals and he enjoyed nothing more than the union of a man and woman on Hogmanay, which was a favourite time for weddings in Glasgow. Traditionally, 'love, honour and obey' were in the vows, but Ross (significantly ahead of his time) insisted on using 'cherish' rather than 'obey'. What is even more noteworthy is that when asked to perform the ceremony, he would agree, but asked the couple to promise that after the wedding there would be no alcohol consumed at the celebrations. He married around 1,000 couples over a 25-year period and out of that number only five or six refused to agree to Ross' conditions.

In 1891 Ross wrote to Mr Moody about spending more time in the Highlands, suggesting a campaign from Forres and Nairn up to Helmsdale and Wick – he knew that on the Isle of Skye a revival had taken place and he wanted it to spread eastwards. It would also give him the chance to see his brother Charles, who still lived in the county of his birth.

Occasionally, Ross did manage to get away from Glasgow. In 1885 he went to Sweden, then two years later, he headed off to America. Norway was another destination, and of course he went out to New Zealand to see his brother John (who a minister at Turakina and ran a girls' school) and his wife and their family. It was during 1892, when he visited Toronto as a delegate to the Pan-Presbyterian Council, that he went on to visit his brother in New Zealand. As his ship passed the Samoan Islands, the people on board disembarked and Ross went into a little church where the natives were singing. He heard the word 'Jesus' and he later wrote that it was the most amazing sight that he had ever come across. He was formally welcomed by the Presbytery at Marton in New Zealand and given a cordial welcome by everyone in attendance. Following the usual meeting, in which reports were given about several mission stations and the work that was being done among the Maoris, Ross spoke to the assembled company about his work back in his homeland, which he referred to as the Old Country. He also spoke of his impressions of the work going on in New Zealand, work that he thought was going well, for this, and he received a hearty round of applause. It was also during this visit that he attended the annual distribution of prizes at the Ladies' Classical School in Turakina on 21 December 1892, and presented to, among others, his nieces awards for their outstanding work. He praised his brother for his efforts and told the parents and scholars alike that the education they received and were receiving was equivalent to that which was taught at the higher educational institutes back in Scotland. Ross praised every girl who received a certificate for her endeavours and commitment to the school.

It was also in New Zealand that he held a week's mission at Waganui and addressed a Minister's Conference in Wellington. While staying with his brother, one man travelled 20 miles to hear Ross preach in Gaelic. But Ross' trip was marred by illness. He became unwell and was cared for by his brother's family. He soon recovered well enough to return home via Australia.

1892 was a momentous year for Ross in another way. It was the 25th anniversary of his becoming a minister. He was honoured for his work in front of his congregation, and many friends – from both Glasgow and much further afield – came to celebrate with him. As a token of their esteem, he was presented with a cheque for £460, which helped pay for his visits abroad that year. A resolution was passed in his honour, stating that 'a little rest from labour may be beneficial to him' and telling him to take six months off from work to 'become familiar with the aggressive and mission work of the churches in other parts of the world'.

An example of the work that Ross did can be found in the story of Danny Fraser – a man who stabbed another to death when he was drunk – and his friend James Allan. On the site where the Cowcaddens Church was built, there used to stand an old public house that was demolished to make way for the church. Here, four men had been drinking and a fight broke out between two of them. Fraser and his companion struggled and Fraser stabbed the man in the heart. He was tried and condemned to death but won a reprieve and served many years behind bars. While there, he learned to be a cobbler. He was eventually freed from prison and took up his trade and made an adequate living from it. It happened that one day, James Allan found Fraser and told him about the Cowcaddens Church. After much persuasion, he attended a service that changed his life. From the pulpit Ross held a service that touched Danny and he became a full member, living the rest of his life quietly, believing in God. Ross touched many lives in this way.

There were occasions when Ross spoke to the people of Glasgow in Gaelic, the language he had been brought up with. The Highlanders appreciated it and Ross himself found that occasionally only a Gaelic prayer would do, as English did not quite fit the bill. He was especially keen when the Highlanders came to visit to speak to them in their own language, much to the confusion of the workers who had no idea what he was saying.

As his time at Cowcaddens passed, Ross found a new mission, which became his trademark. He opened centres that became widely known as 'Pioneer Missions'. The idea had originally been the brainchild of John Galloway of Ardrossan, who had heard of the work that the Salvation Army did in the slums and suggested to Ross that he begin something similar under the umbrella of the Cowcaddens Church. Two women were selected, trained and moved into a small, clean, bright and airy cottage in Bayne's Court, where they held council. The destitution around them was horrific. Poverty was rife and the area was full of despair. What these two women did was invite the poor in and listen to their tales of destitution or stories of how women's husbands had deserted them and left them penniless to bring up their children. They listened to symptoms of illness and the descriptions of the lack of sanitation and food within the homes. But these women helped by providing comfort, food and spiritual guidance. It became a success and soon another mission was set up in Milton Lane, thanks to funding by Mr Galloway and Lord Overtoun. Yet another mission sprang up in Church Place. Dr Norman Walker, who edited the *Free Church Monthly*, visited these missions and wrote that these houses were 'centres of gracious influence'. From these Pioneer Missions, many of those who attended ended up becoming full members of the Church and helped others the way they had been helped. In 1896 the combined total of members at the three missions was 235; and in 1902 there were 317, although these numbers do not reflect the huge numbers who were influenced or helped by the missions.

Ross' health began to decline from around 1895. Before then, friends wondered how he managed to keep going, as an ordinary man would have buckled under the strain. By September 1896, he received help to conduct his ministry in the form of the Reverend James Muir, but he only managed to stay for three years, much to the disappointment of both Ross and his parishioners. In 1897 Ross had a nervous breakdown, due to his incredibly heavy workload. To recuperate, Ross moved away from the grime and suffocating Glaswegian streets for the warmer climes of South Africa. He spent some time at a sanatorium and following his recovery he visited Kimberley and Johannesburg, as well as a flying visit to Lovedale: another missionary station well-known for its work.

In 1899 the three Ross brothers (John in New Zealand, William working in Glasgow, and Charles ministering at Dunbeath) each conducted a service at the Free Church of Dunbeath. Many of those who attended the service remembered these men as children and remembered fondly their mother, who had passed away at the Free Church Manse in November 1881 aged 80. They also remembered Murdoch, their father, who had died in April 1864 aged 69. It was a unique occasion and one that lived on in the memories of the locals for many years afterwards.

Nearer the end of his life, Ross was asked to write a book about his life by Reverend Dr Alexander Whyte, but he told his friend that he did not like to see himself in print. This was put down to Ross being secretive and cautious about what he said. There was little chance he would have had the time to write a book on his ministry anyway, for he was always busy, although in his later years he was also weakening. But Ross did write a pamphlet called *Three Years on the Night-shift* and he scribed articles in his monthly leaflet. His largest work was his edition of the *History of Bute* by John Blain.

William Ross' last sermon was given in March 1904. At the tail end of 1903, he received an invitation to go back to New Zealand, having visited there last in 1892. He had made a huge impression on those he met. Two presbyteries had called for this and the Assembly of the Presbyterian Church of New Zealand sent the official invitation. However, his present work in Scotland prevented him from going. Depsite this, Ross was keen to go, so the date was put forward to 1905 at the earliest. In January 1904 Ross visited Dublin, but he had a breakdown and had to take two weeks or so off work to recuperate. When he went back to work, he was still an ill man. This had begun to manifest during the year before. Many of those who knew him well saw a change in him. He had fainting episodes, shortness of breath and he was no longer the cheery soul he had once been. During one sermon in Kilmarnock, Ross had to stop half way though and asked the congregation to sing a hymn while he rested briefly.

In April 1904 Ross was due to return to Rothesay, so he went over on the boat to begin making arrangements. However, the weather turned on him. A storm arose and he was thoroughly soaked through by the time the steamer made it to the pier. He became seriously ill and the Rothesay mission was postponed. He lay in bed with congested lungs and a few days before he died, a telegram was sent to his brother Charles who came down from Caithness, and his son and daughter-in-law to come to his bedside. His old friend and former assistant Peter Macdonald came to his bedside too and they said a prayer together in Gaelic. The following day he died.

Many in the church mourned his passing. The moderator of the General Assembly, Dr Robert Gordon Balfour, who had served as minister of the New North Free Church in Edinburgh for 40 years, said that the news was like some kind of calamity. As far away as New Zealand where his brother still worked, messages of sympathy came flooding in. John Ross wrote to the family back in Glasgow that: 'you might imagine this coast as part of his parish' such was the outpouring of grief. Following the church service, the funeral procession, led by children, made its way to the Central Station with the local police stopping all the traffic as a mark of respect. Then it reached the High Street. The whole of the street was closed. Bells tolled and every shop and public house had closed down for the day.

As for John Ross in faraway New Zealand, he died 4 November 1912 aged 83. Charles Ross, the minister first of the Free Church of Dunbeath then the United Free Church from 1878, died on 5 June 1924 aged 83. The Ross brothers had made their impact on the world and were all greatly missed when they passed away.

DAVID GRAHAM SCOTT

Documentary filmmaking covers a whole range of subjects from childbirth, rebellious teenagers, medical phenomena and death but drug issues and the impact of them are only now being screened. One man has changed the perception of drug addiction and recovery from it in the hard-hitting documentary *Detox or Die*, which was screened as part of the BBC's *One Life* series in 2004. Today, Wick-born David Graham Scott is working on the follow-up *The Mission* but he has many other screen credits to his name.

David Graham Scott was born in Wick in May 1962, second son of John and Marjory Scott. John worked locally at the radio station after the couple returned to Caithness following a stint in northern England. Educated locally at Pulteneytown Academy Scott entered Wick High School, which at that time was under the auspices of Rector John MacLeod. By this time, Scott had become fascinated with film, thanks to its introduction by his elder brother Ian – the well-known artist now living in New York. During the 1970s Ian bought his brother an 8mm camera. Later, when Scott visited Ian in London, Ian took him to screenings of avant-garde films at the Hayward Gallery, thus reinforcing his interest in filmmaking. The decision to go and study film theory was made and he headed off to the University of Edinburgh where he also studied Art History, before gaining his BA at the University of Kent. By 1985 Scott was married to Denise. Both became addicted to heroin. Also in 1985, Scott's father died. He travelled north for the funeral. His brother Ian heard that Scott was an addict and sure enough, evidence was found in his bag. It was a bitter blow to his mother who feared that she had not only lost her husband but was about to lose her son too.

On his return to the capital, Scott began experimenting with short films about drugs, concentrating on the components needed and death, which became a fixation. In 1988, Scott and his wife split up. Scott headed to Glasgow to try and begin a new chapter in his life and become clean. But the prescribed medication was almost worse than the illegal one. Scott persevered and he got a job as projectionist in the 1990s. He continued to make his own films about addiction to try and understand his own.

Scott's first major success in documentary-making was in the mid-1990s with the short film *Hanging With Frank*. It is the one he is most proud of to date. The film is a study of Barlinnie Prison's execution chamber and the man who worked there. It was a 'real labour of love' as Scott shot it entirely on film rather than video. What inspired him to interview Frank McKue, the former death-watch officer, was an article he found in *The Herald Magazine* that announced the end for the chamber and the loss of its history. He approached the prison governor who told Scott that as long as the documentary was a serious one, he would have open access. Over the coming months, Scott and his crew visited the prison on numerous occasions with 'a truckload of film equipment' due to the fact he had chosen to 'shoot it on grainy black and white film stock', which gives it an atmosphere that is tangible.

Today *Hanging With Frank* is shown in local schools and was chosen recently for Channel 4's website 4Docs as a fine example of good documentary filmmaking. In 1998 it won Best Overall Film at the Reel to Real Festival and was officially selected for the Edinburgh Film Festival the same year. Because of its uniqueness and histori-cal importance it has also passed into the hands of the Scottish Film Archive. Since its making, the death-watch officer Frank McKue has died, which makes the film even more poignant.

In 1999 Scott embarked on the documentary *Little Criminals*, which was runner-up at the Celtic Film Festival in 2001 and was BAFTA nominated in 2002. It is a candid film and follows the lives of a group of people who shoplift for a career to feed their heroin addiction. Following its filming he embarked another historical venture: in 2002 the BBC broadcast *Death on Eagle's Rock*. It concerned the plane crash in which Queen Elizabeth II's uncle, Prince George the Duke of Kent, died in mysterious circumstances. For Scott it meant a trip home to a place he already knew and a piece of history he was already well read in, having lived so near to the crash site. On 25 August 1942 a Sunderland flying boat was en route to Iceland from Invergordon when it crashed into the hillside above Dunbeath. As it struck, it exploded and was engulfed in flames, leaving all but one of the 15 passengers and crew on board dead, including the 39-year-old Duke. The crash was witnessed by David Morrison and his son Hugh, who was sent on his motorbike to alert John Kennedy, the local doctor, and the police. A search party was quickly mustered but visibility by this time was poor. It was just over two hours after the crash that the victims were found. The doctor removed the Duke's watch, believing it to be vital evidence, for it had stopped at 1.42 p.m., the presumed time of impact. But the Morrisons were confused. They had heard the crash much later, at around 2.30 p.m. It was to be one of many mysteries surrounding the events of that day. The bodies of the victims, some of which had been thrown clear and others were still in the burnt-out wreckage, were taken down the hill on stretchers to waiting ambulances, with the Duke's body being taken to Dunrobin Castle. The following day, heartfelt tributes poured in over the death of Prince George. There was confusion for one family. Jean Jack, the sister of Flight Sergeant Andrew Jack of Grangemouth, received a telegram informing her of her brother's death, only for it to be retracted two days later when he was found to be alive. Jack had managed to walk away from the crash with burns and his clothes in tatters. Barefoot, he reached a cottage owned by a widow, Helen Sutherland, where he asked for help, and stating to her that he was the sole survivor. He was taken to hospital at Lybster to be treated. On 14 September, King George VI visited the crash site, where he saw the scorched earth and marks from when the aircraft had impacted. After an inquiry, the captain Flight Lieutenant Frank Goyen – a 25-year-old Australian with a great deal of flying experience – was blamed for the incident. However, Andrew Jack did not believe the findings and was furious that the blame was laid at Goyen's feet. It was something he disbelieved right up until his death in 1978.

Many years later, an account transpired from Captain Ernest Edmund Fresson, the far north of Scotland's pioneer of flight in the early 1930s, which suggested there was a change of captain at the last minute. This delayed the flight and the flight plan changed as well. He had been told that Goyen had given the command to drop lower than necessary to below the clouds, earlier than he should, in order to take a shortcut over the Caithness countryside. He was suddenly confronted with rising ground hidden by the poor weather. The aircraft clock was found to read 1.30 p.m., the same time when Fresson had been flying overhead. However, Jack believed it was actually 29-year-old Wing Commander Thomas Mosely that had given the order to drop altitude. However, the biggest mystery of all had yet to be addressed. Was Adolf Hitler's deputy Rudolf Hess on board that plane? Speculation has been rife for many years that he was on board and historians and laymen alike are no closer to the truth. Was there a sixteenth passenger or was this simply unbridled speculation caused by war? Rumours suggested that Hess was in Scotland at that time and that the plane was deviating from its route to collect him. Hess was allegedly hiding out at Lochmore Cottage on the shores of Loch More in the heart of Caithness. If Hess had been picked up, it was claimed that the Duke would have taken him to neutral Sweden. It is also claimed that the man held in captivity at Loch More following the crash of his Messerschmitt at Eaglesham Moor in May 1941 was not actually Hess. Hess had supposedly been switched with a doppelganger at some stage so that he could leave Britain to seek a peace deal a year later. In all likelihood, there was no mission to Sweden, which would have been dangerous in the daytime over the hostile North Sea, and Rudolf Hess was not on board, but mystery still surrounds the crash at Eagle's Rock due to inconsistencies so may never fully be resolved.

The year 1998 also saw the broadcast of *Beyond the Highland*, a personal journey through the lens of the camera for Scott. Growing up, he had never felt that he really fitted in and this documentary was filmed to address the issue of his methadone addiction head-on by finding out about who he was, and where he belonged. The original idea centred on 'a couple of old ladies living out in the wilds and how they managed to get by', but this fell through at the last minute. Unperturbed, Scott came up with another idea. He suggested to STV that he film himself as a methadone addict on a cathartic journey to find his place in the world before going into detox. Incidentally, the subject of detox later became one of his most well-known documentaries to date: the hard-hitting *Detox or Die*

David Graham Scott
Courtesy David Graham Scott

(see below). The network approved the idea. During filming he met many local characters. There was Peter Stewart, a local crofter; John Angus the Post who was well-known in the Dunbeath area; the Canadian painter Monique Sleidrecht; and Dr Neville Jones and his family. What Scott wanted to do was find out why they were living in Caithness, so far from the hustle and bustle of town life. By doing this Scott hoped he would find out why he felt the way he did about Caithness and that strong feeling of 'home' that it had on him.

The BBC then commissioned the harrowing documentary *Wireburners*, which followed the next year. Scott filmed of a group of homeless people who scraped together a living from scrap metal in Glasgow but for whom street life was the norm.

The year 1999 saw the filming of Scott's most personal and traumatic journey from drug addict to being clean. *Detox or Die* was commissioned by the BBC as part of their documentary series *One Life*, which followed the lives of people in difficult and often harrowing circumstances. It followed Scott's own journey, which saw him ditch his addiction by using the controversial drug Ibogaine. Originally the idea was to follow a group of addicts, but eventually, during the filming, he succumbed. A drug dealer, who knew exactly what he was doing, offered Scott a free hit. Addiction is instant with heroin and dealers make their money by offering small amounts free, knowing full well the people will come back and buy more off them. Scott smoked the heroin and for the first time in a long time, he felt great. This led to him helping the others in the film to inject and unable to resist, he injected himself and on 21 March 1999, 'that was me a junkie again'. The film that had started out as documentary about others soon turned out to be about Scott himself. Over the course of filming, he was charged under the Misuse of Drugs Act and spent half of his wages on drugs. He weaned himself off but the methadone he was receiving from the doctor simply affected his mental health, which in turn caused the breakdown of the relationship he was in at the time.

In the summer of 2003 Scott had cut his methadone down to about half his prescribed dose and travelled north to Wick to stay with his mother and explained to her his plans to get off methadone. In the end, after days of pain and mental anguish, he started taking methadone once more. But it was a turning point. His brother Ian had told him about Ibogaine, a controversial treatment that seemed to succeed in getting addicts off hard drugs in America. In the UK it is legal but unlicensed, so anyone helping an addict has to do it underground. Scott searched the Internet, found information on the drug and decided that was the last course of action he could take if he wanted a dependency-free life. He told his mother what he was about to do with the Ibogaine treatment and allayed her fears as much as he could about the dangers that she had heard were involved. The newspapers got hold of the story and sensational headlines appeared. The journalists simply did not understand the effect the methadone was having on him and he did not want to live the rest of his life taking it. Before he left for treatment in London in August 2003, he recorded his last will and testament. Movingly, he apologised to his mother for everything he had put her through and explained it was his last chance. Treatment followed and he was kept under the watchful eye of the man who administered the drug. A series of capsules were given to him over the course of the day and although it was a bizarre and frightening experience, the Ibogaine worked for him. Towards the end of filming, Scott caught up with his original subjects – some of whom were off heroin but on methadone. The film was aired in 2004 and has since become an invaluable documentary to the many men and women who have given up hope of ever kicking the heroin habit.

Not one to shy away from controversy, Scott filmed those behind Glasgow's vigilante magazine *The Dirty Digger* in 2007, in which he acted as court photographer for a very brief period of time, taking snaps of those who were to be named and shamed as paedophiles or gangsters in the Glasgow area.

In 2008, the Scottish Documentary Institute and Lansdowne Productions decided to gather the best ten documentary filmmakers and give each the task of taking as a subject matter one of the Ten Commandments, it was to commemorate the 60th anniversary of the Universal Declaration of Human Rights. Under the guidelines, Scott filmed Peter Dow, the self-proclaimed Scottish National Standard Bearer for his documentary *The Right to Freedom of Assembly*. The film, along with the nine others, was premiered at the Edinburgh Film Festival in 2008 and broadcast on BBC2 in December 2008. The others were: *The Right Not to be Enslaved* directed by Nick Higgins; *The Right to a Fair Trial* by Sana Bilgrami; *The Right to Freedom of Expression* by Doug Aubrey; *The Right to Life* directed by Kenny Glenaan; *The Right to Liberty* by Irvine Welsh and Mark Cousins; *The*

Right Not to be Tortured by Douglas Gordon; *The Right to Asylum* by Anna Jones; *The Right to Privacy* directed by Alice Nelson; and *The Right to Freedom of Thought* by Mark Cousins and Oscar-winning actress Tilda Swinton.

Scott's thoughts were never far away from his Caithness roots and he came up with a film called *Arcadia* that was to be made on the Thrumster Estate near Wick. Controversy followed and the BBC dropped the film for not being impartial. The ten-minute film was eventually shown in the British Museum in May 2010. It highlights the local community's stance against a proposed wind farm that threatened their way of life. The film itself proposed to demonstrate the impact of the modern world on an ancient landscape that Caithnessians hold dear. Wind farms have proven contentious in Caithness. It was during the filming of this that Scott met Guy Wallace – who lives on the Thrumster Estate, training gun dogs and running a goose farm. Mr Wallace was planning his last big game hunt in Africa and Scott had the idea to film him on this amazing journey.

Currently Scott is filming a follow-up to his personal journey of *Detox and Die* entitled *The Mission*. He cites himself as a controversial documentary filmmaker yet is simply recording people who are on the edge of society. He is constantly driven by the 'overwhelming desire to uncover stories of the marginalised characters of this world' and this shows throughout his work. Caithness itself plays a major part in this. It influences him deeply: 'documentary filmmakers are always on the lookout for subjects and it's amazing how many of these are very close to home'.

One of Scott's hopes for the future was to film the self-styled London dandy, artist and writer, Sebastian Horsley, who was 'perfect material for a great documentary'. However on 17 June 2010, Horsley (whose real name was Marcus) was found dead at his Soho home. Horsley rose to fame in 2000 when he decided to have himself filmed as he was being crucified, without painkillers, in the Philippines in the name of art. He fainted, but the film, photographs of the event and his later paintings depicting the scene, were exhibited. It was his belief that this was the only way to actually feel what he was painting, and by experiencing it, the resulting artwork would be truthful. Just a few days before his death, aged 47, a play entitled *Dandy in the Underworld* opened in Soho, which was based on his candid writings of his heroin and cocaine addiction and his use of hundreds of prostitutes. Horsley had an unconventional life. Born to millionaire Nicholas Horsley, both his parents were alcoholics and after schooling, he wanted to attend the University of Edinburgh to read English but he failed to pass his exams. He became interested in art and writing thanks to a chance meeting with director Danny Boyle. But most of all he was an extrovert, noticeable in Soho because of his flamboyant clothes. He was never without his tail-coat and oversized top hat. He was banned from entering the US for being open about his heroin addiction and claimed that as a concession he removed his nail polish. Soho has lost one of its most vibrant characters and Scott has lost the chance to film his friend.

Through his seminal work *Detox or Die*, Scott has given hope to many addicts and today is an active public speaker on the issue.

To view some of Scott's work, go to www.davidgrahamscott.com.

IAN CHARLES SCOTT

I an Charles Scott lives and works in New York but his roots remain firmly fixed in Caithness and some of his work provides testament to this. Older brother of the documentary filmmaker David Graham Scott, Scott's love of art began when he was a schoolboy and fuelled his meteoric rise in the art world to a renowned position that he has held for decades.

Although born in Whitley Bay in England (where his Edinburgh-born father worked for a time), Scott regards himself as Caithnessian. Most of his young life was spent in Wick and his mother Marjory, who was born in Caithness, still lives in the county town where Scott went to school. When he was in infant school, he won his first art competition thanks to one of his most influential teachers, Mrs Mulraine at Pulteneytown Academy. She enthused about the subject and showed her pupils slides of the work of Paul Gustave Doré, the 19th century artist and engraver who, at age five, was already showing his artistic streak and went on to become one of the best known wood and steel engravers of his time. The competition Scott won was the Walt Disney award, which was open worldwide, and for his troubles he received £750. From then on he was completely absorbed by art, despite the fact that when he went to Wick High School he never studied the subject. However, art was in his blood and he applied to Duncan of Jordanstone College of Art and Design at the University of Dundee where he was accepted on the honours painting and drawing programme. He graduated with a First Class Honours degree and went on to do postgraduate work. When he completed his degree at the Dundee Art College he left with the knowledge that he was the most highly commended student at the time.

Scott lived in Scotland, England and Germany before his move to the United States, where he is a professor at the Hostos Community College of the City of New York University in the Bronx. In 1992 he was awarded one of Scotland's most coveted art prizes, the Alastair Salvesen Art Scholarship, which had been established in 1989. The criteria included the applicants living and working in Scotland, having graduated with honours from one of the four Scottish Art Colleges, and to have worked for three years following their graduation. Around 500 applicants were whittled down to just four who had to face a panel of seven judges. From these four Scott was chosen and won the £8,000 award. With the money, he set off for the United States where he travelled widely and painted at every opportunity.

Over the years, Scott worked in a series of jobs, including spells as a gravedigger and helping people with special needs. One of the most influential jobs he had was at Shotts Prison in Lanarkshire during the mid 1990s where he lectured part-time, teaching art therapy. The prison is maximum security, purpose-built for male long-term prisoners, and is in the countryside near to the village of Shotts. There he met men who were highly skilled, as well as those with little or no education. Yet through art, they began to express themselves. On one occasion Scott recalls a prisoner painting from a copy of the Venetian

Ian Charles Scott
Courtesy Ian Charles Scott

Renaissance artist Tintoretto's *Crucifixion* – Scott later discovered that this man had actually crucified someone and that was the reason for his incarceration. Because of his extremely sociable nature, Scott got on with the prisoners well and on one memorable occasion he was even complimented by one of them who claimed he had been watching him – an expression which had dual meaning but which Scott took to be flattering praise. In 1997 Scott painted *Happening in Shotts Prison Allotment* in tribute to his time working at the prison.

At Hostos in New York, Scott has gained recognition as one of the most prominent members of the college. The college has students from the deprived South Bronx, with some not being able to speak English, but through their own work and under the tutelage of Scott, have managed to express themselves through their art. Deeply underprivileged, the students – who range from the young to the elderly – may have had psychological problems or personal difficulties, but at the college they manage to lose themselves in their art. Exceptional talent has been discovered in these people. His students have said that Scott makes art meaningful and fun, and not only is he hardworking and caring, but he also inspires them – many have turned their lives around thanks to his endeavours. It is due to this work that in 2009 Scott was nominated for the Mayor of New York City's Award for Arts and Culture. Previous winners have included Woody Allen and the playwright Tennessee Williams. Scott is the first person from the United Kingdom to be put forward.

Scott's work has come to the fore back in the United Kingdom too. In 1995 his art was used for the cover of Wet Wet Wet's single *Julia Says*. More recently Scott's art can be found on the cover of James Fleming's latest book *Rising Blood*, as well as in *The History of Orkney Literature* by Simon W. Hall. The former Liberal Democrat Member of Parliament Robert MacLennan, now Lord MacLennan of Rogart, collects Scott's work. Rock legend David Bowie and American musician Moby are also ardent admirers. Only once has Scott ever regretted selling a piece of work – a painting called *Duende*, painted in 1987. This was a portrait of his father John. It was sought by 'several galleries and individuals' but Scott would not sell it to them. Eventually, though, he sold it 'through a gallery on Cork Street, London' and over the years wondered about it and who had purchased it. He even went so far as to paint 'a huge version of it with changes but nothing could compensate for the loss'. There was, however, a twist of fate that favoured him. In 1997, unexpectedly, Scott saw it for sale by Agnew's Gallery of Bond Street in London at an art fair. Scott promptly advised them he was the artist and more in hope than anything else, asked if he could purchase it back at artists' rates. He was astonished when they agreed. The painting now hangs in the family home in Wick.

Scott's mother Marjory had refused to let him paint her, but his brother David has allowed him to draw him. Although many of these works have been discarded for one reason or another, two of them now also hang in the family home. These are one of David when 'he first became a drug addict' then another drawn some 20 years later following his detox treatment, as broadcast in his documentary *Detox or Die* in 2004. However, family aside, Scott's work shows where his inspiration comes from. As he says himself, 'everyone who knows my work will realise no matter where I am in the world that Wick and its environs are my key number one influence'. This is certainly true. His works include *Canisbay Kirk* (1993), *Pentland Taufe* (1987), *Nosshead* (1987), and a study of *Willie Sinclair Harbour Master Wick* (1986). In his 1990 painting *Philoctetes*, the backdrop is the Wick River and part of the town. *Nosshead* was used by the Japanese telecommunications company Teleca on their phone cards following a chance meeting in a lift of a Chicago hotel. The Japanese businessman Satoshi So met Scott in that lift and he was so impressed by Scott's work, he persuaded Teleca to use it.

It is Scott's love of the sea that comes through in many of his paintings. He uses many local characters to enhance this link with Wick and Caithness as a whole. Fishing and fishermen also play a prominent role and there is an element of the Viking heritage of the county in his works. In addition, he has painted and drawn several portraits of the Orcadian poet and author George Mackay Brown.

Scott's art is best summed up as generally being surrealist allegories, using the subconscious to express ideas creatively. Such movement began in the 1920s and has since gone from strength to strength. When looking at his work, it will not be a quick glance, but the viewer will be drawn in by the ideas on the canvas. The strange juxtaposition in the works expresses a psychological element within every piece of art that Scott has created and only by viewing it closely will its full meaning be revealed. The detail is minute and each work takes you to another level of consciousness. Scott's work could also be described as mysterious, for in the main, the subject is not always apparent at first glance.

In his art Scott has been influenced by many, including the 17th century Dutch artist Rembrandt, and the contemporary Norwegian artist Odd Nerdrum, whose allegorical work is deeply controversial in the art world because it is based on figurative work rather than the received wisdom of work acceptable in Norway. Nerdrum stripped away the boundaries of what could be termed decency in his work *Twilight*, where a young woman in the woods is shown defecating, thus bringing into sharp focus the darker and more taboo subject concerning a natural occurrence.

Scott's work has been exhibited and sold in galleries all over the world. However, getting them there has at times, been a challenge. On one occasion, a large diver's head painting measuring 6' by 4' was strapped onto the roof of a car in an upright fashion. A gust of wind caught it during its journey and it freed itself, landing on the car behind and then hitting the road. Damage was done and it was in no condition to be shown. After a week of frantic repair work, it was finally ready to be exhibited and shortly after it went on show it was bought by a leading London collector.

Scott's paintings are currently held in a number of museums and galleries including the Aberdeen Art Gallery, Dundee Museum and Art Gallery, and the Royal Scottish Academy in Edinburgh. Elsewhere, they are on exhibition at East West Gallery and Mercury Gallery in London, the Compass Gallery in Glasgow and the Silverstein Gallery in New York. Scott regularly gave talks on his work and had been on both the BBC and the independent television channels as well as in leading art magazines. In his beloved Caithness his work had been exhibited at the Lyth Arts Centre. He also cares passionately about the local art scene and is a strong advocate of the St Fergus Gallery in Wick, which has faced the threat of closure or transformation into a research facility.

Scott's work can also be viewed online. Some examples can be found at www.kilmorackgallery.co.uk/artists/scott.html and he gives an annual lecture in his hometown of Wick.

SIR JOHN SINCLAIR

Sir John Sinclair was born at Thurso Castle on 10 May 1754. He was the son of Sir George Sinclair of Ulbster and his wife Lady Janet, the daughter of William Gordon, Lord Strathnaver. The couple married in the late autumn of 1740.

The Sinclairs' first child (also called John) was born in 1743, but he died in infancy. The following year, Katherine was born but she died during a smallpox outbreak in 1748, which also claimed the life of her sibling Henrietta, who had been born in 1745. Other children of the couple also passed away, including a stillborn boy in 1752, but John and his sisters Helen, Mary and Janet survived into adulthood.

Sinclair was educated both in Caithness and at the High School in Edinburgh before studying at the universities of Edinburgh, Glasgow and Oxford. He entered Edinburgh University at the tender age of 11 where he studied for four years. At Glasgow he studied law, a subject that landowners of the day needed to know about. His life was rigidly structured. He would study for up to 12 hours a day and took only a couple of hours out for food and relaxation before heading to bed. It was during his time at the University of Glasgow that he attended the lectures of Adam Smith, the Kirkcaldy-born economist, and his interest in economics and philosophy grew. By this stage in his life, Sinclair was already head of the family, following the death of his father in 1776. Sinclair's mother was a 'shrewd, able and managing woman', according to J. T. Calder, the local 19th century historian, and she proficiently looked after her three remaining children who lived with her in Caithness. She was prudent with the money she was left but it fell to Sinclair to take care of the estate. Although he knew little about the running of the estate, one thing he did realise was that the county lacked roads for the transportation of goods and services. However, there was little he could do while still away from home studying. When he completed his studies, he followed in the footsteps of so many Enlightenment thinkers and took a grand tour of Europe. He was joined by his brother James, who had been sent south due to his ailing health in the hope it would improve in the better climatic conditions of the Mediterranean.

However, during their time in Provence James caught a cold and subsequently died. Sinclair returned to Scotland as heir to the family estates. Shortly after his return he married Sarah Maitland, a young lady he had been courting for some time, and they settled at Thurso Castle with Lady Janet.

Aged just 25 years old, Sinclair became Member of Parliament for the county of Caithness. This saw him move away from Caithness and he never again made it his home, although he and his family did return there for most summers until his death. At the time of his election, the American Revolution was in full swing and Britain was at war with France. Unsurprisingly, due to economics in the main, he threw his weight behind the Government. The economy was a subject that he became increasingly interested in as a Member of Parliament. During 1782–83, the harvests in Scotland were poor and there was an increasing sense of a food shortage looming. Sinclair approached the Government for aid to stave off the famine and was duly rewarded when £15,000 was spent on food and supplies. With his political career going well, and now also being a Baronet, conferred on him in 1780, life for the Sinclairs was good. However, in 1785 tragedy struck the young family. In May Sinclair's wife Sarah became ill and she died on the 15th, leaving her husband with two young daughters to care for. It was a devastating blow. He was very much a family man and had few friends. He wrote to William Pitt the Younger, explaining he would not be attending the House of Commons due to Sarah's death and thought seriously about giving up being a parliamentarian altogether. He lost interest in politics, although retained his seat at Lostwithiel, and embarked on a European journey that was to be one of the most pleasurable of his life. Meanwhile, Sinclair sent his daughters – six-year-old Hannah and five-year-old Janet – to Thurso with their nurse to live with his mother. Sinclair visited Holland, Denmark, Sweden, Austria, Prussia and Russia, bringing back with him a wealth of knowledge and an expanded circle of acquaintances. He wrote extensively about his travels.

On 6 March 1788, Sinclair remarried. She was Lady Diana Macdonald, only daughter of Lord Macdonald of Sleat on the Isle of Skye. In all they had 13 children, and Sinclair played an important role in their lives, taking an interest in their education as well as their upbringing. As a concession to Diana, the family moved to the Canongate in Edinburgh, before moving to the prestigious Charlotte Square. Sinclair travelled to London by stagecoach but always managed to return home for the recess and for Christmas. Edinburgh provided the family with all their needs, both medically and socially and their circle of friends grew in the enlightened city. Sinclair went so far as to publish his *Code of Health and Longevity*, which stated that fresh air, cleanliness, a good and varied diet and exercise were paramount for a healthy and long life. Sinclair's dinner parties became legendary for the stories told around the table and the wealth of knowledge that Sinclair had on the Scottish countryside.

With an ever-expanding family, visits to Caithness for the whole brood became impossible, so Sinclair and his sons Alexander, John, George, Archibald, Godfrey and William went to the county themselves. His younger daughters Catherine and Diana travelled only once to Caithness with their father before he died. It was also at this time

Thurso Castle

Thurso Castle

that his daughters from his first marriage joined the family in Edinburgh, following completion of their schooling at Stoke Newington. But it was during the 1790s that Sinclair made his biggest impact on the country.

From his experiences in his home county, Sinclair's interest in agricultural matters had been forged and this led to the forming of the first Board of Agriculture that the country had ever seen. Following its creation, Sinclair began dialogue with the many landowners both at home and further afield on the continent, which led to the publication of the *Code of Agriculture* in 1817. By the 1790s, Sinclair was acutely aware of the fact that wool was imported from abroad because it tended to be finer than the indigenous wool. He recognised that sheep could also be used for their mutton. So in 1788 Sinclair bought Langwell in Caithness for £9,000 and brought Cheviots to graze there. This created the problem of moving existing tenants towards the coastline, which he did, giving each two Scotch acres to work. He also encouraged weaving in the crofters' homes and applied for a grant for spinning wheels and reels for the wool to be wrapped on. He experimented with the sheep, trying to create a Caithness breed and in January 1791, the British Wool Society was established with Sinclair at its helm as chairman. This notwithstanding, he also began looking at setting up fisheries, but the forming of the Board of Agriculture took up more and more of his time.

In 1793 Britain and France were once more at war. War costs money and many businesses went bankrupt because of it, causing Prime Minister Pitt to look for funds elsewhere. It was Sinclair who came to the rescue but with a condition attached – Sinclair knew that Pitt would be in a position to give him exactly what he wanted because of his generosity. Sinclair asked Pitt for a Board of Agriculture. Sinclair estimated the costs to be around £5,000 a year, but Pitt could only spare £3,000 for its running. Discussions took place as to how it would be run – Arthur Young became its first secretary and it met for the first time in August 1793, although Sinclair had started work on it long before this time. Eventually the board undertook surveying of the state of agriculture but the costs involved steadily rose to around £200 for a survey of the counties that gave the most information. Because of this, Sinclair ended up having to prop up the board financially.

Not content with simply improving Caithness and aiding the Board of Agriculture, Sinclair embarked on the most remarkable of feats he ever undertook. It was to become the *Statistical Account* and today it is still a valuable source of information on parishes all over Scotland. Although local clergy had gathered a certain amount of information in the past, it had not spilled over into the whole of Scotland. Sinclair was a Member of Parliament, and he had money as well as the impetus to undertake the work. He was on good terms with the clergy – he was a lay member of the General Assembly of the national church – and suggested to them that he would pay for the printing of the information that he collected and postage costs would be covered under a parliamentary frank, thus saving the ministers money. The clergy agreed. Between 1791 and 1799, Sinclair received information on every parish in Scotland and he read each one. He had a set number of questions and within the first two years, over half the parishes had responded to him. Between 1793 and 1799 the material was more difficult to come by, but Sinclair persisted and eventually he had details of every single Scottish parish. Some ministers had only given short accounts of their local parish, while others went into great detail. The subjects covered included geology, geography, population statistics, agriculture, industry, ecclesiastical state and history. In all, 21 volumes were published of the *Statistical Account* and it gave the Government a snapshot of Scotland. Sinclair himself wrote the account of Thurso, in which he covered the population and referred to 'a great many beggars' in the district, although there was advancement in education with two public schools for boys. Trade and commerce played a vital role, as did fishing, and among the many trades in the town were weavers, shoemakers, boat builders, bakers and coopers. Towards the end of his *Account* he claimed that Thurso was 'well suited for trade, manufactures and fisheries'. Only lack of investment prevented the town at that time from becoming a great place.

Also in this account, Sinclair praised the county of Caithness as a whole with regards to the military. He proclaimed that the county had a long and distinguished history of men taking up arms and becoming professional soldiers, which he believed comparable terms with other counties of Scotland of equal size and population, could not be underestimated. However, by the time of his writing, he did realise the situation was on the wane and men tended to become employed in local industry and enjoy home comforts, rather than taking up arms to do battle in foreign lands. Volunteers were still forthcoming though. The county had nine companies of volunteers, each consisting of 50 men plus officers and non-commissioned officers, amounting to over 600 men. In 1794 Sinclair himself managed to raise two battalions under the patronage of the Prince of Wales, which became known as the Rothesay and Caithness Fencibles. He designed their uniform and spent time with them at Aberdeen where he took an interest in their diet, clothing, health and welfare. His first battalion saw action in Ireland, from where they returned healthy thanks to improvements that Sinclair had instigated.

The *Accounts* were to be the first step in an ambitious plan to collect information on England and Ireland too, as well as an even more ambitious plan to gather accounts for India. However, in England the church was not unified (as in Scotland) and collecting the information would prove difficult. His idea for India was swept aside for being too huge an undertaking and in Ireland, although he believed it would help the country understand its own politics and lessen the divide between the different factions, it too was muted until the Scottish account proved its worth.

Throughout the 1790s as more statistics came to him, Sinclair also had to battle to keep his seat in Parliament. In June 1796 he travelled north to stand for the seat of Orkney during the General Election. He did not get the backing he required, so he wrote to Pitt, hoping he would offer him a seat. Meanwhile the Board of Agriculture held an extraordinary meeting when Sinclair was away and they cancelled all surveys. Sinclair was eventually returned to Parliament in January 1797 when he stood for the seat of Petersfield.

It took a number of years for Sinclair's Board of Agriculture to show its worth. It had been bypassed in 1801 during the first census, and when the matter of doing a survey of the country's crops was proposed, again it was ignored. In the first decade of the 19th century the board struggled to make ends meet, even thought it had grand ideas for completing its surveys, which would be at considerable cost. The turning point came when Sinclair managed to secure new subscriptions from new honorary members. By 1812 Sinclair had the reports in his hands and they were completed in 1814. He alone did much of the work, including the editing. He was a workaholic who enjoyed the challenges he faced. He even found time to visit some of the improved areas of the country, which he wrote about in his volume *Scotch Husbandry* (probably the one publication that he could call his own). Sinclair also edited the Highland Society's edition of Ossian's works in 1807 and wrote numerous articles. But Sinclair's definitive work – the *Code of Agriculture* – was published in 1817, which contained material Sinclair knew intimately. The book would eventually see five editions published.

Yet all this time, Sinclair still had time to deal with his home county. He had high hopes for Thurso – including a new school and infirmary, as well as a decent harbour – but they only got as far as the drawing board. However, Sinclair was successful in the development of Halkirk, the first planned village in Scotland, and Sarclet, south of Wick, although the fishing industry at the tiny coastal hamlet melted away when larger fishing vessels required a larger harbour to seek anchorage.

In the summer of 1804 Sinclair was dismayed upon travelling between Perth and Inverness when he met many Caithness folk heading to Greenock to catch a ship to

America. He realised that one of the ways to keep the county of Caithness' population from migrating was to improve the road system and pave the way for harbours to be built. It was Wick that gained most: having the harbour developed via the British Fisheries Society and new housing was built – Pulteneytown, named after the president of the Fisheries Society. Wick subsequently became a boomtown. All of this hard work and enterprise paid off when Sinclair was elected as Member of Parliament for the county at the 1807 general election. However, four years later he was penniless.

In 1810 Sinclair became a member of the Privy Council, but the following year his debts spiralled out of control. He had hoped for a substantial legacy but it never materialised and he spent vast sums of money on gathering information and improving his estate over the years. Added to that, he lived beyond his means and had done so for many years. Dowries preyed on his mind. Two daughters were already married but he had a further six to think about. He decided to apply for Cashiership of Excise for Scotland and was duly accepted. This eased the burden. In August 1814 he downsized his Edinburgh home and he resigned from the Board of Agriculture due to his age. He was now 60 and was no longer a Member of Parliament – something that he firmly believed the president of the board should be. His Caithness estate was put in the care of trustees. This had little impact in Caithness, as many families had seen financial pressures and he was still supported on the whole. He sold off Langwell and parts of Ulbster to the Hornes

Statue of Sir John Sinclair, Thurso

of Stirkoke near Wick. Following the cessation of hostilities in Europe, Sinclair made a couple of visits there and wrote pamphlets about his visits. In 1819 he and his family left London and settled in Edinburgh permanently. Nonetheless, Sinclair kept busy with Edinburgh society and increasingly took a deeper interest in religion, but never embraced it the way his children did.

In 1831 Sinclair was accompanied by Catherine and Diana north to Caithness to visit his son George, who was now living at Thurso Castle with his wife and children. The county had become more accessible with the roads that Sinclair had envisaged so many years ago now having come to fruition. It was to be his last visit home. Sinclair also spent time in London with his last visit there in the spring of 1835. He was still active in intellectual circles and debated politics and economics. On 21 December 1835 at his Edinburgh home, he died. He was 81 years old. He was buried in the grounds of Holyrood Abbey.

WILLIAM ALEXANDER SMITH

On 22 July 1909 William Alexander Smith of Thurso was knighted at Buckingham Palace by King Edward VII for his services to the Boys' Brigade. As founder of the movement, Smith was delighted to be honoured in such a way and it was one of the proudest moments in his life.

William Smith

William Smith had been born at Pennyland, a farmhouse on the Dounreay Road in Thurso on 27 October 1854. He was the eldest of three sons and one daughter born to Major David Smith and his wife Harriet Fraser. David Smith had served with the 7 Dragoon Guards in the Kaffir War of 1849–50 in South Africa. After he married he left the army, only to join the local Caithness Volunteer Artillery Corps, which is where he achieved the rank of major. When Smith reached the age of five, he attended the Miller Institution for his education. At this time, he was passionate about shinty – a game played predominantly in the Highlands of Scotland involving two teams from different communities, each team consisting of 16 playing with a curved stick called a 'caman' and a leather ball. The game is a fast one and the team that scores the most goals within a certain time frame is the winner.

Being the son of a military man, it was not long before the young Smith formed a small company with friends to do drill and as more boys heard of it, more joined. The children would march up and down with sticks for rifles held firmly against their shoulders.

In 1868 tragedy struck the family. Smith's father David had gone to China on business in connection with the Luban Coal Company, but died in the port city of Swatow, now Shantou, in the Guangdong region, leaving Harriet Smith alone with her four children back in Caithness. She decided to sell the family home and move further into the town rather than being half a mile outside it. Harriet's brother, who lived in Glasgow, offered to take 13-year-old William under his wing. In May, she boarded a steamer with her children and they headed to Glasgow before travelling up to Callander, where the family spent most of the summer coming to terms with life without David. In October, Smith said goodbye to his mother and siblings who returned to Thurso, and he went to Glasgow to work for his uncle, Alexander Fraser as it was too late in the year to re-start school. In January 1869, Smith was sent to the private Western Educational Institution. Here he was until May when he left, aged 14. School life in the city was not easy to begin with. Smith had an accent that was different to the other boys and his clothes were different, in that they were made from rougher materials than those of the Glasgow boys. However he was well-liked as they got to know him. Smith was frank with them in whatever they did or said but he was also very gentle and charismatic which endeared him to the boys.

When Smith left school, Uncle Alexander gave him a full-time position at his company Alex. Fraser & Co, which was a wholesaler in soft goods, with shawls being their principal market. Smith did not give up his education though. He began attending French classes and later Spanish classes. Smith got on very well with his uncle and during the summer months the two would head out to Callander and go fishing, walking and sailing at the local lochs. He would also go north to visit his mother and siblings and at that time he considered Caithness home.

While in Glasgow, Smith never lost touch with his Caithness roots. In January 1872 he joined the Glasgow Caithness Association and soon realised that the city was home to many Thurso folk. In later life he became president of the association. In the autumn of 1872 he joined the YMCA. The year was to prove life-changing for him, as he met and fell in love with Amelia Sutherland, the eldest daughter of the Reverend Andrew Sutherland. The family had returned to Glasgow following the minister's death at Gibraltar and Smith had struck up a friendship with them. He made his intentions very clear but Mrs Sutherland would not hear of an engagement as she felt the couple were just too young. Smith would have to wait.

Smith continued to work for his uncle and learned more about the business, but deterioration in relations between them meant that, in the end, Smith left and set up a business – firstly with his brother, Donald, then his friend James Findlay too. The reason for the split with his uncle was because of Smith's involvement with the 1st Lanarkshire Rifle Volunteers. He had joined C Company in 1873 and became a corporal the following April. Smith took his soldiering seriously and gave it everything he had, and by 1883 had reached the rank of lieutenant, although he had been forced to give it up for two years due to the business. Smith enjoyed the discipline that came with it and took pride in how he and his company looked. Yet his religious zeal also had its place in his life and it was in October that same year that he launched one of the most success- ful boys' organisations in the world. The Boys Brigade had been born.

William Smith's birthplace

At the Free College Church Mission on the North Woodside Road in Glasgow, the doors opened on 4 October 1883 to 28 eager young boys and their three officers, of whom Smith was the captain. The roots of the organisation can be traced back to Smith's time in Thurso when he gathered his friends together.

At the Woodside Mission, Smith had already begun the Woodside Morning Branch of the YMCA with evening meetings for young men too, of which he became president. He had grown up in a religious family and it played an important role in his life: what he wanted to do was mix Christian values and lessons with the discipline of soldiering. Sunday school was fine in teaching youngsters the Bible, but there was a lack of team spirit and this was this essence he wanted to capture. So he put forward his idea to the mission authorities. He suggested to them that he wanted to bring together boys over the age of 12 into what he termed a 'brigade' where they would be taught military drill, physical exercises, be able to obey orders and keep uniforms neat, tidy and clean, and lastly be punctual. It was the *esprit de corps* that would keep each boy doing his utmost to prevent the company being let down. The mission reluctantly gave the go-ahead for the experiment. Smith was delighted.

Smith spoke to James Hill, a Sunday school teacher, who immediately volunteered to help with the new venture. Before the first boys could be registered, rules and regula- tions had to be thrashed out. A meeting took place at Woodside in the home of the future Canon John Hill. Here, the assembled company 'knelt down and committed the future of the scheme to God, asking His blessing on it'. Every detail was decided. The name 'Boys' Brigade' was settled on and the motto for it was to be 'steadfast and sure' with these words on the crest with an anchor. Most importantly of all was its objective and the following phrase was immortalised: 'The advancement of Christ's Kingdom among boys, and the promotion of habits of Reverence, Discipline, Self-Respect, and all that tends towards a true Christian Manliness'. The constitution of the Boys' Brigade was then finalised. All boys aged 12 or over were eligible to join. They were expected to fill in an application form, 'agreeing to comply with the rules' of the Boys' Brigade and by doing so, 'expressing a desire to be true to Christ in their lives'. They were also expected to show other members how to include the Christian doctrine within the confines of the brigade and in their lives as a whole. On the discipline side, all boys were expected to adhere to 'the authority of the Officers and Non-Commissioned Officers' without question. The other issues discussed were what the uniforms should be like; how the brigade was to be organised; funding; and even the style of badges to be worn. Ranks too were decided. There would only be two, captain and lieutenant.

Over three weeks from that first meeting in October 1883, nearly 60 boys put their names forward. All the boys had to be at the hall at 8.00 p.m. sharp. If they were late, even by only a minute, they were not allowed to take part in the drill. In November 35 boys were accepted and became the very first members of the Boys' Brigade movement. In December an exam was prepared with those over the age of 14 that achieved the highest marks being promoted. The first inspection of the brigade took place in the Mission Hall on 24 March 1884 with Captain Kerr of the Lanarkshire Rifle Volunteers doing the honours. In December 1884, the first Bible Class began for the Boys' Brigade. This year also saw the dawn of the uniforms that have become so familiar, although it was not exactly a 'uniform'. The boys wore a brown belt with the crest embossed on it with a white haversack slung over the right shoulder. The cap was small and dark blue, which was

William Smith, Jubilee Reviews 1933

angled on their heads in military style. The reason the uniform was so simple was down to cost. The complete outfit would only be around two shillings.

By the beginning of 1885 there were five companies and it kept growing. Smith and a group including John Hill and his brother James met and drew up a proper constitution. Firstly, the organisation took the name Boys' Brigade, then came the objective of the 'advancement of Christ's Kingdom', followed by the ages of those eligible to join. Number 4 of the constitution gave the brigade the individuality of where the organisation was set up and each company was given a number. This was followed by the proposal that each company worked under a council composed of all officers with the most senior officer allocated as convenor, and these officers were to be gentlemen 'whose appointment shall be approved by the Council in the proportion of one Officer to about twenty boys'. Leading these 20 boys would be a captain who would command the company and who would appoint non-commissioned officers by promotion through the ranks. There would be one sergeant, one corporal and one lance corporal for every 20 boys. Number 8 of the constitution set out the strict discipline that was to be adhered to at all times. The final rule stated that the constitution would not be altered unless the majority called a meeting.

With its adoption, the 1st Glasgow Company of the North Woodside Mission was named, as was the 2nd Glasgow Company of Berkley Street U. P. Church Mission. More followed. By 30 March 1885 there were six companies in Glasgow and the 1st Edinburgh Company was confirmed. By September, the word had spread and over 20 towns in both Scotland and England had made enquiries.

The year 1884 had been momentous for Smith in his personal life, as well as with the Boys' Brigade movement. He had been patient with his pursuit of Amelia and it had paid off when he married her on 5 March 1884 at her home in Hillhead. They honeymooned in Callander. Amelia immediately threw herself into the Boys' Brigade movement by sewing rosettes on uniforms and on Saturday evenings would have the boys round for tea and cakes, one squad at a time. She taught the boys manners and how to conduct themselves, which stayed with them for the rest of their lives. Sometimes she would sing to them in both Spanish – which she had learned when out in Gibraltar when her father was alive – and in Scots. In 1888 Amelia gave birth to their first child, George, and three years later his brother Douglas joined him. Family holidays were often spent at Tighnabruaich during July but occasionally the family would travel north to visit Mrs Smith in Caithness. When she died in 1895, the family instead visited Kate, Smith's unmarried sister who also lived in Thurso.

In 1898 Amelia became gravely ill. Smith was away at a Boys' Brigade meeting in Manchester when he was recalled home. On 10 October 1898 Amelia died. Smith, although devastated by his wife's death, bore the tragedy with great fortitude. A friend visited him shortly afterwards and was astonished to see that he was calm about it. He simply turned to his friend and told him he was sure his wife was happy and he firmly believed that one day they would be reunited. Kate, Smith's sister, travelled down to Glasgow, took over the running of the household and looked after the two young boys.

A last photograph of William Smith

She was not used to children and found it difficult to show affection towards them, and Smith soon recognised the problem. But he also knew that she would help the family and that she would do her best to keep things running smoothly. The boys however, saw their Aunt Julia (Amelia's sister) as the new mother figure. Smith had a great affection for her and she was always affectionate and kind towards the boys.

Following Amelia's death Smith threw himself further into the movement. Again tragedy hit when the influential Henry Drummond died in 1897, whose influence was inspiring to the boys. The following year the Duke of York accepted the invitation to become Patron of the Boys' Brigade and during the coronation of Edward VII, the Prince of Wales reviewed 12,000 boys from all over the country. Smith was also presented to the prince.

In 1904 Smith suffered another blow when the 35-year-old Thomas Cuthbertson, his right-hand man, suddenly died as a result of an accident. Later that same year Reverend Hill, a founder of the pioneer company, also died. A year later, Smith himself was involved in an accident similar to Cuthbertson's, when he was thrown from his horse – but his injuries were minor. Once he had recovered, Smith took part in the camp at Tighnabruich, which was made up of 90 boys and officers. The week was a huge success, with all participating in hill walking, climbing and fishing.

On 10 April 1906 Smith married for the second time. He had met Hannah Campbell, a Sunday school teacher, and the couple were married in Stevenson Memorial Church. Smith's boys welcomed her as their stepmother with open arms. She became heavily involved in the movement, and thoroughly enjoyed her work. In May 1906 the couple set off for the United States where they visited Boys' Brigade inspections at Boston, New York and Philadelphia. They were very impressed by the American Boys' Brigade. On their return home at the end of June, the couple went to Tighnabruich, where the 1st Glasgow Company camp was being held as usual. However, Hannah became unwell on 29 July 1906 and suddenly died.

Smith hid his grief from all but those closest to him. The 25th anniversary of the 1st Glasgow Company was approaching and he threw his energies into that. Old boys attended the parade, as well as over 100 officers and boys from the current roll. Colonel Kerr – the original inspecting officer – was present. Delegates came from all over the world and on 4 September 1908 a cheque was presented to them for the sum of 1,000 guineas from the city's Lord Provost, Sir William Bilsland. But the main event was the parade of over 10,000 officers and boys, which was reviewed by Prince Arthur in Queen's Park, Glasgow. Smith was at the helm and his son Stanley carried the Battalion Colour. There was a special service held in Glasgow Cathedral on the following Sunday and a church parade held in the afternoon. The whole ceremony closed finally with a trip to Tighnabruich, then a garden party hosted by the Marquis and Marchioness of Graham at Brodick Castle. Smith stood to a standing ovation. To top off such an eventful year, a knighthood was granted to Smith, which delighted the Boys' Brigade worldwide. On 22 July 1909 Smith was knighted at Buckingham Palace, but returned to the summer camp at Tighnabruich (where he had been before he had to leave for London).

Just before the outbreak of World War I, Smith attended the Albert Hall for a demonstration on 7 May 1914. Although he looked tired, no one really paid much attention. The following morning he attended a meeting. His son Stanley was also present, his first meeting since he had been promoted to assistant brigade secretary. As Smith tried to dip his pen in the inkstand, he failed twice, which was noticed by those around him. Then he suddenly collapsed in the chair. He never regained consciousness. He died shortly afterwards with his sons by his side. He was 59 years old. There was a deep sense of shock and horror, not only within the brigade, but also throughout the world – he had become so well-known for his inspirational work. His body was placed on the Glasgow-bound train on the evening of Friday 15 May 1914 and he was buried in his beloved Glasgow the following day. A memorial service was held in St Paul's Cathedral before he departed. The place was packed with mourners, including 4,000 boys who had lost their beloved leader. The cortege weaved its way through the streets of London. At the railway station a Guard of Honour was formed. In Glasgow the following day, flags flew at half-mast. Following his burial, the 1st Glasgow Company filed past as one final mark of respect and every boy dropped a white flower into the open grave.

William Smith made such a difference to the lives of boys all over the world that today his idea of a Boys' Brigade is still as strong as ever, and continues his great work. He never lost his links with his friends and family who remained in Caithness long after he left the country, and today as cars drive into the town where he was born his memory is kept alive on the welcoming sign.

ARTHUR ST CLAIR

Arthur St Clair of Thurso became the 9th President of the Continental Congress of the United States on 2 February 1786 and is the only president of Congress to have been born outside of the country. This was a remarkable rise for the young Caithness man who became disenchanted with Britain's rule of her colony and who rebelled against his homeland.

Arthur Sinclair, as his surname was spelt in Scotland, was born on 23 March 1736 at Forss near Thurso, son of William Sinclair, a merchant. It is said that William died at an early age following an idle life and indulging in pleasures. St Clair's mother however, doted on him and gave him a loving home. Following his education locally, he attended the University of Edinburgh where he studied anatomy under the renowned surgeon Dr William Hunter. Even under Hunter's tutelage, university life did not suit the young Arthur St Clair and he left after a year of study to find an alternative career.

In 1757 St Clair joined the army due in part to the inheritance that he received following his mother's death during the winter of 1756–57. On 13 May 1757 he enlisted with the Sixtieth or King's Royal Rifle Corps, also known as the Royal American Regiment, which consisted of four battalions, each with 1,000 men. They had been formed by Prince William, Duke of Cumberland – also known as 'Butcher Cumberland' in Scotland – following his crushing defeat of the Jacobites at Culloden in April 1746, with the First and Second Battalions being the most noted of them.

St Clair became a subordinate in the Second Battalion and was sent to America where he participated in the Seven Years War. Originally the conflict began between Britain and France and involved countries such as India, Canada and the West Indies. It was in America that the British feared the French most, for they already had a 56,000-strong colony that ran the length of the St Lawrence River and the Great Lakes of Canada, and they had begun colonising in America's southern states of Louisiana and Mississippi, which gave rise to the possibility of them cutting off the British colonies. Moreover, the French stirred up the Native Americans against the British.

During the war, St Clair served under General Jeffrey Amherst during the fighting at Louisburg in Nova Scotia, Canada, in 1758. In the run up to battle, the British had managed to blockade the French fleet so her defence of Quebec was severely restricted and this led to the French being outnumbered five to one. In June, the British bombarded the French, but the British suffered heavy losses and were forced to retreat when the French fought back. However, the British waited patiently and General James Wolfe eventually took Lighthouse Point and finally mounted the assault that would see the French capitulate the following month. It was a humiliating defeat. The French were ordered to hand over all their weaponry and equipment and give the British their flags. They were outraged but did this in order to protect the citizens of the town.

During 1759, St Clair was assigned to General Wolfe after he had received his lieutenant's commission on 17 April. He served under Wolfe at the Battle of the Plains of Abraham at Quebec. Here, on 13 September, Wolfe was wounded in battle but the British triumphed and took Quebec. Wolfe died of his wounds the same day. His French counterpart, the Marquis de Montcalm, also died of wounds he sustained in the battle the following day. A year later, France lost control of Canada altogether.

In 1760 St Clair married Phoebe Bayard, daughter of Balthazar Bayard and his wife Mary Bowdoin. They belonged to a large, prominent Boston family and Phoebe was related to the colonial governor of Massachusetts, James Bowdoin, who was her mother's half-brother. St Clair was a charismatic character who had been invited into the Bayard's home and who charmed them with his gracious ways and entertaining conversation. He was also a handsome man. He was tall with chestnut hair, blue-grey eyes and a pale complexion, polite and graceful in company and he could converse on many topics, keeping the assembled company entertained for hours. St Clair had become friends with Major William Ewing during his time in Quebec under General Wolfe, as Ewing was an aide-de-camp to Wolfe. It is thought that it was through Ewing, being the brother of Governor Bowdoin's wife, that the young couple met. On their marriage, St Clair received £14,000 from a legacy left to his new wife from her grandfather James Bowdoin. This – added to his own money that he had saved – meant that they were wealthy and it gave them an influential position in Boston.

The army was no life for the young married couple and St Clair resigned his post on 16 April 1762. A year later, he was given credit for the expulsion of Native Americans from the area. That same year Charles Mason and Jeremiah Dixon from London were asked by Lord Baltimore and the prominent Penn family to draw up a boundary line between Maryland and Pennsylvania, later to be known as the Mason-Dixon Line, which during the Civil War in the 1860s divided the North and South. It was completed in 1767 but gave Pennsylvania a definitive boundary that was seen as important to preserving the state. In 1764 St Clair bought around 400 acres of land in the Ligonier Valley in Pennsylvania, partly using his own money and partly from a grant given to him from the King for his services during the Seven Years War. St Clair settled there and built up a business. It is possible he chose the area because of the number of prominent Scottish families who had already settled in the district.

On 5 April 1770, St Clair was appointed surveyor of the District of Cumberland. This was followed by his appointment as Justice of the Court of Quarter Sessions and Common Pleas and Member of the Proprietary, or Governor's Council, for Cumberland County. A year later, when Bedford County was formed, the governor appointed him Justice of the Court, Recorder of Deeds, Clerk of the Orphan's Court and Prothonotary of the Court of Common Pleas.

The governor of Pennsylvania, John Penn, asked St Clair to become his assistant with a view to him working on the frontier areas of the state. St Clair accepted. He also accepted a position in the Westmoreland County Court although this was not without its problems. For a start, Westmoreland was a new county, taken from Bedford County by an act of the General Assembly of Pennsylvania on 26 February 1773. It included the whole of the southwest corner of Pennsylvania as well as land west of Laurel Hill. Most of the people were happy with the new county but there was a major problem in running it. There was no town hall for conducting official business and people did not want to travel to do their business. It also transpired that in July, people living to the west of Laurel Hill were unhappy with the Government and what they saw as oppression and injustice. St Clair was aware of the disgruntlement but he now saw it as coming to a dangerous head. He blamed factions in Philadelphia for stirring up the trouble, which amounted to the non-payment of taxes. There was only one way to settle the problems with Westmoreland as he saw it and that was to fix boundaries and to see for himself what was happening. He found that most people were unhappy because justice was too lenient but also found that those who had refused to pay their taxes before, had actually begun to pay them as the privileges of the area had been pointed out to them. However, there were those who refused to recognise the jurisdiction of the county and had treated the local sheriff badly. On one occasion for example, he and his deputy were threatened by a number of locals carrying pistols and clubs and told that if they returned to their office they would be murdered in their own homes. The sheriff knew some of them and he believed that it was only because he pulled out his own gun that they had both survived. Sixteen justices of the peace were elected and after much debating, things settled down in the area, albeit briefly. Trouble again was simmering thanks to Dr John Conolly, who put up an advert in the village of Pittsburgh saying that John, Lord Dunmore had appointed him captain, 'Commandant of the Militia of Pittsburgh' and that a new county to include Pittsburgh was about to be set up in order to redress some of their complaints and facilitate the justice which they sought. He asked that 'all persons in the dependency of Pittsburgh ... assemble themselves ... as a militia'. St Clair received a copy of the full advert, which he considered dangerous to the stability of the area. As had already been pointed out, all disaffected men and vagabonds in the area would flock to the captain in great numbers and take up the cause in his name. St Clair acted quickly and issued orders for Conolly's arrest before the assigned meeting time, but over 80 men appeared on the day and marched through the town. They were asked to leave, but said they would be peaceful and were therefore allowed to march. A watchful eye was kept on them but St Clair kept out of their way. Disturbances continued as the area vied for a true boundary.

Pennsylvania and Virginia claimed land around Fort Pitt, which caused conflict that St Clair tried to avert to the best of his abilities. The Native Americans of Ohio, with whom St Clair wanted to trade rather than fight, made him peacemaker in the territories. It is thought his actions with the natives may have stopped the Native Americans from slaughtering those who had settled on the fringes of Pennsylvania during Lord Dunmore's War of 1774. The Virginian governor, John Murray, 4th Earl of Dunmore, had declared war on the Shawnee and Mingo American Indians – who were continually battling the colonists for the rights given to them in various treaties to hunt on land south of the Ohio River, as well as the British who were moving further into the empty lands. This culminated in the Battle of Point Pleasant in October 1774 when the British won and the natives had to give up their hunting rights. In a letter to Governor Penn dated 4 December 1774, St Clair declared: 'The war betwixt the Indians and the Virginians is at last over ... I have not been able to get a true state of the Treaty of Peace; a peace however is certainly made with the Shawanese, one condition of which is the return of all property and prisoners taken from the white people, and for the performance of it they have given six hostages'. Other conditions included the release of all prisoners, including 'negroes and horses', ever taken by them since the outbreak of the Seven Years War; that they were to give up their hunting rights on the east side of the Ohio River; and were to leave white settlers on the west of it alone. When the American Revolution broke out, the Native Americans attacked the colonists in retaliation, which became known as the Chickamauga Wars between 1776 and 1794.

In 1775, seeing himself more as an American rather than a British subject, St Clair accepted a commission in the Continental Army as a colonel. He saw action during the invasion of Canada that year. Earlier in May, a meeting had been held in Hannastown, Westmoreland, where the resident Scots voiced their opposition to British rule. Among them was St Clair and it was a turning point for him. News had reached the town about what the patriots had done at Lexington and Concord on 19 April 1775 and that was the starting point for discussions.

The Massachusetts Committee of Safety had organised its own ammunition depot in the town of Concord, some 18 miles from Boston, where they stored up gunpowder, axes and medicines, and where the supplies were added to daily. It was also thought that the townsfolk were hiding three 24-pound cannons. The British general Thomas Gage knew of the haul and decided to destroy it. On 18 April 1775 under the cover of darkness, he sent out his troops to destroy it. However, the noted American revolutionary Paul Revere got wind of the plan, was ordered to warn John Hancock, later the 4th president of the Continental Congress, and Samuel Adams, a well-known revolutionary, who were in the town, as well as the local militia. They were known as the Minute Men as they could spring into action in what was said to be a minute. Revere and his friend William Dawes rode out and spread the word. Revere reached Lexington and shouted the news to the locals that the Redcoats were coming, while Dawes did the same at Concord. The Battle of Lexington Concord ensued. Local supporters of the British had their homes stormed and many were tarred and feathered. The governors were threatened. As an excuse to rally, they used the pretence of taxation. The local leader Captain John Parker told his men not to fire unless fired upon and ordered them to stand their ground. However, he also warned them that if the British wanted a war then they were to have it. The two sides met at Lexington Green. A crowd gathered to watch. A shot was fired – although no one to this day knows from which side – and this signalled the very beginning of the American Revolution. Battle ensued. Eight American militiamen were killed and ten were wounded. Only one British soldier was wounded with no fatalities on that side. Order was restored, and the Redcoats were allowed to fire a volley in a victory celebration. They then set their sights on Concord to search for the military supplies. The locals had moved or buried most of them. The local militia fought the trained army and to their surprise, they won, although neither side had ever believed that the other would fire. News of the victory spread and the Americans began a struggle that was to last for years, but ultimately they would win their freedom from Britain.

At the Westmoreland meeting, the people knew the British had already declared the residents of Massachusetts Bay to be in rebellion and therefore were determined to stop them by any means possible. St Clair pointed out that such actions 'of tyranny and oppression will be extended to other parts of America' and the only way to deal with it was by immediately forming themselves 'into a military body, to consist of companies to be made up out of several townships' – to be known as the Association of Westmoreland County. This said, St Clair declared that the people were still loyal to the King but 'animated with the love of liberty, it is no less out duty to maintain and defend our just rights (which, with sorrow, we have seen of late wantonly violated in many instances by wicked ministry and a corrupted parliament)'. Therefore, five main aims were set out and adopted. These included arming themselves and forming a regiment 'in such proportions as shall be thought necessary'. They would meet regularly and appoint commanding officers and if any foreign enemy 'or should troops be sent from Great Britain to enforce the late arbitrary acts of Parliament, we will cheerfully submit to military discipline, and to the upmost of our power resist and oppose them'. The assembled meeting also adopted a resolution stating that 'things may be restored and go on in the same way as before the era of the Stamp Act when Boston grew great and America was happy'. Finally, and most significantly, it was put forward that this new association would be disbanded, but only if and when the British Parliament 'repealed their late obnoxious statutes and shall recede from their claim to tax us'. The declaration ended: 'Til then it shall remain in full force; and to the observation of it, we bind ourselves by everything dear and sacred amongst men. No licensed murder! No famine introduced by law!' St Clair was definitely now an American.

Hancock wrote to St Clair and asked him to go to Philadelphia, where on 22 January 1776, he received his orders to raise a regiment that was to serve in Canada. This he duly did and six weeks later, the regiment, consisting of six companies, was ready. St Clair served during the Battle of Quebec, in which control of the region was the objective of the revolutionary army. It was their intention to liberate the province from British rule. The Americans however, were heavily defeated and the British took control. The following year, St Clair participated in the Battle of Trios Rivieres, which was another major defeat of the Americans. They had hoped to stop the British advancing up the St Lawrence but thanks to a local farmer who led them into a swamp, they became surrounded by the British and hastily retreated, eventually ending up at Fort Ticonderoga. Nevertheless, St Clair was promoted again in August 1776. America had made a proclamation to the world in July, which divided the nation.

In May 1775 the Second Continental Congress met in Philadelphia (the first having met the previous year), and although illegal, it was the only kind of governing body the fledgling United States had. Among those present were George Washington, Benjamin Franklin and Thomas Jefferson. They had discussed independence from Britain but the ties that bound them were strong and they were not fully prepared for all-out war. However, this changed the following year when they discovered that the British were employing German mercenaries to fight against their own colonies. Added to that was a pamphlet written by the English-born Tom Paine on *Common Sense*, in which he strongly attacked George III (at the time, the pamphlet's author remained anonymous because he could have been charged with treason). Within three months of its publication 120,000 copies had been sold. In it, Paine claimed that America was strong enough to go it alone and should not be ruled by a tiny island. Besides, America was home to many other European peoples and Britain would continue to drag America into European conflicts. Added to that was the fact that the mother country was so far away, so how was it possible to rule effectively? Paine pointed out that Britain would not change her stranglehold policies and that America was strong enough to go it alone, both politically and economically: she could become a world player. Paine wrote: 'I offer nothing more than simple facts, plain arguments and common sense'.

Congress realised that action was necessary and set up a meeting in which they drafted a declaration that was passed on 4 July 1776. It provided what the American people needed to hear. It justified war and promoted the unification of all Americans in that war. It also set out to attract foreign support, as well as prove to the Americans that they had right on their side. Based on the writings of the English philosopher John Locke, it decreed that people were given the right to choose who governed them and they had the right to overthrow that government if their trust was broken. The document contained 27 grievances, the most important ones being taxation that the British Government did not consult them on, and the imposition of laws, again without discussions. For many years Britain had imposed taxes on the people. The Sugar Act of 1764 for example, imposed an external tax on goods being bought by the people without consulting them: some thought it would ruin the rum trade, but it was widely accepted, although grudgingly. However, it was the Stamp Act of 1765 that caused a much stronger reaction from the colonists. This act imposed an internal tax on stamps that had to be put on legal papers and documents. It extended to marriage certificates, wills, contracts and title deeds. The problem was that it was again imposed without consultation with the colonists, who were already beginning to question the advantages of being part of the British Empire. Regulation trade with acts such as the Sugar Act, or the earlier Navigation Laws, was one thing, but to impose and internal tax on the colonists themselves was something else. This led to the Stamp Act Crisis and the slogan 'No Taxation Without Representation'. The Americans sent a delegate from each of the 13 states to Congress and sent a petition to the Government in England. Not wishing to use military force but wanting to reserve their right to tax the colonies, the act was repealed and replaced by the Declaratory Act, which gave them the right to make any laws they wished on the colonies. The Americans were initially delighted. However, the Townsend Duties were imposed in the act's stead. The Chancellor of the Exchequer, Townsend, knew that he had to raise revenue somehow from America, so he decided to impose tax on tea, glass, paper and lead. The colonists again were furious, and boycotted British goods, but they did send a circular letter from all 13 colonies to London, showing they were co-operating with each other. The duties were repealed in 1770, except for the tax on tea, which was retained to show the colonists that the Government had the right to impose such a tax. In December 1773, tea became a major issue. The East India Company had 17 million pounds of tea in warehouses in Britain and because the company was in difficulties, the Government decided to remove the tax, cutting the cost by half and selling it to the colonies. This in turn would tempt the Americans to remove their embargo on tea, or so it was thought. However, the American tea smugglers resented their loss of business, and legitimate tea merchants worried about the East India Company having the monopoly. Radicals such as Sam Adams and the Sons of Liberty thought this would mean the locals would drop their anti-British stance. When the tea arrived at Boston Harbour, a dispute broke out and a group of Americans dressed up as Mohawk Indians threw 300 chests of tea into the harbour. The British authorities were furious. More acts were imposed on the Americans. The Coercive or Intolerable Acts of 1774 included Boston being stripped of its customs house and colonial government, which was removed to Salem under the Boston Port Act. There was also the Massachusetts Bay Regulating Act, which gave the Crown control over the colony and greater powers were given to the governor; the Quartering Act, which allowed troops to be billeted wherever the gov-

Arthur St Clair

ernor wished; and the Murder Act, which made it impossible for those standing trial for murder to be tried in America. They were to be taken to Britain where the jury would not be biased. Also imposed the same year was the Quebec Act, which meant an end to American expansion north. This act also decreed that Roman Catholics could now hold office and that the governor would rule the colonies along with a nominated council. The Americans were livid. These acts caused massive resistance and this led to the Declaration of Independence two years later.

Many Americans embraced the Declaration of Independence, and called themselves patriots. Others were less enthused by it. The Loyalists had doubts and many still supported the Government, so much so that after its announcement, many left for Canada or Britain, which gave hope to the British Government and caused dismay in Congress.

During the summer of 1776, St Clair received notice that he was to be promoted. In a letter from the President of Congress, John Hancock, dated 10 August 1776, he wrote: 'The Congress having yesterday been pleased to promote you to the rank of Brigadier-General in the Army of the American States, I do myself the pleasure to enclose your commission, and wish you happy'. This followed information from Colonel Matt Ogden who wrote from Ticonderoga to Major Aaron Burr that there was a distinct lack of brigadier-generals in the army. Ogden suggested St Clair, as 'there is no better man'. In response to his promotion, St Clair wrote back to Hancock and thanked him. He said: 'I am extremely sensible of the honour conferred upon me by the appointment'; and he promised 'Congress that they have not misplaced their confidence'.

At the end of 1776 General George Washington sent St Clair to New Jersey to put in order the local militia and prepare them for confrontation. By Christmas, St Clair and Washington crossed the Delaware River and on 26 December the Battle of Trenton took place. It was a victory for Washington. The Hessians stationed at Trenton were defeated and many taken prisoner, so after so many defeats the morale of the Continental Army soared. This new confidence has been credited to St Clair's strategy, which Washington followed. St Clair was again promoted.

The following April St Clair was sent to defend Fort Ticonderoga in New York as part of the Saratoga Campaign. However, he failed in his mission. The fort was strategically placed at the southern end of Lake Champlain – a staging post for defence from the British coming south from Canada – and was known as the Gibraltar of the North. In the high ground above the fort, 'Gentleman' Johnny Burgoyne's troops almost completely surrounded the defences as part of the Saratoga Campaign, and although the campaign ended up a disaster for the British, their first triumph came with the capture of the fort. Two 12-pounders were installed on Sugar Loaf Hill and St Clair decided the best thing to do was to retreat, which they did on 5 July 1777. Under the cover of darkness St Clair ordered the troops to load up the boats with all the supplies they could, and take with them any munitions they could carry. St Clair knew the decision to retreat would be met with hostility. He had a choice: he could save the fort but lose his army in the process, or he could save his men by abandoning it and lose his reputation because of the decision to do so. It was a choice that outraged America. The fort had been thought to be impenetrable. Both St Clair and his superior General Philip Schuyler were blamed by Congress for allowing Ticonderoga to fall into British hands. St Clair had expected nothing less. He had written to John Hancock from Philadelphia in August, expressing his 'pleasure that Congress has determined to inquire into my conduct. My character will therefore be placed in its true light, and a stop put, I hope, to that tide of popular abuse that has run high upon me'. In October Hancock informed St Clair that the 'committee appointed to inquire into the causes of the loss of Ticonderoga and Fort Independence have not yet been able to collect materials and make their report. Resolved: Major-General St Clair be at liberty to attend his private affairs until he shall have notice to attend headquarters, in order to an inquiry into his conduct'. At the court martial over the incident, which took place at White Plains in August 1778, he was charged with neglect of duty, cowardice and treachery in abandoning the post. However, the assembled committee found St Clair and Schuyler not guilty, but their careers did suffer. St Clair did not hold a commanding position again throughout the Revolution and Schuyler had already lost his command by the time of the court martial.

The whole Saratoga Campaign was a turning point in the war. The British plan was for Burgoyne to march south from Lake Champlain to Albany, for General William Howe to march up the Hudson River taking Philadelphia en route to Albany, and for Colonel Barry St Ledger to travel along the St Lawrence to Lake Ontario then march along the Mohawk Valley to meet Burgoyne and Howe at Albany. However, the co-ordination of the three-pronged attack was in complete disarray. Back in London Lord Germain failed to co-ordinate the plan, for he was too busy thinking of his fast approaching holiday. Howe landed in Philadelphia with 1,500 troops and 260 ships but Burgoyne did not realise until too late that Howe was going to take the city first before moving on to Albany. This gave George Washington time to organise his defence and Howe only managed to capture the city in September, when he decided to do nothing. He neither attacked Washington and his men nor did he attempt to move north to meet Burgoyne. St Ledger meanwhile had 2,000 men marching towards Albany but half of them were Native Americans. He failed to capture Fort Stanwix and his army simply began to disperse. Burgoyne meanwhile had captured Ticonderoga from St Clair and everything seemed to be going well, however supplies began to run short and the locals began a scorched earth policy to prevent the troops from eating their food. Progress was incredibly slow, with the men marching about a mile a day. At Bennington Burgoyne lost 900 men in battle and the Americans were mustering forces at every turn. By October Burgoyne was in Saratoga surrounded by General Gates and his men. He had no choice but to surrender. News of the surrender reached St Clair in a letter to him dated 17 October 1777 from Colonel Baldwin.

But it was the French who really turned things around. Two Franco-American treaties were put forward, which changed the whole situation in North America. The first of these was the Treaty of Alliance with France, in which America was to side with the French should Britain attack France during the American war. The alliance made it clear, especially to Spain, that any country which had suffered at the hands of the British would be welcome to fight against them as part of the treaty, subject to negotiation. The second treaty, The Treaty of Amity and Commerce, provided both countries with the protection of vessels and the right to search the ships for contraband, although the due process of law was to be followed should any contraband be found. Assistance was to be given if either nation found themselves at war with another nation: any ships would find a safe harbour and help. The French recognised America as an independent country then entered the war on the American side. Saratoga had given the Americans the confidence boost that they needed. In 1778 Britain declared war on France because of their involvement in America, and a year later Spain declared war on Britain. Holland had taken to trading with America so in 1780 Britain declared war on them too. It was turning into a world war and not just a conflict between Britain and her upstart colony across the Atlantic.

Although St Clair was not allowed to have a command post, Washington asked him to be his aide-de-camp. Washington held St Clair in high regard and the two were at Yorktown in 1781 when Lord Charles Cornwallis surrendered his army. This was another disaster for the British, caused by two generals who refused to agree with each other on tactics and who found it simply impossible to work together. General Sir Henry Clinton, who was promoted to Commander-in-Chief of North America following the disaster of Saratoga when Howe was relieved of his duties as commander, was in New York with around 20,000 men and as Cornwallis entered Virginia, he asked for reinforcements, which Clinton refused. This was because he thought that Washington would take New York if he were absent from the state. Instead, he ordered Cornwallis to fortify the Williamsburg Peninsula so that the British would have control of Chesapeake Bay. Washington knew that Cornwallis was entrenched at Yorktown and the American forces were buoyed up by the arrival of 4,000 French troops under Jean-Baptiste Donatien de Vimeur, comte de Rochambeau, although he also knew Clinton had been given over 2,000 German reinforcements so it made sense for him to attack Cornwallis. Washington liaised with Admiral de Grasse and the French fleet, and they agreed to land an assault in a combined sea and land operation. Washington allowed Clinton to believe that he was going to attack New York, but in secret on 20 August 1781, he led his troops south towards Cornwallis. By late September, he and his men and allies had surrounded the British, who were now trapped. Their only hope was the Royal Navy but the French already had control of the waters in Chesapeake Bay and the approaches too. The British tried unsuccessfully to see off the French fleet, and in October Washington's artillery bombarded the 6,000 British troops. Washington had 19,000 men at his disposal, some of whom were French under Rochambeau and Gilbert du Motier, and Marquis de Lafayette who had taken up positions on Malvern Hill. The British position became untenable and, after a failed counter-attack, Cornwallis surrendered on 19 October 1781. The troops were allowed to march away to the tune of *The World Turned Upside Down*.

In 1873, two years after Yorktown, and as St Clair became a member for the Pennsylvania Council of Censors, the Treaty of Paris – also known as the Treaty of Versailles

– finally ended the American Revolution. The first part of the treaty saw Britain recognise America as an independent nation and the Crown relinquished all its claims to the country. All confiscated land was to be returned. Its border with Canada was set, giving the Americans access to the west. Florida was ceded to Spain, who was never seen as a serious threat to the nation anyway, and loyalists were all guaranteed liberty and the right to emigrate should they wish to do so. Many, however, lost their property as a result of that loyalty to the British crown. Fishing rights were also guaranteed off the coast of Canada and each country was to have the right to access the Mississippi River, as it was a vital trade route. The second part of the treaty was signed between Britain and France, but the French gained little from it except the guarantee that its citizens that lived on the islands that were not be returned to Britain (such as Grenada and Montserrat) were to be left in peace. Britain still held on to Canada, India and the West Indies.

In 1875 St Clair was elected to be a delegate to the Congress of Confederation in New York where he served from 2 November 1785 until 28 November 1787, during which time he became the 9th President of the United States Congress on 2 February 1787. His tenure as president ended on 29 October that year. The Congress had little power, but did manage to pass some laws – the most notable of which was the Northwest Ordinance. In 1787 the Congress also appointed St Clair as the first governor of the Northwest Territory, following the passage of the Ordinance law. He was responsible for an area that today includes Ohio, Indiana, Illinois and Michigan, parts of Wisconsin and Minnesota. St Clair named Cincinnati in Ohio and it was there that he made his home. It was also during this time that the United States Constitution was enacted. Following a meeting of delegates, seven articles were agreed. These were legislative power, executive power, judicial power, states' powers and limits, amendments, federal power and ratification. This final article recommended that only nine of the 13 states would have to ratify it. In the end, all 13 states ratified it, although Rhode Island only did so by two votes and New York by three. One of the main amendments was the Bill of Rights.

Things did not run smoothly for St Clair during his time as either president or governor. In early 1787, Shay's Rebellion was in full swing. Following the end of the war, there was severe economic depression, which led to hardship for the general population. Farms were seized due to debt levels and in Massachusetts, Daniel Shays, a former army captain, began to use force to prevent the courts from sitting in judgement in debt cases. Like so many compatriots, Shays found himself in court over debts he had amassed. The local militia managed to quash the rebellion but local landowners, frightened that this sort of action could happen again, saw the need for a national government to avoid it in the future. Land disputes were also commonplace and few people wanted to contribute to the new American Government, simply because they did not have the means to do so.

St Clair's second problem was the Northwest Territory. With help from William Maxwell, publisher of the first newspaper for the territory, St Clair formulated the first written laws for the territory, known as *Maxwell's Code*. The book was the first to ever be published there. It contained a comprehensive legal and civil code, which St Clair had thrashed out with two judges: John Cleves Symmes and George Turner. It contained 37 laws that had already been passed in at least one of the original 13 states. It set out to protect locals from paying excessive taxes and was based on English common law.

But St Clair's main problem in the area rested with the Native Americans who opposed the white settlers that were taking over their land. In 1789 St Clair invited them to sign the Treaty of Fort Harmar – but many had not been invited to participate in the negotiations or they had refused to take part. The American Government had no money to muster an army against the natives but Henry Knox, the Secretary of State for War, told St Clair to sort out the dispute once and for all. St Clair set up a meeting at Fort Harmar. Here, the best the natives hoped for was a reservation on which to live comprising of land west of the Muskingum River and north of the Ohio River. But St Clair refused point blank. He wanted them to accept the terms of a previous treaty: that of Fort McIntosh, which had already established a boundary in 1785. The chiefs put forward that they would attack if the boundary was not changed, but St Clair bribed them with $3,000 worth of gifts. The chiefs signed the treaty that simply reinforced the earlier one. However, those who chose not to be present did not accept the agreement and attacked the white settlers. War ensued in what became known as the Northwest Indian War or Little Turtle's War, which lasted from 1785 until 1795.

In 1790, St Clair dispatched an army to western Ohio to build defences against the natives and ordered General Josiah Harmar and his 1,500-strong army to destroy a Miami Indian settlement in Indiana. Harmar's men met strong resistance and were defeated by the Shawnee chief Blue Jacket and the Miami chief Little Turtle in October 1790. St Clair was ordered by George Washington to take matters into his own hands and defeat the Native Americans himself. During the summer of 1791, St Clair scraped together a contingent of men and supplies but had no time to train the soldiers properly. Also, General Butler had not managed to join him, nor had the quartermaster. Furthermore, he was lacking horses that should have been ordered by an agent, so he took it upon himself to see 800 animals were purchased. He and his men left Fort Washington in Cincinnati on 17 September 1791, building Forts Hamilton and Jefferson en route to the Miami villages on the Wabash River. During the march, some of St Clair's men deserted and supplies began to run low. It did not help matters that although it was autumn, the temperatures were low for that time of year and they suffered rain and snow, which demoralised them even further. On 21 October 1791 from Camp Sixty-Eight and a Half Miles Advanced, St Clair wrote a stern letter to the quartermaster-general about the lack of support from the agents employed to deliver provisions to his men. St Clair stated: 'I have the greatest reason to fear a disappointment, which may render the whole campaign abortive'. He asked the quartermaster-general to go back to the agent and ascertain a 'precise account from him, of the measures he has taken to afford a certain supply of provisions for the army'. St Clair then said that: 'they have failed entirely in enabling me to move with forty-five thousand rations and ...the agent seems not to expect to move any beyond this place'. Regardless of cost, St Clair required help and needed it soon.

During this period St Clair had taken ill, although was now recovering. He had suffered from something akin to a 'bilious colic and sometimes as a rheumatic asthma' that changed to 'a gout in the left arm and hand, leaving the breast and stomach perfectly relieved and the cough, which had been excessive, entirely gone'. However he still had to deal with his disobedient men. On 23 October 1791, three of his recruits were hanged: two for desertion and one for shooting another soldier. By the end of the month, about 60 men had deserted. On 28 October, clothing finally arrived at Fort Jefferson where they were now encamped and it was duly distributed. This boosted morale. Flour and horses arrived at the same time.

In November they camped near what is today Fort Recovery in Ohio. However, the defences surrounding the camp were weak and at dawn on 4 November 1791 a 2,000-strong force led by Little Turtle attacked the unprepared camp. According to Major Ebenezer Denny, St Clair's aide-de-camp, throughout the night there was frequent firing of the sentinels, which gave the officers some concern. Guards reported that the Indians were 'sulking about in considerable numbers'. As usual, the troops paraded on time but they were dismissed. Denny wrote: 'the sun not yet up ... the woods in front rung with yells and fire of the savages. The poor militia, who were but three hundred yards in front, had scarcely time to return a shot – they fled into our camp'. Denny went on to describe how the enemy managed to encircle the camp and cut off, and then killed, the guards. The smoke from the camp-fire helped the Indians as they flitted from tree stump to log in complete silence. The only noise to be heard was from the firing of muskets on both sides. After three hours of fighting, St Clair gathered together the survivors, ordered them to have one last bayonet charge against the natives, force their way through the enemy lines and make good their escape. The Americans were totally annihilated: it was America's worst defeat in battle against the Native Americans, with over 800 men killed. Those who made it through the charge retreated to Fort Jefferson, some 29 miles from the battleground. They had no provisions or medical supplies. The injured were treated with what they could find and they holed up in the fort. The natives made an attempt to catch them at first but after three miles returned to the camp and looted it.

At Fort Washington on 9 November 1791 St Clair wrote to the Secretary of War, General Henry Knox, and gave his version of events. He explained that following the Second Regiment's charge and the serious wounding of Major Butler, in all only three men survived the assault, and he knew it was time to abandon the camp. All horses had been killed so very few supplies were taken. He listed the most high-ranking casualties as Major-General Butler, Lieutenant Colonel Oldham, Major Ferguson, Major Hart and Major Clarke. He made no excuses for the failure, except to mention the illness from which he had been suffering and the lack of discipline among his men. He wrote that in his opinion, 'the weight of the fire, which was always a most deadly one, and generally delivered from the ground, few of the enemy showing themselves afoot except when they charged' was the reason for the Native American triumph and he knew there would be a public outcry at the loss of so many men. To ease this backlash he wrote that each man that fell – especially General Butler and Major Ferguson – had fought gallantly in the execution of their duty.

The whole affair was given numerous names, including 'St Clair's Defeat', 'St Clair's Massacre' and 'the Battle of Wabash'. An enquiry into it was to be held. On St Clair's return to Philadelphia, he had to explain what happened. He blamed his quartermaster and the army for the route. Washington demanded that St Clair resign, which he did on 7 April 1792. In his letter to Washington, St Clair wrote: 'Although I was very desirous, sir, to hold my commission of Major-General until the enquiry by the committee of the House of Representatives should be over, for the reasons which I assigned … I do, therefore, now formally resign the appointment of Major-General'. However, St Clair retained his governorship of the Northwest Territory.

Life was no easier there for St Clair. The Native Americans were still fighting in the northwest and

MAJ. GEN. ARTHUR ST. CLAIR

Drawing of Arthur St Clair

there seemed to be no end in sight. In 1794 Washington ordered General Anthony Wayne to defeat the natives once and for all, which he finally did at the Battle of Fallen Timbers in August. In a letter to Colonel Sproat in April 1795, St Clair declared that hostilities between the United States and the Indian nations to have been suspended, and hope for a lasting peace was initiated. He asked that the militia in the territory be disbanded, except for the woodsmen who also acted as scouts. He congratulated Sproat and 'all the inhabitants of the county, of whose zeal and alacrity in the service of this country I have a very high sense'. On 2 August 1795 the Treaty of Greenville was signed, in which the natives gave up their lands to the white setters of the state, except for a corner in the northwest of Ohio. General Wayne wrote to St Clair two weeks later. A Cherokee chief and four of his young warriors had approached him with news from Coonanisky, also known as Big Spider, and promised him that none of his people would attack or harm any United States citizen. The chief also told Wayne that his people would leave and return to their own nation, which he knew as fact for he had received word that they had already declared their intent to Governor Blount and had proclaimed that peace would return to the area. This meant that the 'mischief that has been done up the Ohio for some time past, was by the party of Shawanese … in retaliation for the aggression of Mr Massie'. The Shawanese chiefs also told Wayne that they now sought peace and those who had executed the attack would be brought to account. 'Peace', Wayne continued, 'with all its train of blessings, will attend the citizens on the frontiers of the United States in future, unless prevented by their own misconduct'.

Over the next few years Ohio moved towards declaring itself a state. St Clair opposed this and it was his opposition that caused President Thomas Jefferson to remove him from office in 1802. It was to be a difficult year for him. At the end of January, Thomas Worthington wrote to President Jefferson about St Clair's conduct as Governor of the Northwestern Territory. He claimed that he had usurped legislative powers and used his position to pass laws, as well as having complete control over the proceedings of the judiciary. He was also unpopular because he assigned the office of attorney-general to his son and used people who lived out of the area in offices that dealt with internal matters. The local militia too had been neglected – for over 18 months a law had been in place in which officers should have been appointed to organise and discipline the men but St Clair had ignored it. Each tavern licence that was granted paid $4 to St Clair directly. Marriage licences and ferry licences were granted for a guinea. Towards the end of the letter, Worthington wrote that Governor St Clair had urged that: 'the then administration [in 1800] should procure a division of the population of the Territory so as to prevent any part from becoming an independent state; because when they did, they would oppose the views of the administration'.

St Clair knew there was a faction waiting to bring him down. He too wrote to Jefferson, acknowledging that he had learned of 'persons now endeavouring ... to ruin me with you' and begging Jefferson 'not to give implicit credit to their suggestions', professing he had done his best for the people of the territory. By March 1802, rumours were rife that St Clair would be removed as governor. In April, the House of Representatives passed a bill admitting the territory into the Union, should the people wish it and by May it was passed by the Senate. On 8 December 1802 in Cincinnati, St Clair addressed the people of the Northwestern Territory. Devoted followers had asked St Clair to become the State Governor of Ohio, which he thanked them for, but he declined. He went on to say how he had seen the state flourish but he had neglected his own private affairs, which he now wished to turn to. He ended: 'I will take my leave, assuring you that my best wishes will ever attend you, hoping that you may never have cause to look back with regret to the time when I was at the head of the political family'. He received formal word in late December that the President had relieved him of his duties. When Ohio finally became the 17th state in February 1803, it was thanks to St Clair's work with *Maxwell's Code*, which gave it a strong legislature.

St Clair, meantime, retired to Pennsylvania where he took time to get his personal affairs in order and spent time with his family. He had hoped the Government would help him out financially. He had helped Washington's army during the Revolution with money from his own pocket, and without this the army would not have survived. Added to that, he had used his own money during the time he was Governor of the Northwestern Territory to keep supplies moving, as the Government did not give him enough to cover the costs. But he was let down and never recouped all the money he was owed. In order to make ends meet in old age he was forced to sell his properties, including a piece of land on which a mill and a fine mansion house was situated, as well as farm outbuildings and his smelting furnace. In all he received just $4,000 for his property, which was actually worth more than ten times that amount. He was forced to use this small sum to pay off debts incurred on him from the US Government. The beautiful home he had built for his family was consigned to their memories and they were forced into poverty. All he was left with were some books 'and a bust of Paul Jones', which he had sent to him. Hearing of the great difficulties the family and the former president of Congress endured, many of New York's patriotic ladies sent money to St Clair, which he gratefully acknowledged. His plight even reached the politicians in Washington but the Republicans voted down an amendment that was put forward, in which it was suggested that some of the debt owed should be placed squarely at the feet of the Government. Instead he was awarded an annuity of $300, which was raised in 1817 to $600.

Also during these years, St Clair was still active in the local Freemasons, to which Benjamin Franklin, who also initiated him, introduced him. Many prominent men in the US were Freemasons; this is borne out by the fact that the Declaration of Independence was signed by no fewer than nine masons, and the Constitution by eleven. Washington inducted St Clair into The Society of Cincinnati, which was founded in 1787, and later he was one of the petitioners for a charter for a lodge in Cincinnati in 1791. At some stage, Washington also presented St Clair with a hand-painted silk masonic apron.

On 31 August 1818 Arthur St Clair from Thurso died. He was heading to the neighbouring community of Youngstown a few days beforehand, when he fell from his wagon, hitting his head on the ground. The road was rough and dangerous. A wheel from the wagon hit a rut and the wagon flipped over, throwing St Clair to the ground. He never regained consciousness. He was found and carried back home, where his beloved daughter Louisa waited for him, but neither she nor the medical profession could help him. St Clair had achieved greatness in his lifetime, but it had sadly fallen away following his removal as Governor of the Northwest. The years of the Revolution and the loans and gifts that he had endowed meant that by the end of his life he was poverty-stricken. A further example of this sees St Clair advancing William Butler $1,800 so that Butler could re-enlist in the army. When Butler died without repaying the loan, St Clair tried to get compensation from the Government. They refused.

St Clair was buried in St Clair Park in Greensburg, where a short time after, his wife too was buried. She survived him by only 18 days.

Before he was finally laid to rest, a dispute had erupted between Ligonier and Greensburg. Both wanted to have his body interred in their respective cemeteries. Colonel Ramsay, one of the oldest citizens of Ligonier appealed directly to St Clair's daughter, urging her to bury her father there. The argument was that St Clair had stronger ties with that town than Greensburg because he had once been the captain of the old fort. Ultimately Greensburg became St Clair's final resting place.

The Arthur St Clair legacy still remains in the United States. In states up and down the country there are parks, towns, and counties all named after the 9th President of the

Continental Congress. And near the remains of their log cabin home on the old state road that links Bedford and Pittsburg, at Chestnut Ridge about five miles west of Ligonier, a bronze tablet was erected in honour of him. And at the place where the tavern stood where St Clair worked during the last years of his life, is a stone monument in honour of him. The spelling is American but it reads:

St Clair Hollow
Named in Honor Of
Gen. Arthur St. Clair.
The Source Of This Hollow Is
A Large Spring Two Miles
South, Where Gen St. Clair, In A
Log Cabin, Spent His Last Days.
He Was
A Major General In
The Revolution.
President Of The
Continental Congress.
First Governor Of The
Northwestern Territory.
A Pioneer Ironmaster In
Western Pennsylvania.
Born 1736 – Died 1818.
Buried In Greensburg.

General Arthur St Clair is best summed up by the biographer of General Lewis Cass who wrote: 'General St Clair was a most interesting relic of the revolutionary period; tall, erect, though advanced in years, well educated, gentlemanly, thoroughly acquainted with the world, and abounding in anecdotes, descriptive of men and scenes he had encountered in his eventful career'.

Almost 40 years after St Clair's death, his surviving family finally received a considerable amount of money from Congress in recognition of the financial injustices he had endured.

JOHN FRANCIS SUTHERLAND

In 1912 at Tain in Ross and Cromarty, the death was announced of Dr John Francis Sutherland, the deputy commissioner for lunacy in Scotland. He had an illustrious career and the loss of the Lybster man was keenly felt not only at home but in Europe as well.

John Sutherland was born in Lybster on 29 May 1854. His parents were Benjamin Sutherland and Isabella Henderson. At that time Lybster was home to a booming herring industry with hundreds of boats using its harbour to land their catch. The tiny harbour built there in 1810 brought in trade and in 1829 Temple Sinclair, owner of the Lybster Estate, financed the building of a new, more substantial harbour designed to take many more boats. Between 1850 and 1860, around 3,000 local people were employed in the industry. These included coopers, curers, gutter and packers, labourers and of course a wealth of fishermen. It was a vibrant and exciting place and according to statistics, by the end of that decade more than 350 boats were registered with the Lybster Fishery.

For Sutherland, going into the fishing industry was not an option. Instead, he decided to train as a doctor. He studied at the Universities of Edinburgh, Glasgow and Paris. While at Edinburgh he worked under Dr Joseph Lister who noted Sutherland very early on in his career as 'a very distinguished member' of his class. Twenty years later Lister wrote that Sutherland had worked 'assiduously at the subjects of hygiene and welfare of the insane' and that his work had been recognised as being of a very high standard both at home and abroad. During Sutherland's student days, some of his clinical notes were sent to the General Medical Council by Sir Andrew Douglas Maclagan, a Fellow of the Royal College of Surgeons in Edinburgh, as an example of case notes taken at the Royal Infirmary. In 1880, Sutherland graduated from the University of Edinburgh with the highest honours possible and becoming an M.D. Edin. The thesis he wrote during his degree was later published as *Hospitals: Their History, Construction and Hygiene*. This work gained a lot of attention as it came at a time when the administration of hospitals was in absolute chaos. A petition was sent to the House of Lords by the Charity Organisation

Society, which quoted much of what Sutherland had written in the thesis. Their aim was reorganising both hospital administration and clinical practice where hygiene was lacking.

During Sutherland's career he worked as deputy medical officer for the training ship *Mars*. The ship became a famous landmark in the city of Dundee during the 19th century and changed the lives of hundreds of boys aged between 12 and 16 who might have otherwise ended up in prison. It had been built in 1848 and was used as a coastal defence vessel but with the emergence of new technologies, she was soon sent for scrap. However, she was saved and used as a training ship instead. Not only did boys from Dundee spend time there, but also from Glasgow and Edinburgh and onboard the boys all learned new skills. They had school lessons in the school-room then spent time learning carpentry and seaman skills, as well as swimming and life-saving skills. The carpentry took place at a building near the Woodhaven Pier where the boys made everything from stools to intricate detailing on staircases. Moreover, they were taught simple hygiene which led to the ship having a reputation of being one of the healthiest. Sickness levels were low thanks partially to the good diet. When many of them arrived on the ship, they were undernourished and underweight but with porridge for breakfast, a soup thickened with rice for lunch and bread and jam for supper, they soon became healthier. They were given a chance to better themselves and stop the vicious cycle of turning to petty crime and following a life of criminality. However, they lost their identity. During their time on the *Mars*, the boys were each allocated a number on admission and it was this number that they were known by at all times, even when talking to each other.

Life on board was strict but most of the boys had lacked discipline and it helped to build their confidence for when they left. Their day began at 5.00 a.m. with a prayer and the singing of hymns and ended at 9.00 p.m. with a prayer. Each boy had to be in his hammock by 9.30 p.m. Routine was paramount for a safe and well-run ship. The day was spent cleaning the ship, running errands, school-work and finally some time to play games with the other boys. One particular pastime gave the boys a chance to show off their skills, not only in Dundee and Edinburgh but also as far away as Thurso. A band had been formed and in 1882 a contingent of 50 members arrived at Thurso Town Hall where they gave a recital, having been transported on the *Mars*, which had docked at Wick. They were heartily greeted by the crowd, who thanked them when they had finished by applauding them loudly. However, this was long after Dr Sutherland had left the *Mars* and had gone on to doing other things.

Following his stint on the *Mars*, Sutherland was then appointed resident medical officer to the British Hospitals in Paris. It was during his time here that he met and made a lifelong friendship with Sir John Rose Cormack, Bart. M.D., the editor of the *Association Medical Journal* and author of *The natural history, pathology, and treatment of the epidemic fever prevailing in Edinburgh and other towns* in 1843. While living in the French capital, Cormack translated and published the work of Armand Trousseau, the famous French internist doctor who had written extensively on the diagnosis and treatment of serious diseases such as pleurisy, malaria and cancer. Cormack and his wife Eliza stayed in Paris with their children during the Franco-Prussian War, aiding the wounded on both sides after the rise of the Paris Commune. What remained of the National Guard joined the insurrection with whatever weapons they had. The National Government at Versailles tried to restore order but it was in vain. The troops refused orders and joined their fellow citizens in the uprising, culminating in a bloody confrontation in May. French troops annihilated the defenders of Paris with more than 15,000 dead and many more wounded. On the Government's side around 1,000 lost their lives with over 6,000 wounded. It was these men that Cormack attended to, dressing their wounds and feeding them whatever he could. For this he received the Legion of Honour from the French Government in 1871 at the cessation of hostilities, and Queen Victoria knighted him the following year for his services to the British residents of Paris who found themselves caught up in the chaos of fighting. He remained in Paris until his death in 1882.

Another lifelong friend that Sutherland made was the Hon. Alan Herbert M.D., son of the 3rd Earl of Carnarvon. He had also embarked on a medical career in the French capital, becoming physician to Hertford Hospital in Paris, which had been founded by Sir Richard Wallace in the 1870s. The hospital was intended to serve the British community living and working in Paris but later also allowed French citizens to make use of it. Interestingly, it was Wallace who also provided the people of Paris with drinking fountains following the siege of the city. For his work during the fighting in 1870–71, Herbert also received the Legion of Honour in recognition of his services to the wounded French. During the conflict he had become heavily involved in ambulance work, which Sutherland too became interested in. Again, this was due in part to Wallace, who had donated an ambulance to the 13 Corps and gave enough money for two others to be refitted. Sutherland realised the importance of the ambulance service and knew it would be an invaluable commodity in years to come.

In 1880 Sutherland was appointed medical officer to H.M. Prisons in Glasgow by Sir William Vernon Harcourt, the Home Secretary in Gladstone's Liberal government. In 1887 the Marquis of Lothian, Schomberg Henry Kerr, as Secretary of State for Scotland under Lord Salisbury's administration, appointed Sutherland consulting medical officer to the General Prison Barlinnie. Sutherland spent 15 years in Glasgow where he became deeply involved in insanity, inebriety and criminology and it was here that he promoted radical penal reforms following his research. He first came to notice during a murder trial and it was during his questioning as a witness for the defence that his ideas on drinking and how it affects the brain and therefore a person's culpability came to the fore. On that occasion the judge ignored his ideas, but later in life the Lord Justice Clerk of Scotland considered them. Thanks to his work, Sutherland managed to secure two royal commissions and a departmental committee on habitual offenders and inebriates. In 1894 he was invited to become a member and the secretary of the committee by Sir George O. Trevelyan, the Secretary of State for Scotland. Glasgow's Lord Provost Sir James Bell referred to the 'continuous efforts of Dr Sutherland to bring this crying evil to a point at which the Government could take it up and treat it as a disease'.

While researching his work, Sutherland concluded that many factors contributed to criminality, insanity and alcoholism and how each could be related to the other. He looked at certain age groups and the crimes of which they were convicted. He looked into their background and found a correlation between where they lived, their education and whether they were in employment or not. Moreover, he looked in depth at both nature and nurture to see which one had the greatest impact on people. He looked into genetics to see if there was a history of insanity, criminology or intoxication within the home environment, as well as taking into account factors such as poor housing, parental neglect and unemployment causing lack of money to buy decent food and clothing. The local environment too played its part: he believed that if a child saw immoral behaviour out on the streets, such as prostitution, drinking, and gambling, this could lead a child into that world and therefore lead to criminal behaviour. Education also was looked at. He studied children who played truant or who were illiterate and found this had an impact on their adult lives. As he once said, 'It does not require Sherlock Holmes to distinguish the *bona fide* tramp with tatterdemalion, unkempt locks, gaping boots and grimed skin from the *bona fide* labourer in search of work'.

Also while living and working in Glasgow, Sutherland took an interest in the locale. He became a deacon in the United Free Church and played a major role in the forming of the Association for Improving the Social Condition of the People. This notwithstanding, he was also the vice-president of the West of Scotland Free Education League and a member of a committee involved in the Industrial Exhibition which was held in Glasgow.

In 1895, Sutherland's name was put forward to Queen Victoria for senior deputy commissioner for lunacy. He got the post and was entertained by the people of Glasgow before he left to take up his new post in Edinburgh. The Lord Provost of Glasgow, the Conservative Sir John Ure Primrose, addressed the assembled company, stating that they were gathered together to 'pay a tribute of admiration to one who has commended himself to us all, and whose good qualities are tonight receiving that recognition at the hands of his fellow citizens which is very precious to any man of honest intention'.

For many years, Sutherland was invited to address various scientific conferences and societies throughout the United Kingdom and beyond. In June 1890 he addressed the Reformatory and Refuge Union Conference in Glasgow on *Habitual Offenders: Failure of Existing Police Enactments*. In 1901 he delivered an address on *The Ratio, Growth and Geographical Distribution of Insanity in Scotland* to the British Association for the Advancement of Science; and in the *Edinburgh Judicial Review* a paper by Sutherland was published on the *Jurisprudence of Intoxication*, which received wide acclaim. His published work included papers on criminology, psychology, and penal reform, as well as the construction of hospitals and asylums. His most popular work, *Ambulance Pupils Vade-Mecu; Notes on First Aid*, ran to 41 editions. In 1908 Sutherland published *Recidivism: Habitual Criminality, And Habitual Petty Delinquency; A Problem In Sociology, Psycho-Pathology And Criminology*. 'Recidivism' was a word that he had picked up in France. It refers to a criminal who has been reprimanded for a crime or has had treatment to change the behaviour but persistently relapses. It strongly relates to psychopathic behaviour, such as repetitive criminality purely for gratification. It was thought that repetitive spells in prison or trying to reform an inebriate at home just proved to be a waste of time, therefore the best form of treatment was legislation to place these people into some form of mental institution – although a problem did arise when the person in question categorised as a delinquent was a borderline case. At the heart of treatment was cost, and it would not be cheap to have them sectioned. But Sutherland made the distinction between a recidivist and a lunatic, which was fundamental into understanding behaviour. A lunatic, as people with mental disorders were termed – including everything from euphoria, mania and depression, could be cured. A recidivist was altogether more difficult to treat, if at all. At home, a lunatic's family had no idea how to treat them, whereas in a clinical environment such as the local asylum, doctors knew exactly what to do. They understood the condition to the extent of up-to-date medical knowledge at that time, and although their liberty had been taken away, the lunatics (it was thought) preferred the sanctuary away from those who were ignorant of the condition. A recidivist, on the other hand, was seen as a perpetual offender where nothing could cure them. Those who studied recidivists believed that they were happy to keep returning to prison in defiance of any judge or prison authority. In prison they were fed, had a roof over their head and were privy to medical attention at no cost to themselves. They made up the largest percentage of the prison population at the turn of the 20th century. They were divided into separate classes: everything from vagrants and petty offenders to hard-core criminals such as those who used violence; yet they were intelligent and fairly responsible people. When this kind of recidivist was in prison, he tended to get on well and this would eventually lead to his release. With the Prevention of Crime Act 1908, the recidivist was tackled in a new way. Punishment and reform were to be dealt separately at different institutions. Punishment was to take place in a conventional prison but the rehabilitation would take place in a preventative detention establishment where the recidivist was to be re-educated both morally and religiously, and taught new skills such as carpentry and crafts. Rewards would be given and each one would get better with each new level attained. It was a carrot and stick approach but it seemed to work for some.

Sutherland became a fellow of the Royal Statistical Society of London, which had been established in the 1830s and had gained its royal charter in 1887. He also became a fellow in Edinburgh and from Europe received distinctions from the scientific societies in Paris, Moscow and Madrid. New York too honoured him for his work.

In his personal life, Sutherland married Jeanie Mackay, the youngest daughter of the Free Church minister the Rev. John Mackay of Lybster and his wife Williamina Sutherland. Sutherland and his wife had two sons and a daughter. His eldest son Halliday, born in Glasgow in 1882, followed in his father's footsteps, taking up the medical profession after gaining a Bachelor of Surgery from the University of Aberdeen in 1906. He became well-known in his own right for his work on the control and prevention of tuberculosis and died in London aged 77 in 1960.

By the time he was 57, John Francis Sutherland was living in Tain at a house on Scotsburn Road. He and a friend decided to go out on a shooting expedition one day with his beloved dogs. He was a good shot and often would trample over the moors for hours on end looking for birds. However, this was an expedition he would not return from. He died suddenly on the moor and it was the end of an era.

Following his death the *Journal of Mental Science* reported that following a meeting of the Scottish division of the Medico-Psychological Association on 15 March 1912 in Glasgow, the members expressed their deep regret on hearing the news. Sutherland had 'been a member of the association for fifteen years' and as such, the secretary was instructed to send a copy of the minutes to Sutherland's widow so that 'their sympathy with members of his family in their bereavement' could be passed on.

Sir John Barr, who became president of the British Medical Association in July 1912 and was another associate of Sutherland's echoed the sentiments in the obituary that was printed in the *British Medical Journal*. He fully endorsed 'the kind words' that had been written. He referred to a photograph that also appeared with the article and noted that although it had been taken some years before, it showed that Sutherland was a deep and thoughtful individual – which he was – and he also highlighted that in life he had been 'genial' and 'vivacious' around his friends and family. Barr also wrote that Sutherland was a man of 'sterling merit' and of 'high moral character', as well as having a natural ability in his chosen field of work. However, Barr had a sting in the tail in his notice. He claimed that Sutherland had never received the recognition that he deserved from the work he had done and that his 'brilliant intellect had been cramped by official surroundings'.

DONALD SUTHERLAND SWANSON

In 1888 London's East End fell victim to a murderer who has never been found nor brought to justice. The Ripper Murders took place between late August and early November that year, with five women known to have been his victims, although some believe there were more. The Metropolitan Police came under fire for not doing enough to stop the man nicknamed Jack the Ripper, due to a letter signed 'Jack the Ripper' that was sent to the Central News Agency on 27 September 1888 – the mentioning of clipping a lady's ear gave credence to the note for a time. But for one detective the hunt never ended, despite the fact that he believed he knew who the killer was. The detective was none other than Thurso-born Donald Swanson.

Donald Sutherland Swanson was born on 12 August 1848 to John Swanson, a brewer, and his wife, Mary Thomson at Geise. John and Mary already had numerous children. Swanson was christened in Thurso two months after his birth on 2 October 1848. The family lived in Durness Street. Swanson attended the Miller Institution under the direction of Mr James Waters, where he was a good scholar and a bright student. When Swanson left, he took up a position as a school-master, firstly at the Miller Institution then at the school in Castletown. However, he soon realised that teaching was not a profession with prospects of promotion. After giving his future some thought, Swanson decided to join the police force and left his native Caithness for London.

Early in 1868, Swanson worked as a clerk at 8 Catherine Court in London and on 20 March he wrote a letter of application to the police after they had advertised vacancies in the *Daily Telegraph* that day. In the letter Swanson stated that unfortunately his 'employer will give up the business in a few weeks' and that if he was called for interview he would be able to provide 'unexceptionable references as to character, education and ability'. Swanson closed the letter stating that he did not 'so much desire a large salary as a good opening at a moderate one'. Enclosed with his letter of application was a glowing reference from his employer Mr Meikle, which stated that he recommended him 'where intelligence, activity, honesty and steadfastness will be appreciated'.

Following his letter of application, the Metropolitan Police asked for two witnesses to sign the Form of Recommendation. The signatories were both from Thurso: George Gunn of High Street; and James McLeach of Brabster Street. They stated they had known him from 1862–67. On 31 March 1868, Swanson was found to be fit following his medical examination. His medical records showed that in his entire career with the force, he was off sick for less than 60 days. Among the ailments were pharyngitis, tonsillitis, influenza, and on one occasion he had to take ten days off due to a strained ankle. He entered the police force on 27 April 1868 in a career that would span 35 years and see him involved in one of Britain's most notorious criminal cases.

When he was accepted into the force he was attached to A Division and had to abide by the rules contained in *Conditions upon which each Constable is admitted*, which he duly signed. Among these conditions the number one priority was the 'Police service' at all times, and members of the force are 'not to carry out any trade nor can his wife be allowed to keep a shop'. His pay was 19 shillings per week and would rise by increments of two shillings until he reached the position of first class, when he would be paid 25 shillings. A uniform was supplied to him and he was given an allowance of 20 lbs of coal in the summer and 40 lbs in the winter, as he was single. Married officers got double. A pension scheme was also available to him which could only be 'granted by the Secretary of State', according to certain conditions being met. It was condition number 15 that Swanson held in highest regard for promotion in the future. It stated: 'Every Police Constable in the Force may hope to rise, by activity, intelligence, and good conduct, to the superior stations'. Soon he impressed Superintendent Williamson, a fellow Scot and head of CID, and a man he was to follow into that position.

When he was fairly new to the force, some infractions did go on his record. On one occasion he was 25 minutes late for roll call and turned up in plain clothes rather than his uniform. For this he was fined a shilling. On another occasion, he clambered over railings at King Street Station because he was late for roll call and was fined two shillings, but on the whole he was rewarded for his work. On 15 June 1880, whilst at D division, Swanson was awarded 25 shillings for active enquiries on a murder case; and on 30 November he was again rewarded, this time £5 for his 'energy and zeal' in pursuing enquiries. He was also sent to Scotland at one stage, where he apprehended and brought to justice a swindler and received £3 for his endeavours.

By 1881 Swanson had married Julia Ann Nevill and they had an infant son. The family lived at 1 Grove Cottages in Lambeth, Surrey. The couple went on to have two more sons and two daughters. That year saw Swanson involved in the arrest of Percy Lefroy Mapleton, alias Arthur Lefroy, who was accused of the murder in a railway carriage of Mr Isaac Gold (a retired stockbroker from Brighton) on 27 June 1881. It was labelled the 'Brighton Railway Murder'. Gold had been shot and savagely attacked with his throat slashed and his body thrown from the carriage into Balcombe Tunnel. Thomas Jennings and his nephew, labourers on the railway, discovered it and robbery seemed to be the motive. Gold travelled regularly on the train to collect takings at a baker shop that he owned at Walworth. At the inquest into the death, a local doctor, Benjamin Hall of the Sussex County Hospital, gave evidence that Lefroy, a journalist, had been admitted to the hospital that same day with wounds consistent with a struggle or fight. There were splatters of blood all over his face and neck and dried blood on his waistcoat. He claimed not to remember how he received the wounds he displayed. Later he said there had been two assailants who had jumped from the train while it was travelling at speeds of up to 50 miles an hour with goods that they had stolen. The police questioned Lefroy and even when they found two Hanoverian flash sovereigns, a gold watch and chain in his boot, they still let him go home. The officers thought about his statement and immediately dispatched men round to his house in Wallington. In the intervening minutes he had disappeared, only to be caught 12 days later at Stepney in London.

Lefroy stood trial and the jury found him guilty of Gold's murder after only a very short time deliberating the facts of the case. Lord Coleridge passed the death sentence on him. Lefroy told the jury that one day they would realise that they had murdered him. He was hanged at Lewes (by the executioner William Marwood) just after 9.00 a.m. on 29 November 1881. He was 21 years old.

In the same year as the Gold murder, Swanson also arrested a merchant navy captain named George Drevor, who had sent threatening letters to the wreck commissioner, Mr Rothery, following the suspension of his certificate for six months. Drevor said he believed he had been told by God to find the illusive sea serpent and the suspension of his certificate would impede that mission.

The year before the infamous Ripper murders took place, Swanson was promoted to Chief Inspector of the Criminal Investigation Department at Scotland Yard. CID was fairly new. It was set up in 1878 by C. E. Charles Vincent, a lawyer who had investigated the Parisian police force and was asked to report to the British Home Secretary R. A. Cross on his findings. Cross was so impressed that he appointed Vincent to head up the new CID. Swanson's promotion placed him in good stead for the Ripper Murders, which would happen less than a year later.

Swanson was the senior investigating officer for the murders. He was highly educated and was described by a contemporary as being 'one of the best class of officers'. He read every single document relating to the murders and was the foremost authority on them at the time. He spent hours reading witness statements, post mortem reports and sifting through other evidence as it came to him. His task began with the murder of Mary Ann Nichols, who is widely seen as the first of Jack the Ripper's victims.

Before Nichols was found dead in Whitechapel, other murders were being investigated – but these were never linked to the Ripper case. These murders, along with the bodies of four other women and also including the Ripper bodies, became known collectively as the Whitechapel Murders. On 3 April 1888, Emma Elizabeth Smith was assaulted and robbed of her possessions in Osborn Street in the district of Whitechapel. The next victim was that of Martha Tabram, whose body was found at the George Yard Buildings in George Yard, Whitechapel, and whom some historians now believe was the Ripper's first victim. Both women had suffered abdominal mutilation. Next was Mary Ann Nichols, the first clear Ripper victim.

Mary Ann Walker was born in London on 26 August 1845. In January 1864 Polly, as she was known, married William Nichols and they had five children. However Nichols' relationship with her husband was stormy and over the years she left him as many as five or six times. In 1881 she left him for the last time. Between the time Nichols left her husband and the time she was found murdered, she moved from workhouse to workhouse. During a stay at the Lambeth workhouse she made friends with the woman who would eventually identify her body. On 12 May 1888, Nichols finally found work as a domestic servant and left the workhouse. However, she only lasted two months in the position. On 24 August 1888 she moved into the White House in Flower and Dean Street, where men and women openly had sex within its confines.

Late on the night of 30 August 1888, Nichols was seen soliciting for trade in Whitechapel Road. An hour and a half later she was seen leaving the Frying Pan Public House at around 12.30 a.m. on the 31st. She returned to a house on Thrawl Street. Here she was told to leave the house because she had no doss money. She pointed out her new black bonnet to the man and told him to save a bed for her because she would be back. At 2.30 a.m. she met up with Emily Holland, who later testified that Nichols was extremely drunk and she had told her that she had been paid three times that day but spent the lot. The last Holland saw of her was when she was walking down Whitechapel Road.

Just over an hour later, Charles Cross and Robert Paul found Nichols' body. One of them thought she was still breathing, but because they were hurrying to work they decided to tell the first police officer they came across, which they did. In the meantime, Nichols' body had been discovered a second time; this time by P.C. John Neil. She was identified by her friend Mary Ann Monk from the Lambeth Workhouse and William Nichols. Her throat had been cut and on her abdomen there were several incisions caused by the same knife. She was 43 years old and at the inquest into her death no one had a bad word to say about her. She seemed to be well-liked even though she was an alcoholic.

Inspector John Spratling of J Division (based at Bethnal Green) wrote the initial report on the Nichols case. In it he described how P.C. John Neil, the beat officer, had found her as well the preliminary police activity at the scene. It also detailed her injuries, her appearance and what she was wearing.

Just two days after Nichols' funeral on 6 September 1888, another victim, Annie Chapman, was found in the back yard of 29 Hanbury Street in Spitalfields. Like Nichols, her throat had been cut.

Annie had been born in September 1841. When she was 28 she married John Chapman, a coachman, and they had three children, although their eldest daughter died of meningitis aged 12 and their son John was sent to a home because he was a cripple. Family life took its toll on the Chapmans and Annie and John separated in the mid-1880s. Both of them were heavy drinkers and it is thought this contributed to the break-up of the marriage.

During their separation John would occasionally pay Annie 10 shillings, but when he died on Christmas Day 1886, the money dried up. By this time Annie Chapman was living with John Sivvy but the relationship did not last. She is then known to have had a relationship with a bricklayer's mate, Edward Stanley. But since the death of her husband, she had begun to turn to prostitution for money.

At the time of her murder Chapman was staying at Crossingham's Lodging House on Dorset Street, Spitalfields. On the evening of Friday 7 September 1888, she sat in Crossinghams with another lodger drinking until 1.00 a.m. when she decided to leave. It was thought that she had gone to bed. She returned to the house sometime after 1.30 a.m. but did not have enough money for her bed, so told the deputy Timothy Donovan to hold the bed for her and she would be back. She left and was seen walking towards Spitalfields Market. Four hours later Elizabeth Long saw her with a man outside 29 Hanbury Street. Long heard them talking. A short time later Albert Cadosch heard a woman say 'No' then heard something falling against the tall wooden fence. He thought nothing of it at the time. Just before 6.00 a.m. John Davis, a resident in Hanbury Street, discovered Chapman's body. At the inquest, details of her mutilated body were made public. Her throat had been cut 'with a thin narrow blade ... at least 6" to 8" in length', and her uterus and upper part of her vagina had been removed. This caused leading pathologist Dr George Phillips to believe that the person who had carried out the attack had a fairly sound knowledge of anatomy and surgical skill to some degree.

On 19 September 1888, Inspector Frederick Abberline of Scotland Yard – who was assigned to lead the 'on the ground' investigation – wrote a report on both the Nichols and Chapman murders. Within that report he mentioned one of the early suspects in the case, Joseph Isenschmid. The report also detailed the identification of the two victims and noted the questioning of witnesses.

By the end of the month, another two Ripper victims were to meet the same fate, but this time he struck twice on the same day. Elizabeth Stride, known as Long Liz, was Swedish by birth. In 1865 she decided to apply to move to the Swedish parish in London. She was granted permission and registered in the city the following summer, having secured a position with a family. In 1869 Elizabeth married John Stride and the couple ran a fairly successful coffee shop until it was taken over in 1875. However, the marriage failed. It is known that she lived apart from her husband: she spent time in the Whitechapel Workhouse while her husband was still alive, but he died in 1884 and the following year she was known to be living with Michael Kidney, a labourer. Yet she spent time away from him, often on drinking bouts in the city.

Between 1886 and 1888, Stride received money from the Swedish church, but it seems that she probably spent most of it on alcohol – over the period of 20 months before she died, she appeared before magistrates no less than eight times, charged with being drunk and disorderly. Michael Kidney last saw Stride alive on 25 September 1888. She was absent when he returned home from work, which was nothing unusual, and he assumed she would return in time. She turned up at 32 Flower and Dean Street in the hope that she could stay there. She told one of the lodgers there that she had fought with her partner and needed somewhere to stay. At the inquest a witness, Dr Thomas Barnardo, later confirmed Stride as being at this location. He had entered the kitchen that day where a group of women were discussing the murders and one of them had supposed that it could be one of them next. Barnardo remembered the discussion distinctively and when Stride's body was found, he identified her as one of the women in the kitchen.

In the early evening of 29 September 1888, Stride had been out drinking as usual, and then had returned to her lodgings before heading out again to ply her trade. Over the next few hours, she was seen with a few different men, the last one of which was seen with her at approximately 12.45 a.m. James Brown said at the inquest that he had seen her with a stout man with a long black coat. Fifteen minutes later, Louis Diemschutz entered Dutfield's Yard with his horse and cart. The horse acted strangely, which alerted him to something not being quite right. He probed with his whip as the yard was in darkness and assumed the body he had hit was a drunk or someone sleeping. He entered the International Working Men's Educational Club to get some help. Two men offered, but when they arrived they discovered that Stride was dead. Her throat had been cut. All three knew this had happened very recently as the body was still warm, although the hands were cold. It is thought the arrival of Diemschutz disturbed the murderer. She was pronounced dead at 1.16 a.m. by Dr Frederick Blackwell. She was 45 years old.

That same night, Catherine Eddows, also known as Kate Kelly, had been thrown in the cells at Bishopsgate Police Station for being very drunk after being found in a heap on the pavement. At 12.15 a.m. on 30 September, Kate could be heard softly singing from her cell and she called out to the gaoler P.C. George Hutt asking when she would be released. He replied: 'When you are capable of taking care of yourself', to which she replied: 'I can do that now'. She was found to have sobered up and was released at around 1.00 a.m. About half an hour later, witness Joseph Lawende saw Eddows talking to a man. Lawende later identified the clothes she was wearing. Ten minutes after this, P.C. Edward Watkins discovered Eddows' body in Mitre Square. Her throat had been cut, and during the post mortem it was discovered her left kidney had been removed. Dr Frederick Brown, the police surgeon who carried out the post mortem, believed that whoever had removed the kidney had a great deal of medical knowledge and that he had acted alone.

On 19 October 1888 Swanson wrote a summary of the Elizabeth Stride case. By this stage he was in overall control of the collective Whitechapel Murders. He summarised the events surrounding her death and the subsequent police enquiries and managed to sort out the sequence of events from the various witness statements. By the end of the Ripper case, he was the one person who knew it best.

Sir Charles Warren, the Commissioner of the Metropolitan Police, had given strict instructions that Swanson should be given his own office and that 'every paper, every document, every report, every telegram must pass through' Swanson's hands. Yet Warren himself was forced to resign his position in November 1888 because of his difficult relationship with the Home Office and the fact that he had not caught the Ripper. He was a controversial figure at the Met and in a report for the Home Office on the Stride and Eddows cases that month, he had to explain why he erased a chalked message which had been on the wall near to a suspect's house on Goulston Street.

At the same time, Swanson was preparing another report, this time into the Eddows' case. It was dated 6 November 1888, just two days before the Ripper claimed what was thought to have been his last victim. Because the Eddows' case fell under the jurisdiction of the City Police, Swanson had to relate all the known facts to them, including details of a letter known as the Lusk Letter and the accompanying package, as well as having to give details of the man the witness Lawende described who was with Eddows before her death.

The last of the 'canonical five' murders was that of Mary Jane Kelly, a native of Limerick in Ireland but whose family had moved to Wales. In 1884 she decided to move to London, and on her arrival began working in a high-class brothel. At some point Kelly took to drinking. When drunk, she was unpleasant. When sober, she was well-liked. She lived for a while with Joseph Barnett who she met in April 1887 and who also had Irish lineage, but the couple failed to pay their rent at Little Paternoster Row and they were evicted, also for being drunk. They took lodgings in Brick Lane then Miller's Court but in August, Barnett lost his job and Kelly took to prostitution once more. On 30 October 1888, Kelly and Barnett split up. However, Barnett still visited her every day.

On Thursday 8 November 1888, as usual, Barnett had visited Kelly before heading back to his lodgings, where he played cards until after midnight before retiring to bed. It is unknown where Kelly was for much of the evening, but she was seen at 11.45 p.m. walking with a stout man who was carrying a pail of beer. She was also seen talking to him outside her room and was heard to bid him goodnight, before singing to herself. At around 2.00 a.m. Kelly asked George Hutchinson for a loan of sixpence, but he had spent all his money, so she declared that she was going to find some. He noticed Kelly talking to a man carrying a small parcel who he had passed earlier. The couple then walked off. Hutchinson got a good look at the man and described him as 'Jewish' in appearance. He decided to follow Kelly and the mysterious gent but at 3.00 a.m. he left them to it.

At around 10.45 a.m. John McCarthy, the owner of where Kelly was lodging, sent Thomas Bowyer round to her room to collect her rent money. There was no reply, so Bowyer peered in the window. He saw Kelly's body on the bed. He ran for McCarthy who came immediately, saw the body and ran to Commercial Street Police Station. Accompanied by Inspector Walter Beck, all three returned to the room. After waiting for the bloodhounds to come, McCarthy was told by Superintendent Thomas Arnold to smash down the door.

Kelly's body was lying on the bed. Every organ in her abdomen had been removed, and her face had been hacked beyond recognition. At the post mortem, it was concluded that the actual cause of death was the severed carotid artery.

It was Inspector George Abberline who prepared the report on the Mary Kelly case on 12 November 1888. He gave great credence to George Hutchinson's witness statement and details from both the inquiry and inquest were also included in the account.

During the investigations house-to-house enquiries took place and lists of suspects were made up, followed by interviews and the collection of forensic evidence. In Whitechapel, as the number of murders increased, a vigilante group was set up under the leadership of George Lusk. Lusk received a package containing part of a kidney and what was to become known as the 'From Hell' letter. Whoever sent the letter and half kidney claimed to have eaten the other half, which he had taken from Catherine Eddows.

The Metropolitan Police had four suspects, having discounted the rumours surrounding the likes of Prince Albert, the Duke of Clarence and George Chapman (who poisoned three of his wives – for him to have slit the throats and mutilated all these women would have been a huge step for this serial killer to take, so he was discounted). Of the four remaining suspects: Montague John Druitt; Michael Ostrog; Francis Tumblety; and Aaron Kosminski, Chief Inspector Swanson favoured Kosminski. Druitt, Ostrog and Tumblety were Sir Melville Macnaghten's prime suspects for the killings, although out of all of them, Macnaghten favoured Montague Druitt. Macnaghten had joined the Metropolitan Police in June 1889 as assistant chief constable and was second in command of the CID. Druitt was a well-educated man from Dorset. He was a barrister and also worked at George Valentine's Boarding School for boys; a position he was dismissed from shortly before his suicide on 1 December 1888. Just at the time of his disappearance, the last of the Ripper's murder victims had been found and (in private information relayed to Macnaghten) this led the assistant chief to promote Druitt to prime suspect in 1894. Inspector Abberline however, dismissed him as a suspect, because at the time of Mary Ann Nichols' murder, Druitt was miles away in Dorset playing cricket, as verified by witnesses. Druitt's mother had suffered from a psychiatric illness and Macnaghten may have assumed it had been passed on to him.

Little is known of Macnaghten's other suspect: Michael Ostrog, a Russian; except he had spent time in jail for fraud and had been a surgeon in the Russian navy. This fact alone was enough to arouse suspicion – but that in itself was not enough.

Finally, there was Francis Tumblety, an Irish American from New York State. A 'herb doctor', he had been suspected of the deaths of a number of his patients and was actually charged in Canada, but he had evaded justice and fled. He arrived in England in 1888. He was arrested for gross indecency on 7 November 1888 but given bail and while he was awaiting trial, he fled the country. The Metropolitan Police tried to get him returned from the United States by sending officers over to retrieve him, but it was in vain. Their reasoning behind it was that there were no more Ripper murders after he had left the country. Tumblety died in hospital in 1903.

It was the head of CID and close friend of Swanson's – Dr Robert Anderson – who favoured Kosminski as the identity of the Ripper and convinced Swanson of it. Aaron Kosminski was born Aron Mordle Kozminski on 11 September 1865 in Klodawa, Poland. The reason Swanson believed that Kosminski was the murderer was that at the time of the killings he had lived very near to where each one took place. Added to this was evidence found at his house in Goulston Street. A piece of blood-stained clothing belonging to Catherine Eddows, was found in a doorway and he had no explanation as to how it got there. Just above the piece of apron was a piece of graffiti saying: 'The Juwes are The men that Will not be Blamed for nothing'. To this day, no one knows the full truth behind this, but for Anderson and Swanson it made some sense. They had a witness who was a Jew, who claimed that he had been perfectly positioned to see the murderer, however he was not willing to testify against a fellow Jew. This pointed the finger at Kosminski once more. Macnaghten himself had reason to suspect Kosminski in that he knew the man had a 'great hatred of women ... with strong homicidal tendencies', as he wrote in a memorandum.

Many years after the murder, Anderson published *The Lighter Side of My Official Life* in 1910. Anderson was the second assistant chief with the Met from 1888 until 1901. Originally he was a barrister until he was called to London to investigate the murder of a policeman in Manchester during a Fenian jail-break and in 1868 he was asked by the Home Office to advise on political crime. In 1877 he was appointed secretary to the new Prison Commission. In 1887 he assisted James Munro, assistant commissioner in crime at Scotland Yard, and in 1888, when Munro was promoted, Anderson became assistant commissioner. In 1901 he retired from the police force and was knighted. Swanson had a copy of the book and as he read through it he pencilled in the margins that he believed Kosminski was the Jew who had been identified at a 'Seaside Home'. Swanson wrote about the Jewish witness: 'because his evidence would convict the suspect' he would not be able to reconcile the fact that Kosminski would have been hanged for the murders and he, the witness, would have difficulty in living with the knowledge that it was his testimony that had sent him to the gallows. Swanson continued: 'he knew he was identified'. Kosminski was returned to live with his brother in Whitechapel but the police kept a close eye on him and in 'a very short time the suspect ... was sent to Stepney Workhouse and then Colney Hatch', a lunatic asylum. Mistakenly Swanson thought that he died shortly afterwards, but in fact Kosminski lived until 1919.

The case of Jack the Ripper never closed and mystery still surrounds it today. Swanson continued to work for the police and received yet more commendations. On 22 March 1892 the Secretary of State for India commended him for his 'valuable assistance' in the case of a breach of the Official Secrets Act. Again, in August 1896 he was highly commended by the Director of Public Prosecutions during the arrest of a number of people in connection with offences under the Foreign Enlistment Act and his questioning of witnesses in the case.

Over the whole course of his career, Swanson became involved in other notable cases, and travelled to Gibraltar, Egypt and Canada. He worked on the case of the suppression of Fenianism in Ireland, encountering Michael Davitt – the Irish republican nationalist who went on to become founder of the Irish National Land League and became an MP at Westminster. Swanson was also involved in the Dunecht Mystery. This concerned the embalmed remains of the late Earl of Crawford and Balcarres, which had been missing from the family vault for 14 months. The earl had died in Florence in 1881 and his body was embalmed and returned to Scotland. It was placed in three coffins. The outer one was made of wood, an inner case of wood and a leaden shell. The outer coffin was heavily decorated in silver but none of it had been tampered with and it was thought the body was therefore not removed by a petty thief, in order that a ransom or reward would be paid for its safe return. One day a man called Charles Souter claimed in a drunken stupor to know where the body was. But when he sobered up and was questioned by the police, he said that he had been out poaching on the estate and had come across a gang of men who were burying an object – and that he was sworn to secrecy. Souter maintained his innocence all his life but in 1882 he was sentenced to five years in prison.

There was another side to Swanson: on one occasion when he was working at Leyton he got to know a blind man who sold alms on the bridge at Lea. One day Swanson loaned the man some money for rent at his lodgings. The man thanked him for the half-crown and promised to pay him back, which he did. But more than that, he gave Swanson some information about a group of men who were planning to meet at a local public house – two of whom were known criminals and Swanson suspected they were going to plan a job of some kind. Swanson relayed the information to his superiors back at the station and he was ordered to attend the premises in plain clothes. Soon he knew the movements of the gang and they were all arrested on various charges.

One of the more bizarre cases that Swanson worked on in the 1890s concerned a man who professed to make silver into gold. What this man did was to use smoke as a screen. This threw the witnesses of this supposed miracle off their guard, especially because the smell of the smoke caused discomfort when it was inhaled. People went back to him time and again with their silver coins, only to come away with what they thought was gold. The fraudster lured them in further so that the more silver they brought and left with him the more gold they would theoretically get back. One day of course, the so-called alchemist suddenly disappeared with the money. This went on for years. At last he tried his magic on one of the world's leading metal experts, who incidentally was working undercover for the police. The magician was caught. Swanson found it one of the most amusing cases he had ever dealt with.

One other case of note that Swanson was involved in was the theft of a Gainsborough picture. Swanson worked with the prestigious American detective agency Pinkertons. An American called Adam Worth was in London in 1876 and was head of a forgery syndicate. One of his colleagues was arrested in Paris and extradited to England to stand trial for forgery and that put him in jeopardy. The only way out was to free the man in prison somehow, and he formulated a plan. As he walked down Bond Street with his friend Jack Phillips, he saw a crowd and wondered what they were looking at. It was a Thomas Gainsborough portrait of the Duchess of Devonshire, which had just been sold at Christie's auction house for £10,500 just a few days before. Quickly a plan was hatched. The next day was foggy, which helped, and with the help of Joe Reilly (another associate of Worth's), they managed to steal the painting, rolling it up and escaping into the fog.

The following day – 27 May 1876 – London was abuzz with the news of the stolen painting. A reward of £1,000 was offered and the police issued description of the men involved. Reilly and Phillips began to question the theft. After all, they could hardly return the painting for the reward as their description had been circulated. But Worth was thrilled. He told the men he knew of someone, an unscrupulous solicitor, who would help them. He planned to give this solicitor a small piece of the Gainsborough for him to take to their colleague who was holed up in Newgate Prison and he in turn would profess to know where the painting was. In return for this, a bail bond would be set up, which meant that the man would be released under those conditions. He could then flee, thus not implicat-ing any member of the gang in the £4,000 fraud that had already taken place in France.

However, this plan went awry: a technical error in the extradition papers meant that he was released anyway, and he fled the country as soon as he could. The Gainsborough was now a burden. No one could claim the reward and Worth's accomplices started to blackmail him. Eventually Worth gained the upper hand and, following his thrashing of Phillips at the Criterion Bar (Phillips had waited the previous day with two police officers to catch Worth with the painting), the group parted company. Worth kept the painting. Many years later Worth wrote to William Pinkerton and the two spoke over the telephone. Worth admitted to him all his crimes and recalled the time when he stole the painting, but asked that no details would be published until after his death. A deal was struck that would ensure the return of the painting. Pinkerton got in touch with his brother Robert in New York, who in turn contacted Swanson at Criminal Investigations Department in New Scotland Yard. Swanson sent a telegram to Pinkerton's office, instructing them to negotiate the safe return of the artwork and telling them that Worth's terms were acceptable. Worth left America and returned to England on a steamer. Pinkerton received the news and cabled Swanson in London. He in turn cabled back, saying that Mr C. Agnew and his wife (the owners of the painting) had left for America onboard the *Etruria*. The Agnews finally arrived in Chicago on 27 March 1901. In a hotel room the following day, a package arrived and when opened, a perfectly preserved portrait of the Duchess of Devonshire unfolded. It had been missing for 26 years. Agnew confirmed it was the painting that had been stolen from his father's gallery. Nothing was reported about the painting until the *Etruria* docked back in England.

In 1895 Swanson was sent to the island of Jersey in order to apprehend Leonard Harper – who had been accused of fraud back in New Zealand. Harper was remanded in custody and bail was set at £10,000, a sum that was available to him. Extradition was granted in August and Harper was anxious to return to answer the charges before him. He was committed for trial on 11 October 1895 and had several cases brought against him, which amounted to over £11,000. By November Mr Justice Denniston set the trial date for 2 December before a special jury. In March the following year Harper was acquitted of all charges of fraud.

In 1896, Swanson became involved in a robbery that involved an American millionaire who promised a reward that was not forthcoming. Earlier that year, New Yorker Mr I. Townsend Burden had around £20,000 of diamonds and jewellery stolen from his house by two of his employees, the butler, Mr Turner; and footman, Mr Dunlop. The Burdens were at the opera when the robbery took place and the culprits fled to London, where they thought they could sell without any problems. They took their haul to a Bond Street diamond merchant by the name of E. W. Streeter who was suspicious and called Scotland Yard. Needless to say, police officers were dispatched promptly and the two thieves were apprehended. All of the stolen jewellery and diamonds were recovered, including that which had been taken to back-street pawn-shops and an East End jeweller's shop. Burden and his wife made the journey over the Atlantic and identified the goods. He then publicly announced that the reward would be considerably higher than first reported and he wanted to give it to Scotland Yard for their efforts. He also admitted the jewels were worth much more than the £20,000 he had stated originally. But he left England without drawing the £2,000 cheque that was to be divided between the officers and Mr Streeter of Bond Street. Mr Streeter was to be awarded £500, as was Swanson for his part in the proceedings, and Inspectors Hare and Frost would each get £500 – from which they were to give money to sergeants and others who had helped under their instruction. When Burden was contacted, he simply refused to pay up. He even refused to pay the £100 shipment and insurance costs for the jewellery to be returned to New York. Mr Streeter wrote to him politely but to no avail. He claimed he was being sued and did not have the money. In London, one of the men due some money died and another married on the grounds of receiving a sum of cash. More letters were sent to Burden and eventually he compromised, following lawsuits. He would send over £1,300 with £650 being sent over on the next steamer. It is unknown if the men received the rest of the payment.

For all the years he was away from his home county, Swanson holidayed there every year, spending time fishing on the rivers, lochs and on the sea. He never lost his love for Caithness nor did he lose touch with his friends.

On 1 July 1903 Swanson retired from his appointment as superintendent. He was given a pension of £280 per annum and the leaving certificate noted that his conduct throughout his career was 'exemplary'. He spent much of his time reading or tying flies for his fishing expeditions.

Donald Sutherland Swanson died on 25 November 1924 at 3 Presburg Road in New Malden, Surrey, a house the family had moved into in 1912. He was buried at Kingston Cemetery. His wife Julia died on 6 May 1935 at the age of 91.

WALTER ROSS TAYLOR

Walter Ross Taylor became a church minister in Thurso in April 1831 and is one of the Far North's most notable ministers. He was related by the marriage of his daughter to another Far North minister of note, Alexander Auld of Olrig, and his only son, also named Walter Ross Taylor, followed in his father's footsteps and became a prominent minister of the Free Church in Glasgow.

Walter Ross Taylor was born in Tain, Ross-shire, on 11 November 1805. He was the eldest son of the Sheriff Clerk of Cromarty, James Taylor and his wife Flora Ross. Her brother, Colonel Walter Ross, left his entire estate to her, so following his death the family moved to Nigg. Walter, named after his uncle, was christened on 25 November 1805. In all there were nine children, but the youngest girl, Willina, passed away aged 13 in August 1822. She died as the result of an accident at home and this had a profound effect on Taylor, as it did on the rest of the family.

Taylor was schooled initially at the parish school in Cromarty before the move to Nigg. When at the school in Cromarty, he became friends with Hugh Miller, the eminent geologist. It was to be a lifelong friendship until Miller took his own life in 1856.

At the age of 13 Taylor applied to study at the University of Aberdeen, where he was accepted. He graduated four years later and it was around this time that his thoughts turned towards the ministry. During a visit to his family in Cromarty he decided to study divinity and by the following January had begun his course in theology at the University of Aberdeen. He had to attend Divinity Hall in Glasgow to complete his studies. Here on 1 January

Reverend Walter Ross Taylor, Thurso

149

1825 Taylor wrote in a diary how the locals were misguided in their revelry at the dawn of the New Year and how instead they should be giving serious thought to the solemnity of the season.

Three years later Taylor completed his degree and early in 1829 he was called to be minister for a small congregation in London – although he was not ordained until he returned to Scotland in the autumn of that year. He spent the best part of two years in the city at the Chadwell Street Church, but when he happened to be visiting friends in Ross-shire, he received a letter from the Thurso Parish Church committee. They were without a minister and had heard all about Taylor from his former professor at Aberdeen, Mr Tulloch, so decided to invite him to become their minister. He visited the church and preached there on two occasions. The congregation were greatly taken with him and in April 1831 he finally settled in Thurso, aged 25. He was very youthful looking, slim and slightly smaller than average, but he endeared himself to his parishioners by being courteous and listening to their points of view – although he made clear his own thoughts on the matter in hand. At his induction at St Peter's Church, the parish church, were other prominent ministers from Caithness, including Reverend Alexander Gunn of Watten. The ceremony was given in both English and Gaelic. However, his time at St Peter's was limited, because the church was old and beginning to crumble. He was the last minister to preach there on the final Sunday of December 1832.

St Peter's had been established in the 12th century. Following the Reformation there was the addition of the north aisle, with the south aisle then being added in the 17th century. By this stage the church had doubled in size. It was also during this century that the church was involved in a battle between the congregation and a group of Highlanders that were headed by the freebooter Donald MacAlister (an Irishman who had settled in Strathnaver). He had wanted to send an aggressive message to the town and gave orders for the church to be burned to the ground. The townsfolk got wind of it and attacked. Neil Williamson was killed in the fracas but the church survived. MacAlister's men were routed, killed, and buried at the roadside near to the Water Gate.

In the 18th century Thurso's population doubled. To accommodate the increased numbers of parishioners, a loft was erected above the town aisle. Later, another one was built over the nave. By the end of the century the church had little space left for expansion. In the 1820s repairs were needed. The General Inspector of Works, James Bell, found the decay was worse than anticipated and the cost rose steadily. The whole roof structure had both wet and dry rot and many beams inside were in serious decay. The slates on the roof were all in a poor state through age and weathering. The masonry too was at risk as the lime had turned to dust, making the walls dangerous. It was following this report on the poor state of the church that a new church was proposed and on the last Sunday of 1832, over 700 years of Christian worship ended in the church.

During that final sermon at St Peter's, Taylor commented on how the church had been used for many generations as a place of worship. He spoke of how 'the pure light of the Gospel shone' and that 'with these walls the Gospel has been long and often preached'. He made reference to 'many a longing soul [that] has been satisfied, [and] many

Old St Peters

a mourner comforted'. The church had also witnessed such wonders as sinners entering into it, curious about salvation, and subsequently becoming members of the congregation. The congregation could go away in the knowledge that St Peter's was the place where they 'met God', where God spoke to his people and where they themselves had 'sealed and ratified' their covenant with Him. Taylor ended the sermon in a reflective mood, knowing that many of the parishioners were reluctant to leave but reminding them that a new place was waiting to house them and that God was not 'confined to this or the other place'. This 'other place' was the newly-built St Peter's Church in the centre of Thurso and his first sermon there took place on the first Sunday in January 1833. The local congregation had asked the builder to construct a plain church that could seat up to 1,800 people with good acoustics so that the minister could be heard. In the end, the number it could hold was considerably smaller.

When the old church was abandoned, many of the relics – such as the communion cup, the baptism basin, and the bell engraved 'The Church Bell of Thurso 1740' – were all lost. The ornate pews and pulpit were abandoned, but the bowl from the medieval font was saved, as was a large key said to have been from the church. But the ornate artwork as mentioned in Calder's *History of Caithness* has all but disappeared.

Taylor settled in to parish life well. Every Sunday he would preach two sermons in English and another for the native Gaelic speakers in their own tongue. He would also hold weekly prayer meetings and a monthly fellowship meeting. It was the children of the parish in which he took most interest. He insisted on taking part in the Sunday school, where he would give them the lesson of the day and conduct the final prayer before they

151

were dismissed. In addition to this, he also took Bible Class on Wednesday evenings. He was always available to the congregation and took time to answer any letters that he received from them. He also travelled widely over the parish, except when epidemics hit the town, when he realised it was best to contain the illnesses in a particular area. Like so many others, Taylor succumbed to illnesses, but when he made a full recovery he went back to work as soon as he could.

Taylor became attached to Isabella Murray, whom he married on 9 May 1833. The marriage proved to be a long and happy one, and they had a family of four daughters: Christina, Flora, Esther, and Jemima, and a son, Walter. Christina married the Reverend Alexander Auld of Olrig, while Taylor Jr followed in his father's footsteps and became a well-known minister in his own right.

During Taylor's first ten years in Thurso, the church had a crisis that had a profound effect on the Scottish kirk. The national church had always sought to be free of the state and be in charge of its own affairs, such as appointing their own ministers. However, patronage played an increasing role within the church and was widely seen as interference by both ministers and congregations. In 1834 the evangelical division of the church won the right to pass the Veto Act, which meant that if a parish had a minister put in place by their patron that they thought was inappropriate, they had the right to reject him. This came to a head on 18 May 1843 when over 450 ministers decided to leave the church and set up the Free Church of Scotland, which would not adhere to any patron or government, but only be answerable to God and Jesus Christ – who they believed was its head. Many ministers immediately lost their livelihoods and homes but they were determined and the Free Church managed to find money to fund itself – and so it was established in its own right. Taylor and the Reverend Cook of Reay went all over Caithness in a bid to inform parishioners of their stance. In freezing conditions they stood outside and preached their message. The Church of Scotland ministers refused them entry to use their own churches as a platform for this revolution. Even Sir George Sinclair tried to pass a bill in London to avert the breaking up of the Kirk but it was rejected. Taylor participated in that day in May in Edinburgh when Dr Thomas Chalmers led the ministers from the General Assembly meeting. His wife meanwhile took the prudent step of finding the family a home before they were removed from the manse, which was attached to St Peter's.

New churches had to be built to accommodate the new Free Church ministers, as well as manses in which they would be able to live. In Thurso the parishioners who followed Taylor were able to use the Independent Church until their new church was built. In June 1844 Taylor conducted his first sermon in the new church, which later became the West Church, in Sinclair Street. The congregation also contributed to the cost of finding the Taylor family a manse, which they duly did at Castlegreen. Here Taylor lived for the rest of his life. The manse was situated on the remains of Ormlie Castle and later became the United Free Manse. The Free Parish School was then set up and Taylor took charge.

In the later 1850s an evangelist named Mr Brownlow North visited Caithness at the behest of Sir George Sinclair. During his visit, he preached at many neighbouring parishes, which Taylor used to ferry him to. He enjoyed listening to him, as did many of the parishioners, and those who were dissatisfied with the particular church they adhered to suddenly found a voice and joined the Free Church.

In late 1859 Taylor visited Ulster where the revival of this same religious fervour that had been introduced to Caithness was underway and many Catholics were turning to the Protestant faith. He found this an exciting time and recounted his visit to many people when he returned home.

During the 1860s as the population of Thurso further increased, so did the number of parishioners who attended Taylor's church. It was time to build a bigger one to accommodate the swelling numbers and this was done at a cost of over £5,000. This church was called the First Free Church and had its founding slab lain in the autumn of 1868 by Sir George Sinclair. Two years later, with a magnificent church in Olrig Street finished, Taylor delivered his first sermon in the new premises on 31 July 1870. This was the fourth and final church in which Taylor preached in the town. It was also the first time father and son preached. Taylor preached in the morning while his son preached in the afternoon and evening.

Walter Ross Taylor Junior became well-known in his own right. Born in the manse on 11 April 1838, he was christened when he was eight days old and schooled at the Thurso Free Church School. Following this he studied at the University of Edinburgh. He was a good student, took first place in many of his classes and received a medal in moral philosophy. He went on to receive the Stratton Scholarship. In 1857 he entered New College to study for the ministry and four years later he graduated and became a minister. His first appointment was to Lochmaben in Dumfries and Galloway then after just six months he was called to East Kilbride where he took up the role following the departure of Principal Oswald Dykes (who had been transferred to Free St George's Church in Edinburgh). In 1868 his time at East Kilbride came to an end when he was called to Kelvinside Free Church in Glasgow. He took over the post the following year from the Reverend William Traill – a position Traill had held for five years – at a time when that church was heavily in debt. Taylor Jr was always willing to help out in his father's parish so when Taylor asked him to come north, he did so without hesitation. The parishioners enjoyed his Thurso sermon on that summer evening in 1870.

Back in Glasgow, Taylor Jr injected new life into his church. He was young, friendly, approachable and above all, a good orator. In just ten years the number of parishioners almost trebled, although money was still a problem. In October 1878 the City of Glasgow Bank failed spectacularly and this had a profound effect on all the churches in the area. Out of 1,200 or so shareholders, 80% of them were financially ruined when it was found that the directors – who had made poor financial investments in America and Australasia – had lied about the bank's position. On a more personal level however, Taylor Jr had by this time married Margaret Paterson, who helped him cope with the difficulties he had to endure. The couple went on to have three sons and two daughters.

In April 1879, in the 50th anniversary year of Taylor Sr becoming a minister, his old university conferred a Doctor of Divinity on him, which he gratefully, but humbly, accepted. On Christmas Day that year, a gathering was held in Thurso Town Hall for him.

The artist Norman Macbeth painted a life-sized portrait of Taylor and it was presented to him at that gathering. His parishioners had commissioned it as a vote of thanks for all his hard work over the years, and his commitment to them. The hall was full: parishioners, family, friends and other ministers and elders attended. Donald Mackay, the oldest of all the office bearers and a man who had worked diligently under Taylor for 48 years, presented him with the oil painting. The inscription on the painting read: 'Presented to the Reverend Walter Ross Taylor, D.D., by the congregation of the First Free Church, Thurso, and other friends, on the fiftieth anniversary of his ordination'. Both the town council and the local magistrates also addressed him and gave him high praise for all his efforts in the local community. However, Taylor was to receive one more calling. As usual, he rose to the occasion, but not before tragedy struck.

Taylor's eldest daughter Christina married the Reverend Alexander Auld on 2 September 1857 in Thurso. On 25 February 1859 she gave birth to a son, Walter Ross Taylor Auld. The Aulds, and Taylor of course, had high hopes for this new addition to their family, believing that he could follow in his father and grandfather's footsteps. When he was less than two years old, he had learnt The Lord's Prayer and could recite some Biblical texts. A friend of the family was astounded because the young Walter seemed, even at such a tender age, to have an understanding of what he was repeating. His honesty also came to the fore at a young age. In her memoir about her son, Christina wrote:

'One evening that I brought him from Thurso a much desired toy, as a reward for rocking the cradle when the nursery was busy, he, instead of coming forward to claim it, kept out of sight. At last, I said "Walter, where are you? Here is your steamer." Rushing out of his hiding place, he looked at the gaily painted steamboat, and bursting into tears, said "I cannot take it; I was building my bricks [small wooden squares] in the window and did not rock the baby the minute he moved and he awoke."'

In the end the toy was put away and given to the baby Alexander a few months later.

When Walter was five years old he became gravely ill, causing much concern for not only his parents, but his grandfather too. Dr James Mill from Thurso believed that the child would pass away. As the days wore on the congestion in Walter's lungs grew worse. One night, as he lay unconscious, his father said his goodbyes and gave his soul to God. In the morning, a message was sent to the doctor, who came out to the manse where he was astonished to see the child still alive. The cook, Bell, had made a poultice and it is believed it helped him. The doctor noted the change and placed leeches on Walter as his fever was high. This gave him some strength. Within hours the leeches had done their work and Walter regained consciousness.

In the autumn of 1874 both Walter and Alexander were sent to the University of Aberdeen where Walter passed his examinations at the close of the session. However, his parents did not send him back to complete his studies at Aberdeen, and instead kept him at home where he read widely on history and kept up his knowledge of both Greek and Latin. The following year Walter headed off to the University of Edinburgh. By December 1877 Walter was writing down his thoughts about Christ being the Son of God. He wrote: 'However dim and feeble my conception of it is ... I do believe that He came forth from God; and he that believeth in Him shall be saved. Hope for a sinner!' The maturity of his thought became self-evident to friends.

Walter wrote to his family just before the College Session closed that he would be returning home and would like to look for a position as a tutor. He left Edinburgh on 18 April 1878 bound for Caithness. During his stay, he attended a sermon in Wick with his mother to see Dr John Kennedy of Dingwall preaching. During that summer, he took a Sunday school class before he had to return to Edinburgh to continue his studies.

In March 1879 Walter wrote home to his parents that he had caught a cold, but explained that many students had caught it. However, Alexander wrote a few weeks later to say that a doctor had been called as Walter's health had become worse. The doctor diagnosed mild bronchitis and told him not to attend classes for a few weeks. Walter was asked to come home, which he did. Another attack saw him laid up for a few weeks but over the summer his health improved enough for him to go out for walks, although the cough never left him. His intention was to go back to Edinburgh and complete his maths exam and gain his diploma. However, the cough returned in earnest and he was advised to stay at home for the winter. Over that winter, he spent time reading the Bible and newspapers. He also read *History of Protestantism* by Dr James Wylie 'with much interest'. Walter's desire was to enter the ministry, to follow in the footsteps of his father and grandfather, but it lay heavily on his heart as to the prospects of the Free Church in Scotland, so he spent a fair amount of time speaking to his mother about it. In April, Walter made his decision and joined the Free Church, much to the pleasure of Taylor who still had hopes that his grandson would follow in his footsteps, but he knew how ill Walter was. Over the course of the winter, Walter's health deteriorated further. By March 1880 he was able to leave the confines of his bedroom but still could not go outdoors, even though the weather was mild at the time. One Thursday, his mother heard him coughing violently through the night. She found him sitting up in bed gasping for breath and coughing up blood. In the morning Dr Sutherland was sent for and he 'gave him some astringent, and wished him to be kept cool and quiet'. Walter kept coughing up the blood and became weaker and weaker. On 19 April 1880 Dr Sutherland examined him again and during the consultation, Walter complained about a darting pain near to his heart. Dr Sutherland told Christina to keep her son warm but not to expect him to live much longer. Prayers were said and at the dawn of the next day, the window shutters were opened and as Christina wrote: 'Our darling Walter, drawing one long breath, and drooping his head upon the pillow, yielded up his spirit to God who gave it'. He was 21 years old and was buried in Olrig Churchyard.

A few years later in November 1883, Taylor was chosen from a list of candidates for the position of moderator of the Free Church. The candidates included: Principal David Brown of the Free Church College in Aberdeen; Reverend Dr Alexander Somerville of Glasgow; and the Reverend Mr John Laird of Cupar in Fife. This news came as tragedy struck his family again. Isabella, Taylor's wife of over 50 years, suddenly took ill in March 1884. The winter had affected her health badly and while Taylor attended the annual Sunday school gathering, his wife collapsed. Soon after, she died. The family were in shock at the death but after managing to come to terms with his loss, Taylor began turning his thoughts towards his duty and his impending time as moderator. His candidacy had been put forward by his predecessor Dr Horatius Bonar and seconded by Mr E. A. Stuart Grey of Kinfauns. During his nomination speech Bonar said that Taylor was one of 'the worthiest men that our church contains ... one on whom life's sunshine has rested for more than half a century', that he was an accomplished minister, full of justice, and one of the most hard working of all ministers, but who was at this time 'sorely tried'. It was a passionate speech, which went down very well with the assembled company. Taylor was warmly welcomed by all when he took the chair as moderator.

In his opening address to the General Assembly in 1884, Taylor told them that he was both 'surprised and disquieted' at his appointment. His surprise was because he felt that he did not deserve the position but disquieted due to the 'responsibility and anxieties connected with the discharge of its duties'. He thanked them for placing him at the helm and expressed his faith in the assembly and in the work it was doing. He mentioned some ministers who had passed away, such as Dr Kennedy of Dingwall, Dr Thomson of Paisley and Mr Fraser of Rosskeen, but went on to call for those left to devote themselves with 'earnestness to our appointed work'.

At the close of the assembly he again made a speech, this time with reference to the other Presbyterian churches, intimating that they should not be forgotten. He said: 'It is surely most desirable that the reproach of our divisions were wiped away, and that Scotland again became united, not only in testifying for Christ's crown and covenant, but in yielding to Him the homage and service [that God had given Him]'. He continued: 'Our land has been highly favoured of the Lord', referring to the Reformation and the Covenanters who changed the face of religion in Scotland. He ended his address by once again thanking his fellow 'fathers and brethren' for giving him the position of moderator, and brought the proceedings to a close.

When Taylor's time as moderator was up, he proposed that the previous candidate Principal Brown (who had in fact been runner up in the election when Taylor was chosen as moderator), be his successor. Taylor had known him since his student days and the pair had often met since. When Taylor left, having served his 12 months, he returned to work and continued to conduct services twice every Sunday, even though he was now in his 80s.

In 1887 Taylor remarried. She was Isabella Macdonald from Pennyland in Thurso. By 1893 Taylor had been forced to seek a colleague to help him in his duties and cut back on his heavy workload. In the winter of 1893 Taylor had a stroke, from which he recovered over the following six months. But in this time a new minister had been chosen. He was the Reverend George Morrison and in August 1894 he moved to Thurso to take some of the burden of office from Taylor. Two years later Taylor attended the General Assembly where Thurso-born Reverend William Miller of Madras College India was now the moderator. Taylor had baptised him when he was a baby and he was very proud of him. On his trip south Taylor was accompanied by his son-in-law, Sutherland-born William Mackay, a farmer and chief magistrate of Thurso. He was also a chief office bearer of the First Free Church who often held sermons in the outlying districts of Thurso and took Bible classes. He was highly regarded by those whom he taught and received many letters from his former students over many years. Mackay married Jemima Taylor in August 1871 in Thurso and died suddenly aged 59 in 1903. His widow died ten years later.

When Taylor returned from the assembly, many people noted how frail he looked – although, as always, his spirits were high. Two months before Taylor's death, he gave a sermon at Olrig without notes and without help from anyone, but he was weak. Over the coming weeks, Taylor gave a lot of his time to reading and praying and began to spend a great deal of time in his room. On 5 October 1896 Taylor died. The funeral was held in Thurso and was attended by hundreds of people. He had touched the lives of so many Thurso folk over the years and they found themselves wanting to pay their respects to this most noted minister of the Far North of Scotland. He was buried in Thurso cemetery.

Taylor's son, Walter Ross Taylor Junior, further followed in his father's footsteps, a few years after his father's death (in May 1900), when he became the moderator of the Free Church General Assembly. That year was significant because the Free Church joined with the United Presbyterian Church to form the United Free Church and Taylor Jr, as moderator of the Free Church, had the privilege of leading the first-ever General Assembly of the United Free Church. Two years earlier, Taylor Jr wrote a book that outlined the differences between all the churches in the United Kingdom. He wrote in some detail about the split in the church at the Disruption when the Free Church wanted to revive spiritual life in the country and not be governed by decisions made by civil courts. He explained how the congregations no longer wished to be compelled to take a minister forced upon them by a patron and how a new spirit had taken over. This spirit prompted the building of more churches. The turning point occurred in Auchterarder, when a vacancy arose for a new minister. The Earl of Kinnoull appointed a minister that the congregation just could not accept. Out of 3,000 people only two were happy with the new appointment. A petition was made and the Presbytery felt they could not proceed, so 'they rejected the presentee'. This 'presentee' appealed to the Court of Session, with the backing of Kinnoull, which found in his favour by a majority of eight to three and cited that the 'Presbytery were bound to give effect to the patron's choice'. It was found that the 'call' was nothing more than a mere formality and the Church 'had no freedom or authority in the matter beyond what it received from civil statute'. This posed the question of who actually had authority within the Church of Scotland: 'the law of Christ, or the dictate of the civil power?' It was not a new question but this case brought it to the fore. Added to this, when the General Assembly appointed ministers to parishes where other ministers had been suspended, the 'Court of Session stepped in with an interdict, prohibiting those appointed from preaching in these parishes'. The Church had no choice but to approach the legal system about what it saw as 'assaults made on its liberties and rights'. In a statement, the Church outlined its independence and its jurisdiction as far as religious matters were concerned, quoting from various Acts of Parliament in the process. Many Scottish MPs understood what the church was saying and agreed by a majority with its claim, but after two days of deliberation, the Church's claims were rejected by Westminster. It was a devastating blow, which resulted in rebellion. The Church could not bring itself to accept State Establishment and put civil law above Christ's. On 18 May 1843 the Government got its answer: the 'most venerated and trusted members of the ministers of the Church of Scotland, to the number 474, gave an emphatic No'.

The first problem to be surmounted by the new church was funding, but Thomas Chalmers had already thought of this before he led the ministers out of the General Assembly in May. The rich would be most able to pay and the poor were only expected to contribute what they could. In the first year, the central fund raised over £68,000, with each minister receiving £105. By 1898 this had risen to in excess of £170,000 a year, with ministers receiving £160. The Church of England and the Established Church of Scotland also later adopted this Sustention Fund. Within ten years the Free Church had raised over three million pounds for the building of churches, manses, halls and schoolhouses – all raised from the generosity of the congregations. The number of ministers grew and 'a great Home Mission movement' began whereby young ministers were sent out into parishes to bring people into the Church. Taylor Jr cites 'Dr J. H. Wilson, of Edinburgh, a veteran in Home Mission work', who raised thousands of pounds 'for the promotion of the work in mining districts'. There were also foreign missions established in Europe, India, South Africa, Syria and elsewhere.

What Taylor Jr held to be the essence of the Church was its progressive nature. In the 1870s, an article appeared in the *Encyclopaedia Britannica* about the Bible by a Professor Robertson Smith. It raised questions that the Free Church 'had not hitherto been called upon to face and investigate ... therefore it had not pronounced any judgement'. They asked for an inquiry and for any disciplinary action to be taken against the professor to be delayed, but the majority within the Church believed that he had committed heresy. However, over the next few years the professor was acquitted as the Church moved forward and the case was dropped. By this time he had written another, defiant article and he was told his services were no longer required. This, according to Taylor Jr, was a mistake and 'the Free Church deprived itself of its most gifted scholar'. Smith gained a position at the University of Cambridge where he taught Biblical students for the rest of his life.

This case brought debate to the Free Church. Dr Marcus Dodds had a sermon published, which brought into question the traditional views still held by many. Even so, Dodds was elected unanimously to the Chair of New Testament Exegesis at the New College in Edinburgh, thanks to his 'proposer', who said that the position he had taken up 'was the only, safe, sound, and Scriptural position on the subject'. According to Taylor Jr, these controversies were purely on the surface, but 'beneath them lie fathomless depths, calm and untroubled, of pervading reverence, trust and love'. He continued: 'He who has been pleased to lay it upon the Free Church to bear ... the strain of the theological questionings of our time, has not failed to grant that rooted sense of certainty regarding the truth as it is in Jesus, which enables a Church to stand firm'.

Towards the end of his piece, Taylor Jr turns to the union of the church with others. The first of these occurred in June 1852 when the group known as the 'Original Seceders' joined the Free Church. Following this union, the Reformed Presbyterian Church joined in 1876. During the 1860s, union was sought between the Free Church and the United Presbyterian Church but after the initial frenzy of activity, 'mistakes and misapprehensions got into circulation, prejudices were aroused' and 'opposite camps were formed'. The moves to join the churches were abandoned. In 1897 new negotiations began when the United Presbyterian Church declared it still wanted to join them. At his time of writing, Taylor Jr believed that the continued separation could no longer be justified 'and ought, as a matter of obvious Christian duty ... be brought to an end'. Taylor Jr also desired a union with the Established Church. He wrote: 'How much nobler it would be ... if the Established Church had the brotherliness and courage to say – "We would rather be in union with our brethren and fellow-workers in Christ, and make common cause with them in warfare with sin and vice, than hold aloof for the sake of State favour and prestige!"' In 1900 the Free Church and the United Presbyterian Church finally joined as the United Free Church of Scotland.

In recognition of his work at Kelvinside, the University of Glasgow conferred the degree of D.D. upon Taylor Jr in 1891. However, his work was not limited to Scotland. He travelled far and wide to places in Europe, Africa, and North America. Taylor Jr's congregation presented him with his portrait in 1902 in recognition of his life's work, just as the parishioners of Thurso had done for his father. Taylor Jr had also been chairman, then vice-president, of the National Bible Society; chairman of the Glasgow United Free Church College Committee; and chairman of the Mission to the Chinese Blind. He also was a member of the first Govan Parish School board: education was important to him. In November 1904, Taylor Jr travelled back to Caithness to hold a service in the manse at Olrig. It was at this time that his brother-in-law the Reverend Alexander Auld passed away.

In 1906 Taylor Jr had an operation from which he never fully recovered and he died on 6 December 1907.

SELECTED BIBLIOGRAPHY

Auld, A. (1911) *Memorials of Caithness Ministers* (W. F. Henderson)

Auld, C. (1896) *Memorial of Walter R. T. Auld* (J. C. Pembrey)

Begg, P. (1992) *The Jack the Ripper A–Z* (Headline)

Begg, P. (2004) *Jack the Ripper: The Definitive History* (Longman)

Begg, P. (2006) *Jack the Ripper: The Facts* (Robson Books)

Bicheno, H. (2003) *Rebels and Redcoats* (HarperCollins)

Black, G. F. (1921; 2007) *Scotland's Mark on America* (BiblioBazaar)

Boyd, D. H. A. (1998) *Amulets to Isotopes* (Bookcraft Ltd)

Brown, C. G. (1997) *Religion and Society in Scotland Since 1707* (EUP)

Brown, J. (1891) *The History of Sanquhar* (J. Anderson & Son)

Calder, J. (2003) *Scots in Canada* (Luath Press Ltd)

Calder, J. T. (1861; 1887) *Sketch of the Civil and Traditional History of Caithness* (William Rae)

Conway, S. (2000; 2002) *The British Isles and the War of American Independence* (OUP)

Corlett, E. (2002) *The Story of Brunel's SS Great Britain: The Iron Ship* Conway (Maritime Press)

Davidson, A. (1923) *Flora of Southern California* (Times-mirror Press)

Devaliant, J. (1996) *Elizabeth Yates: The First Lady Mayor in the British Empire* (Exisle Publishing)

Fodden, F. (1996) *Wick of the North* (North of Scotland Newspapers)

Gibbon, F. P. (undated) *William A. Smith of the Boys' Brigade* (Collins)

Grant, D. (1966; 1967) *Old Thurso* (John Humphries)

Gunn, R. P. (1998) *Inventors and Engineers of Caithness* (Whittles Publishing)

Hayman, J. (1989) *Robert Brown and the Vancouver Island Exploring Expedition* (UBC Press)

Hewitson, J. (1998) *Far Off in Sunlit Places* (Birlinn Ltd)

Humphries, J. (1965; 1977) *Henry Henderson, Bard o' Reay* (John Humphries)

Jones, R. (2008) *Jack the Ripper: The Casebook* (Andre Deutsch Ltd)

Lister, M. H. (1949) *Journals of Andrew Geddes Bain* (The Van Riebeeck Society)

Little, K., *et al* (1898) *Our Churches and Why We Belong To Them* (Service & Paton)

MacLeod, J. L. (2000) *The Second Disruption: The Free Church in Victorian Scotland and the Origins of the Free Presbyterian Church* (Tuckwell Press Ltd)

McCullough, D. (2006) *1776: Britain and America at War* (Penguin)

Marston, D. (2002) *The American Revolution* (Osprey Publishing)

Middlekauf, R. (1982; 2007) *The Glorious Cause* (OUP)

Mowat, J. (undated) *James Bremner Wreck Raiser* (J. S. Duncan)

Omand, D. (1972; 1973) *The Caithness Book* (Highland Printers Ltd)

Peacock, R. S. (1954) *Pioneer of Boyhood: Story of Sir William A. Smith* (Boys' Brigade)

Rhind, A. H. (1856) *Egypt: Its Climate, Character and resources as a Winter Resort* (Thomas Constable)

Rhind, A. H. (1862) *Thebes Its Tombs and Their Tenants* (Longman)

Ross, J. M. E. (1905) *William Ross of Cowcaddens* (Hodder and Stoughton)

Smiles, S. (1878) *Robert Dick Baker, of Thurso Geologist and Botanist* (John Murray)

Smith, W. H. (1882) *The St Clair Papers* (Robert Clarke & Co)

Smout, T. C. (1986; 1997) *A Century of the Scottish People 1830–1950* (Fontana Press)

Springhall, J. (1983) *Sure and Steadfast: History of the Boys' Brigade 1883–1983* (Collins)

Stephen, D. (1891) *Gleanings in the North* (William Sinclair)

Stuart, J. (1864) *Memoir of Alexander Henry Rhind of Sibster* (Neill & Co)

Sugden, P. (2002) *The Complete History of Jack the Ripper* (Robinson Publishing)

Williamson, J. A. (undated) *Mr Robert Dick Naturalist and Baker* (John Humphries)